DATE DUE		

WAR
MEMORIALS
ᴬˢ POLITICAL
LANDSCAPE

WAR MEMORIALS AS POLITICAL LANDSCAPE

THE
AMERICAN EXPERIENCE AND BEYOND

JAMES M. MAYO

PRAEGER

New York
Westport, Connecticut
London

Grateful acknowledgment is made to the following for permission to reprint previously published material: Ann Landers, Los Angeles Times Syndicate, Excerpt from Ann Landers, *Kansas City Times*, June 21, 1976, p. 12a.

Every reasonable effort has been made to trace the owners of copyright materials in this book, but in some instances this has proven impossible. The publishers will be glad to receive information leading to more complete acknowledgments in subsequent printings of the book, and in the meantime extend their apologies for any omissions.

Library of Congress Cataloging-in-Publication Data

Mayo, James M.
  War memorials as political landscape: the American experience and beyond / James M. Mayo.
  p. cm.
  Bibliography: p.
  Includes index.
  ISBN 0-275-92812-8 (alk. paper)
  1. War memorials—United States. 2. Architecture—Political aspects—United States. 3. Symbolism in politics—United States.
  4. United States—History, Military. I. Title.
E159.M43   1988   87-22328
973—dc19

Library of Congress Catalog Card Number: 87-22328

ISBN: 0-275-92812-8

First published in 1988

Praeger Publishers, One Madison Avenue, New York, NY 10010
A division of Greenwood Press, Inc.

Printed in the United States of America

The paper used in this book complies with the
Permanent Paper Standard issued by the National
Information Standards Organization (Z39.48-1984).

10 9 8 7 6 5 4 3 2 1

To my Mother and in memory of my Father

CONTENTS

ILLUSTRATIONS

CHAPTER FIVE

CHAPTER SIX

CHAPTER SEVEN

ACKNOWLEDGMENTS

This book would not have been completed without the help of colleagues and friends. Philip and Birgit Ambrosius, Richard Branham, Ralph Clement, Susan Elkins, Marcia Feldman, John Forester, Eileen Grabow, Stephen Grabow, Elizabeth Grossman, Herman Hattaway, John B. Jackson, Hobart Jackson, Lawrence Perkins, Michael Nutkiewicz, James Rowings, David Saile, Elizabeth Schultz, Roger Shimomura, and Thomas Shutt were particularly helpful to me. William Ryan, Director of Operations and Finance for the American Battle Monuments Commission, willingly provided information and material from the commission's files. Gordon Holland made a special attempt to develop good photographic prints from my own photographic work. Gera Elliott and Cindy Muckey spent countless hours typing and retyping the book. Elizabeth Scalet proved to be a most understanding editor in sharpening my ideas. I owe a special debt to the University of Kansas for providing a summer grant and sabbatical leave to complete this book. Finally, my wife Shirley Harkess and my daughter Meredith have to be congratulated for surviving the ordeal with me.

PREFACE

The purpose of this book is to understand as fully as possible the relationship between politics and design. My own past work, as well as that of others, has treated this subject more at the theoretical level than at the practical level of emotions. It became apparent that if I looked closely at parts of the American landscape that are more obviously political than others I might be able to demonstrate the symbolic connection between politics and place—not only theoretically but also in the realm of feeling.

War memorials affect people's emotions at a deep level. In fact, the decision about how a particular war will be memorialized is often an emotional decision in itself. When you compare the relative costs of war memorials with other civic projects, a greater amount of time and more arguments occur when memorials are at issue. War, with its cost in human life, is the most drastic political act a nation can make. Consequently, Americans have demonstrated that sacred memorials are an unassailable investment in which no economic return is expected.

Because of the vastness and diversity of the national landscape, Americans tend to lose sight of how much war memorials actually permeate the environment. Untold millions have been spent by state and federal agencies on the construction and maintenance of war memorials on thousands of acres, both at home and abroad. American tourists annually spend significant portions of their savings to visit them.

At the local level, commemorative street names and public building dedications help to create a web of remembrance. All of these local monuments considered at a national level, though, have a collective power. The Minuteman Statue, the Liberty Bell, the Vietnam Memorial, the Tomb of the Unknown Soldier, the Marine Corps Memorial of the famous flag-raising at Iwo Jima—these and many other monuments have become part of the national psyche. They express symbolically our political and emotional response to war and peace, victory and defeat, justice and destiny, or horror and revolt.

While there is a diverse literature on war memorials, almost nothing has been done to consolidate the American experience. Most publications treat the war memorial as an artistic artifact. Travel books and maps tell us where they exist, and in a few cases, individual histories of monuments and battlefields are available. Political interpretation of war memorials is rare, indeed.

A study of American war memorials provides an interesting opportunity to reflect upon how war as a political act has been expressed symbolically. This book, however, necessarily went beyond the American experience. So many critical events in world history occurred outside of the United States. The Holocaust and other atrocities from the Second World War are included in order to understand humanitarian commemoration and because of the unique memorials designed to remember these tragedies. It would have been easier not to address those horrors, but this book is more meaningful because it has.

WAR
MEMORIALS
AS POLITICAL
LANDSCAPE

CHAPTER ONE

WAR MEMORIALS
AS SYMBOLIC MESSAGES

THE STRENGTHS AND WEAKNESSES OF A SOCIETY are demonstrated in war, and memorials to those wars often mirror those qualities. War is the ultimate political conflict, and attempts to commemorate it unavoidably create a distinct political landscape. The war memorial—a statue, a place, a building, or a combination of these and other things—is, at its simplest, a social and physical arrangement of space and artifacts that keep alive the memories of those who were involved in a war.[1] As an artifact a memorial helps create an ongoing order and meaning beyond the fleeting and chaotic experiences of life.[2] These simple definitions suggest some boundaries for the examination of memorials in the built environment, but they are not sufficient to explain the historical, social, and symbolic circumstances that give memorials their meaning.

A HISTORICAL PERSPECTIVE

War memorials originated during the Classical Age of the Greeks and Romans. As these cultures developed, attempts were made to translate societal values into built form. The two dominant themes portrayed in war memorials were religious expression and proclamation of victory, but mourning and re-creation of the human spirit were also present.[3] A victory for the empire was a victory for the gods, and these values were manifested in the architectural achievements of the Classical Age.

The Greeks introduced a variety of war memorials. In Greek culture, temples were intrinsic forms of memory which related religion and victory. Arnold Whittick, an architectural historian, argued: "The whole Acropolis, which includes a temple dedicated to Nike, the Greek goddess of victory, must be regarded partially as the great Athenian War Memorial."[4] The Parthenon, the most famous building on the Acropolis, was in part an expression of thanksgiving to Athene for the Athenean triumph over Persia. In the Hellenistic period public altars, such as the altar of Pergamon, were erected in thanksgiving for victory.[5] Many now familiar Greek sculptures were originally created for use in war memorials. *Winged Victory*, which represents Nike, is one of the most famous; it is now in the Louvre. The Greeks also employed victory columns and placed statues atop them, such as those in Delphi and Olympia where remains still exist.[6]

Not all Greek victory memorials paid homage to the gods. Funeral monuments, such as the tablet of Dexilos in the cemetery of the Cerameicus at Athens, commonly displayed a cavalryman riding over a defeated enemy.[7] Since remembrance in Greek society commonly occurred within the geographical confines of the city, there are relatively few memorials located at actual battle sites. An exception was the Battle of Marathon, which was commemorated at the battlefield with an earthen mound.

The Romans continued many of these Greek traditions. Religious faith and the proclamation of victory continued to be important themes, but the Romans made innovations of their own in the expression of these concepts. Memorial columns were typically larger and used more frequently than in Greece. The most famous remaining example is Trajan's Column in the Roman Forum. Its huge size reflects the more grandiose scale that typified the Roman Empire, but more importantly, this monument was used as a prototype for other victory pillars erected to honor various Roman generals.[8] The most unique memorial structure developed by the Romans was the triumphal arch. The first monumental arches date from about 200 B.C. and were erected to commemorate emperors, generals, and victorious campaigns.[9] The Arches of Titus and Constantine are among the best known remaining edifices celebrating Roman victories.

With the fall of the Roman Empire, the Classical Age passed into history and so did its values as expressed in the architecture of empire. The Medieval Age in Western civilization was a time of Christian expression in architecture. War memory was not portrayed through monuments but was instead part of the functional city landscape. City walls, moats, and castles were necessary for defense. Castles and cities which were besieged and marred provided physical reminders of war. Churches were even desecrated, as when Oliver Cromwell's armies defaced religious figures on

English cathedrals. Because Europe was mainly a collection of fragmented states which could hardly be called unified nations, war memorials as a focus of national identity were not significant during medieval times.

In the Medieval Age, the design elements of war and remembrance were perhaps best sustained in funerary architecture. This form of memorial is exemplified by the tomb monuments of Edward the Black Prince in Canterbury Cathedral and Thomas Beauchamp, earl of Warwick, in St. Mary's Church in Warwick.[10] Sculptures atop their tombs portrayed those men in fighting armor to symbolize their reign and their honor. Their portrayal as honorable warriors was more important than the historical truth of whether or not they had actually fought. Other noblemen in England and Europe were also commemorated in this fashion, and such tombs provided a design concept for war memorials in later times.

The revival of war memorials came with the Renaissance. Nationalism emerged as a prevailing political force during this age. In Paris, the Porte St. Denis was built to commemorate victories under Louis XIV, and the Arc de Triomphe de L'Etoile honored Napoleon's conquests. In London, Lord Admiral Nelson's monument and Trafalgar Square became symbols of the British Empire. Although Germany did not become a unified nation until the nineteenth century, the Brandenburg Gate in Berlin indicated the growing military power of a Prussian state that would ultimately expand its boundaries. While war memorials of the Renaissance were designed much like those of the Classical Age, one innovation emerged. The equestrian monument first appeared in Italy and then spread to the rest of Europe as a means to honor military commanders. The earliest remaining example is Michelangelo's equestrian statue of Marcus Aurelius in Rome's Capital Plaza.[11] The European empire-building of the Renaissance inevitably led to military conflicts on a national scale, and thus to the first real emergence of war memorials since the Roman Empire.

The U.S. experience with war memorials was greatly influenced by these European developments. Initial efforts to provide monuments were decidedly modest. The United States was certainly no empire, but when monuments were built, the classical style was as popular as it had been in Europe. As the nation expanded politically, geographically, and economically in the nineteenth century, war became commonplace. Americans wanted to commemorate those who died, and for the first time, the nation's growing wealth made it possible to construct memorials for all U.S. wars, from the American Revolution to the Spanish-American War. As the United States became a leading world power in the twentieth century, the number and variety of its war memorials increased, and American innovations in commemoration developed that went beyond classical approaches in concept and execution.

As memorials evolved from the Classical Age to the American present, so also did the perceptions of what war memorials are and can be. The classical notion of the war memorial is a monument. This view still persists, but there are other ways in which war memory can be related to place.

SENTIMENT AND UTILITY IN WAR MEMORIALS

War memorials derive meaning from the sentiments and utilitarian purposes we impose on them. Choosing a particular sentiment and a particular purpose provides alternative possibilities for the remembrance of past wars.

Sentiment in memorials can be either sacred or nonsacred. The nineteenth-century sociologist Emile Durkheim once characterized religious thought, what we should believe to guide our moral life, as the difference between the sacred and the profane.[12] The sacred is a proclamation of virtue while the profane is not. The transformation of these ideals into space, however, creates new meanings. Mircea Eliade, a philosopher, identified profane space as having amorphous meaning; people have fragmented life experiences in a profane place. In contrast, sacred space as a place has a distinct, spiritual meaning amidst chaos.[13] Brian Robinson, a geographer, astutely remarks that the sacred is beyond unique individual experiences.[14] To become spiritual about a place requires some consensus, a communal notion of good. There are social expectations regarding personal behavior in a sacred place. To keep a place sacred, social sanctions must exist that allow the space to be ritualized temporarily or to remain sacred when we must be elsewhere. While sacredness enables a place to be defined as having moral value, it does not follow that what remains outside it is immoral and disorderly. The profane and the immoral are so often seen as the same, but to call all places and rituals that are not sacred profane is an overstatement. The designed landscape is mainly nonsacred; it is orderly without a moral message. Sacred or not, people associate historic memories with places and things that they design or experience. As a result, they make memorials, from personal acts to institutional proclamations. Tradition may suggest that war memorials and rituals are the only sacred messages that are part of the spatial fabric, but this is untrue. Not all memories of war are treated sacredly, nor are all the places and things associated with those memories. Any war memory that is bound to a place or artifact can be a war memorial.

All memorials have utility, however modest. They can be used solely to remember the past. On the other hand, buildings constructed for other human activities, such as schools and hospitals, may have a secondary identity as memorials. This provides an added layer of meaning to these structures.

The combinations of sentiment and utility chosen for memorials allow them to be separated by types. As shown in Figure 1.1, memorials can be sacred or nonsacred and can have low or high utility. Bernard Barber, a sociologist, says: "The compatibility of utilitarian activities and symbolic

Utility	Sacred Sentiment	Nonsacred Sentiment
High	Public service	Business and war remains
Low	Shrine and commemorative ritual	Collection and recreation

Figure 1.1. Types of War Memorials

functions in a war memorial is determined by the degree to which the utilitarian values are expressive of the same set of values which are being memorialized."[15]

Shrines and commemorative rituals are war memorials that emphasize sacredness but not utility. They commemorate those people who fought to preserve certain human values. Not heavily laden with uses which may compete or conflict with the message, these spaces and artifacts become hallowed ground, and any blemish, such as trash or graffiti, is a sacrilege. Similarly, ceremonies that commemorate the past are expected to be performed flawlessly. Special efforts are often made to designate a place for fallen soldiers, and it is enriched through written and artistic means with ceremonial performances to express desired human values. This is the most common conception of war memorials, and war shrines and commemorative rituals constitute historically the most frequently used approaches to remember past deeds.

Public service memorials are used to emphasize both sacredness and utility. The public service purpose of such memorials reinforces the values and aims represented by the sentiment of commemoration. In this century, the public has called for memorials that provide a community service rather than only a symbolic and aesthetic gesture.[16] At the same time, the values associated with the service are expected to be compatible with those expressed in the memorial. For example, dedicating a school or hospital as a war memorial reflects the desire to better the human condition. The worthy values of war are put into practice through humanitarian services.

Nonsacred memorials may also have high utility, such as businesses related to war or actual war remains. Tourist enterprises near sacred memorials market war memories for profit. Army-Navy stores, war militaria shops, and other enterprises rely intrinsically upon items used in war. A nation that goes to war unavoidably accumulates artifacts and places that are no longer usable when peace is achieved. These war remains are sometimes abandoned landscapes, and new ones are created to store artifacts that are returned from war. Some war remains are refitted for other practical uses. While all of these businesses and remains evoke memories of war, their practical purpose is one of profit or use, not one of sacredness, that is, commemoration.

The collection of war memorabilia and the use of war as a theme in recreation both constitute nonsacred memorials with low utility. Collectors buy or trade weapons, medals, and other items out of personal interest rather than as a means to make a profit or to serve others. These artifacts become nonsacred memorials by default, because they were used in war rather than intended as designs to commemorate war endeavors. For recreation, people often participate in memorabilia shows, battle reenactments, and war games to use history selectively or to imitate it. Objects and events are separated from history, good or bad, and such behavior expresses war history without explaining or justifying a war's cause.

SOCIAL PURPOSES OF WAR MEMORIALS

War memorials are distinguished not only by combinations of sentiment and utility but also by their social purpose. Some forms of social purpose are valued more than others, and they represent a select hierarchy of human values. As shown in Figure 1.2, war memorials can purport identity, service, honor, and humanitarianism, and this ascending hierarchy of social purpose depends upon the chosen combinations of sentiment and utility.

Communities are pluralistic, and all types of memorials can potentially coexist within a community. These memorials help to form the community's identity. By law, communities must allow any legitimate activity to occur within their public boundaries. Within this territory, however, sacred memorials can be partitioned from those activities that may arouse public indignation. Even nonsacred memorials are controlled. Private enterprise is confined to approved commercial land uses, and personal collections of war memorabilia are voluntarily confined to residential homes. Synthetic rituals which use war as entertainment are often not allowed to be held on sacred turf. While the sacred and nonsacred may be separated, every war memorial has an identity that can evoke memory of past wars and these evocations may have competing or conflicting meanings.

Service as a social purpose in memorials goes beyond identity because of the need to make them part of the public realm. Personal collection has no place here since people are not obligated to share their artifacts. Service could be one social purpose of both a business which trades on war memory and a school, which serves a public function, named after a war hero. Memorabilia shows and war dramas also offer an opportunity for people to attend or participate in them. In all these cases, war memory is less important than how the public wishes to be served. Shrines include service as well, although this aspect is seldom emphasized. Monuments are often

Social Purpose	Sacred Sentiment		Nonsacred Sentiment	
	Shrine and Commemorative Ritual	Public Service	Business and War Remains	Collection and Recreation
Humanitarianism	●			
Honor	●	●		
Service	●	●	●	
Identity	●	●	●	●

Figure 1.2. Social Purposes for War Memorials

used to beautify cities as much as they are built as commemorations. They often become emblems that people use to justify the preservation of historic commercial districts, especially when honor rituals reinforce their meaning. In this sense, memorials are used as a borrowed landscape to serve another public use.

The addition of honor as a social purpose separates the sacred from the nonsacred. Honor cannot be bought or collected. It can only be bestowed. Of course, public services do charge citizens. People are taxed to pay for schools that honor people and events, and memorial hospitals must charge patients to continue operation. Honor in war, however, is collectively associated with government. A nation that goes to war can commemorate those who fought since its government jointly obligated itself to protect and to defend its citizens while simultaneously calling upon them to fight. Government repays its citizens through honor. While local and state governments do not declare war, they operate under the confines of national law and implement it. Like the federal government, lower levels of government can bestow honor, because the public assumes that local commemorations are congruent with the national purpose of honor.

Governmental support and dedication of all monuments clearly convey honor, but not all public services are honored as war memorials. Schools, parks, hospitals, and cemeteries can be considered as possible memorials, but water plants, sewer plants, or garbage disposal sites are not acceptable. Two reasons divide these functions. First, honor in these memorials can exist only as long as commemoration is bestowed upon a place that has a social function. People learn in schools, play together in parks, share in healing in hospitals, and gather for funerals at public cemeteries to remember loved ones. All of these positive activities further advance the positive values for which wars are fought. Second, honor cannot be associated with the unclean. To be unclean is to be without honor, and it is impossible for people to conceive of processing plants and garbage sites as clean. While such facilities functionally enable society to separate the clean from the unclean, these places are ultimately conceived as vaults of the awful. In the end, honor in memorials and rituals can only occur in places where people can conceive that human betterment can be presented or can take place in a social context.

The highest social purpose in commemoration is humanitarianism. Most war memorials stop at honoring those who died or served. While praise is important, it is sometimes insufficient in proportion to the events which must be remembered. Humanitarianism in war memorials is as much a questioning of war as it is a statement. Some monuments not only honor those who fought but also offer a plea for peace. A few memorials go even further, because what is being remembered demands a concern for humanitarianism. Prison camps, execution factories, and massacre sites are often commemorated as statements to counter inhumanity with humanity. All levels of social purpose are expressed here. Identity denotes that something out of the ordinary happened at this place, and service is expressed through education about those events and their origins. Honor is bestowed upon those who suffered, and humanitarianism introduces the plea that society should neither forget nor allow such inhumanity to repeat itself. Rituals of remembrance can make these places even more sacred. Understanding what happened, what must not be repeated, can be verbally expressed in ways that monuments cannot convey visually.

The hierarchy of social purpose enables society to separate the sacred from the nonsacred and allows distinctions to be made within the realm of sacredness. But these are only expectations, and people may have their own conceptions of past wars which lead to different expectations. When these differ, social conflicts can arise. The conflicts often center on how objects as memorials are related to history versus how they are used. People who are angered by the inhumanity of the Holocaust are often disturbed by collectors of war memorabilia, who see their possessions as a means to satisfy their self-identity through a hobby. The gap in social purpose between humanitarian purpose and nonsacred memorials is too great. Even simpler is the circumstance in which a public service has a memorial building, but the community considers that the service is poorly delivered. War memorials are limited by their social purpose, but the plurality of expectations often leads to conflicts in social meaning.

HISTORY AND MEANING

While war memorials themselves may be preserved, the society around them changes, and so does its history. These changes can lead to alterations in the perceived meaning of war memorials. First, historical interpretations may remain the same but be enriched with new knowledge, and symbolic meaning in memorials is then enhanced. Second, historic events and interpretations of them change the course of history, and people reinterpret the dedicated meanings used in memorials for past wars. These new interpretations of history can be contradictory, and memorials are then seen as having conflicting meanings. Finally, certain wars and events are considered less important, and they are largely forgotten. As a result, meaning in their memorials fades away.

These three influences of history upon war memorials are not altogether independent, because people can simultaneously enhance, reinterpret, and forget various facets of war history. People will neither hold the same interpretations of history nor will they share the same combinations of meaning for war memorials. Personal bias comes into play regarding what actual history is and what should be remembered and commemorated. Multiple messages in war memorials are unavoidable for they serve a variety of audiences who interpret history differently. Such pluralism may seem democratic, but it can create serious conflicts in remembrance, particularly for sacred memorials. People can accept and may even want a suspension of the truth in the nonsacred, but sacred meaning is expected to represent truth. Knowing actual war history is realizing the truth. When people lack knowledge or disagree over true history, it is difficult to commemorate the past. They may be sincere in their desires to remember past wars, but their assumptions and understanding of history can make commemoration inauthentic.

When historical studies continue to demonstrate that a nation's cause was just, war memorials can be enhanced in their meaning. In the case of the American Revolution, the most famous historic sites were declared national monuments. Further historic aspects of this war were documented, and as a result, many other sites have been saved and marked. Collectively, all these memorials add an aesthetic richness to historic meaning that enhances the righteousness of the American Revolution. Even Civil War memorials, both northern and southern, are place documentaries that make Americans realize that the nation experienced a transformation in its beliefs about basic human rights, from the right to own slaves to personal freedom for all. Many Civil War memorials simultaneously articulate and enhance this change. Some monuments are enhanced by being recommemorated to the continued willingness of Americans to fight for their country. Both the Tomb of the Unknown Soldier in Arlington National Cemetery and the famous Marine Corps War Memorial of the flag-raising at Iwo Jima are monuments that are now recommemorated after every war. These memorials reinforce historical beliefs that the United States is a just nation regardless of a particular war's cause. Enhanced beliefs in the nation may not always be congruent with historic facts. War memorials can enhance memory, either through the historic belief in the nation or through verified history. But enhancement is most meaningful when war memorials and documented history both declare the same beliefs and deeds.

The meaning of a war memorial can change as a later war forces its reinterpretation. Many World War I memorials have lost their meaning due to the war's perceived role in history. In the 1920s and part of the 1930s, it was popularly called and thought to be "the war to end all wars" or "The" Great War. These public labels of finality made it difficult for any World War I monuments and ceremonies to have a different meaning even if the labels were not used in inscriptions and rituals. Some designers tried to include the value of perpetual peace in these memorials, a value they could not reinforce in real life.[17] World War II devastated the symbolism intended or placed upon these commemorations. They became commemorative anomalies to bygone beliefs. In time, a number of these memorials have added a public service or have been newly identified as part of an urban renewal area. They have become resymbolized. Hubbard says: "Monuments tell us that the moment we become unwilling to do the actions that an idea entails, at that moment the idea dies: It becomes a 'form,' a thing to be paid lip service, or a target of cynicism."[18]

The meaning in a war memorial is often reinterpreted when historians change their interpretations of the true nature of historical events. History attempts to give us the facts, but like other fields of knowledge, it is often positivistic—historians seek arguments for truths that fit their values and interests. Interpretations of history change as more facts are brought into account. When dedicating a memorial, people make honest attempts to commemorate historical accounts of war. Military leaders can be glorified, and a nation's reasons for entering war may be justified. In time, the actual worth of these leaders may be seen to be significantly less than the honor bestowed upon them. More critically, a nation's purposes for declaring war can be questioned and ultimately found to be unjustified. When people reject previous interpretations of a war's history, they can easily take the next step and challenge the validity of meaning in memorials dedicated to that war.

War memorials lose the forcefulness of their meaning when past wars and events are forgotten. Rose Coombs's study on World War I memorials presents this dilemma in her book's title, *Before Endeavors Fade*.[19] Even when a nation cherishes the memory of a particular war, people and places are forgotten when their monuments are not preserved and honor rituals are no longer held. Coombs notes that after World War I, memorial markers disappeared when battlefields were reconverted into farms and bomb blast holes became fishing ponds.[20] The astute observer can connect these remaining remnants with war events, but disinterested passersby are now unaware of what they are seeing. These are shadow memorials, environmental shapes without monuments or periodic rituals to clarify their history. Memorials in a war may be preserved but ignored when that war is increasingly perceived as insignificant. The Spanish-American War was short-lived, but a number of memorials were dedicated to remember it. Yet, its importance is pale when compared to the issues fought over and the number of servicemen killed in the Civil War and World War II. Some events of a war and memorials to them may be forgotten while other monuments for the same war may sustain remembrance. But sometimes an entire war can be largely forgotten, and the commemorative meaning of memorials for that war fade away until they are only footnotes to a local historic guide.

WAR MEMORIALS AND SOCIETY

The appropriateness of war memorials is structured by societal expectations. People are not obliged to have war memorials; they want them. Yi-Fu Tuan, a geographer, tells us: "Experience as it occurs has immediacy, but no permanence; its value is ephemeral. . . . Artifacts are thrust into the world. They have the power to stabilize life, and sacred rituals reinforce them. Transient feelings and thoughts gain permanence and objectivity in things."[21] Because memorials endure as places and rituals, communities are consciously made to confront wars that are a part of their history.

The brutal fact that friends and neighbors fought, suffered, and were often killed brings forth genuine feelings of remorse and the need to remember them, if only modestly. War memorials may even be a necessity. In speaking of sacred sites, Christopher Alexander, an architectural theorist, pleads that: "People cannot maintain their spiritual roots and their connections to the past if the physical world they live in does not also sustain these roots."[22] More specifically, J. B. Jackson, a landscape historian, insightfully notes that the memorial is a reminder of promises made and of origins we are inclined to forget.[23] Public institutions initiate or lend support to these altruistic emotions. In time, nonsacred memorials follow and often feed upon this altruism as far as the public will allow. Yet, inhumanity in war, such as maltreatment in prison camps, does not support our value standards, and we avoid remembering them if possible. We are often shamed into commemorating these events.

The following chapters attempt to show how symbolism in war memorials is expressed and how these memorials fit into their spatial environments. Not all memorials are successful, and failures are often due to improper symbolism or inadequate definitions of purpose in the scene. Inadequate articulation is not always just an improper use of design decisions and techniques, because historical and political circumstances of war often determine what can and should be remembered.

Chapter Two attempts to demonstrate how sacred and nonsacred memorials have become part of everyday life and celebration in our communities and in the nation. It describes how many of these places in the landscape are unrecognized as war memorials yet still have the power to evoke war memory, however subliminal. These evocations often present conflicting messages because they frequently lack the clarity of history.

Chapters Three, Four, and Five explore how America's wars have been commemorated. The historic reasons for the United States entering war have been uneven. Sacred memorials may honor all those who fought equally, but not all American wars are equally honorable, nor was America always victorious. Chapter Three discusses America's "good" wars—the American Revolution and the world wars—in which victory was equated with justice. Chapter Four describes wars of national expansionism, justified or not. These Manifest Destiny wars—The War of 1812, the Mexican wars, American Indian wars, and the Spanish-American War—resulted in enormous gains in territory and power. Defeat has also been a part of the national experience. Chapter Five discusses three wars—the Civil War, Korea, and Vietnam—which, while interpretations may vary, are perceived as wars that the United States did not win. Although the Union was preserved, the southern Confederacy was defeated in the Civil War, and their loss is reflected in commemorations of that war. The Korean War was at best a stalemate and at worst no victory. The nation's longest war, Vietnam, resulted in the loss not only of a great many lives but also of a sense of national virtue. While there are common forms of sacred remembrance for all of America's wars, there are also unique forms of commemoration for each one. These differences reflect not only the historical context of the war itself, but also the development of the arts in this nation.

Chapter Six goes beyond discussions of honor for those who fought to examine commemoration for victims of war. U.S. war victims both have been commemorated (at Andersonville Prison) and forgotten (in Japanese-American internment camps). The United States can claim no special status, for it has mistreated prisoners and been involved in massacres, but the most important commemorations are beyond the American experience. There is no equivalent to the execution factories and other crimes against humanity carried out in Nazi Germany. It is important to be aware of these acts of inhumanity and how they have been remembered in order to understand the meaning those commemorations have for the living. While these lie outside the American experience, their lessons cross all national boundaries.

Chapter Seven presents a political critique of commemoration for the past and the future. The nation's wars are put into perspective according to how Americans have come to remember or to forget them. It is not only wars that have been forgotten. Some Americans who deserve to be commemorated have been systematically ignored. Humanitarian understanding of the past is discussed as an educational experience, as exemplified by Holocaust centers in the United States. War memorials are then seen as artifacts that can be critiqued through their own medium, art. In conclusion, questions are posed about the future of war and the resulting future of war memorials.

War memorials in the landscape are part of a nation's political history. How the past is commemorated through a country's war memorials mirrors what people want to remember, and lack of attention often reflects what they wish to forget. War memory as sacred remembrance typically enhances a nation's image; neglect defames it. In either case, memorials speak to a country's political history.

CHAPTER TWO

WAR MEMORIALS IN THE LANDSCAPE: EVOCATIONS OF HISTORY

PEOPLE ARE REMINDED OF WAR when a sight or event stimulates their memory. Seeing a war monument at the town square, for example, could evoke a personal memory, even if only for a brief moment. However, war memorials of whatever type are meant to cause more than accidental reverie. As J. B. Jackson has said: "A landscape without political history is a landscape without memory or forethought."[1] Whether a memorial is defined as sacred or nonsacred, it is intentionally designed to evoke war memories, often forcefully.

War memory and place are brought together with particular sentiments in particular settings. As shown in Figure 2.1, there are two basic social settings for war memorials, everyday life and celebration. Most people daily see some thing or some place that is either directly or indirectly related to past wars. On certain occasions, people escape the normal routine and celebrate particular war-related events. They may tour memorial sites, attend ritual events, or participate in them. In these circumstances, people may go to places and events where war memory is the primary theme or where the activity is warlike in character. Everyday life and celebration help to define socially how people can remember war, but sentiment, sacred and non-sacred, determines how war memory is appreciated and prescribed in physical settings.

Sacred space is usually associated with a public landscape. Everyday recognition of past war endeavors is provided in our communities through

Social Setting	Physical Setting	Sacred Sentiment	Nonsacred Sentiment
Everyday life	Home	Home as patriotism	Home as private collection
	Community buildings	Public institutions	Business establishments
	Signs	Public signs	Private signs
	Community open space	Public greens and cemeteries	War remains
Celebration	Museums	Public war museums and battlefields	Museums as commercial tourism
	Ritual sites	Public ceremonies	Synthetic dramas

Figure 2.1. War Memorials in the Landscape

public buildings, greens, and signs. Sacred space can also be created in the home by reserving a special place for mementos of loved ones who fought in a war. Sacred celebration more clearly focuses war memory in place. Battlefields, public war museums, and public ceremonies are all designed for audiences who want to commemorate past wars. The concept of honor for those who fought is required in all these places, if remembrance is to be sacred.

Nonsacred places are not designed to evoke authentic feelings of honor and recognition of past deeds. In everyday life they often belong to the world of private business establishments and signs associated with them. Memorials in the home can also be nonsacred. Private collections of war memorabilia are merely private interests. They may be collected without profit in mind, but they are not associated with honor. Not all nonsacred places are in the private sphere. Abandoned military sites and stored weapons are remains of past wars, but they are not forms of public recognition. Not all celebrations of war are sacred. At many commercial war museums war memory becomes entertainment for profit. People may also attend gun or war memorabilia shows, battle reenactments, and warlike sporting events. None of these nonsacred places and events honors the past, but they do give an identity to place which evokes memories of war history.

Whether memorials are sacred or not, they subtly permeate our lives and affect us more than we realize. A drive down Memorial Avenue, past Veterans Park, which has a World War I cannon in it; a stop by the county courthouse, which has a Civil War monument on its lawn; and a walk by the American Legion Hall where one meets an old schoolmate from Douglas MacArthur High School all represent experiences that help shape what we remember about past wars and influence how we want to express those memories symbolically in our communities. Just as in these everyday encounters with war memory, celebrations are taken for granted, because they are expected. No one is surprised when friends tell them about visiting a battlefield and nearby museums on their vacation. Everyone expects a parade on the Fourth of July, and most people are not too surprised to see announcements in the local newspaper for a gun show with war memorabilia, an air show with old war planes, or a battle reenactment at a nearby battlefield. All of these sacred and nonsacred memorials provide a set of reminders so constant that they are taken for granted.

HOME

Home as Patriotism

The home may seem an unlikely place for a war memorial, but people often have mementos, both serious and innocent, which give added symbolism to the household. Respect for people and commemoration of past history are values that are expressed at home.

Yard areas can be used for national celebration. Some people raise an American flag in the front yard on Memorial Day or the Fourth of July to celebrate the occasion. This display expresses patriotism and pride in those who fought for their country. It is a simple way to make sacred turf to commemorate past war endeavors. Some cynical passersby may be put off by what they view as "superpatriotism," while others may agree with its symbolism.

Inside the home, war commemoration can hold deep meaning. People often set aside a place in their home to remember loved ones who served or were killed in a war. The commemoration may be a photograph in a prominent place, such as the fireplace mantle, or it may be more complex, including displays of war citations. There may be the special drawer where military medals and citation certificates are carefully kept. These artifacts take little space but these precious places are memorial altars, and family members treat these miniature sanctuaries with great respect. Adding the inscription "In Remembrance" to these settings is not only unnecessary but also inappropriate, because families cannot help but remember. These places signify the great sacrifice that the family made, and the loss of a loved one can hardly be treated lightly.

During World War II, families brought symbolism into their homes by placing a gold star in a living room or kitchen window for every family member who went to the war. It was a sign of family sacrifice, a demonstration that they were "doing their share." The ritual is no longer practiced, but many families have replaced the star with a picture of their son or daughter in uniform in some prominent place within the home.

The home as war memorial can reflect a range of emotions. Flying the American flag is a patriotic gesture that the family can enjoy. In contrast, a Purple Heart medal for a family member killed in war represents a family tragedy. In both of these remembrances, however, there is pride in the past. The special places that families create, from the flagpole to the special drawer for military decorations, to the gold star in the window, are expressions that combine honor and patriotism.

Home as Personal Collection

The collection of war memorabilia, known as militaria, is not a commonly chosen hobby, but a few people maintain this selective interest in history. Some collectors may be nostalgic veterans, while others enjoy the collected objects themselves. But some romanticize the heroic past as an escape from the present. Collecting of any type disassociates the object from its historical place. It is withdrawal with personal control, a way for people to reconstitute their self-wholes. As Yi-Fu Tuan said:

Life that has grown too complex in the public sphere encourages people to withdraw. The problem is how to withdraw without withdrawing from life; how to nurture a sense of self without losing touch with other people all together; how to escape from the world and yet still be in the world—a world, however limited, of one's own design, or a world over which one has some control.[2]

Personal collections of war memorabilia allow collectors to express selected history by exerting their personal values. They remake themselves by creating this personal world. Tuan bemoans these acts as private compulsions which rob things and external events from much of their value, vitality, and objective standing.[3] History is reconstituted through war militaria, yet it is not really separate from the real world.

Displayed collections within the home are often altarlike assemblies.[4] While home altars have traditionally been religious in nature or have honored revered people,[5] a display of war militaria does not serve these purposes. It is a landscaped altar for a collector's unrestrained ego and feelings. However, collectors—especially collectors of Nazi militaria—are sensitive to outsiders who criticize their hobby. They are selective about whom they allow to see their artifacts in order to protect their personalized world from attack. The collector's display of artifacts is an altar for personal enjoyment and identity, but if it is likely to be criticized by outsiders, it is a protected haven shared only with friends and other collectors.

Militaria hobbyists who collect enemy memorabilia are often criticized for keeping alive the spirit of inhumane political ideologies. In the past,

2.1 Home as Personal Collection of War Militaria (Author's Collection)

designed displays have given credence to political ideology, legitimate or not.[6] Quite simply, some people believe that a person who owns Nazi militaria may be a Nazi or may be oblivious to the past wrongdoings of the Nazis. But these hobbyists vehemently claim that their collections are for entertainment and investment and not for the promotion of inhumane values. As one collector wrote: "It is the fashion in certain quarters nowadays to decry all interest in things military, as though collecting badges, buttons, or firearms will bring forth a race of homicidal maniacs. I disagree."[7] Militaria collectors separate the artifacts from their history. They see evil done in the past as finished, and feel that evil history has no influence on collecting. Collectors typically are quite aware of war history beyond their hobby, and they do not approve of war crimes by any nation. Critics of these collections do not separate the history from the artifacts, and as a result of this, collectors and their critics keep divergent paths.

Others may not collect artifacts but rather further their interest in war history by collecting books about specific or general aspects of war. Certain shelves in their bookcases may be reserved for books on fighter planes, warships, some specific war, or a combination of war-related subjects. While actual artifacts, such as medals and guns, may be seen as an unusual hobby, book collections do not carry the same stigma. The more these books are perceived as intellectual excursions of self-interest, the more legitimate the collection becomes to outsiders. Such books keep alive the memory of war without disassociating it from the present.

COMMUNITY BUILDINGS

Public Institutions

Few public institutions are designated strictly as war monuments, but some structures have a recognized secondary identity as memorials. Since people want an economical way to commemorate past wars, they may use an inscription or other symbolic overlay to create a public war memorial and still balance the city budget. Public buildings can be designated as memorials in a variety of ways, such as naming a school after a military leader or putting up a plaque in the courthouse for soldiers who died in battle. In some communities, veterans have instigated public bond issues to raise funds for public facilities to remember dead comrades. Especially after World War I, veterans used bond issues to build civic auditoriums, popularly known as soldiers and sailors memorial halls. These buildings may have a commemorative title, but more often they have memorial plaques. Some are more opulent than others, with statues and small museums to honor veterans.

Many colleges and universities have memorials dedicated to students who died in previous wars. Some campuses have statues, campaniles, chapels, plaques, and marble monoliths to commemorate their dead. Memorial student centers, however, are the most common form of remembrance. These buildings typically display a dedication plaque, and the word "memorial" is usually part of the center's name. However, most students are indifferent to the memorials and identify them with university tradition rather than with war. At armed forces academies and other colleges with a military orientation, these memorials are more closely identified with their symbolic meaning.

The federal government also has local facilities that have been dedicated as war memorials. National guard armories, for example, are dedicated to "dogface" soldiers—privates, corporals, and sergeants who distinguished themselves in battle. A plaque within the installation describes the soldier's wartime deeds. Reserve centers also may have war surplus tanks, artillery, or aircraft on the building's front lawn. These artifacts convey the soldier's message: "We stand ready to defend our country as we have in the past."

Some communities have veterans' hospitals, which are functional memorials to past deeds. Some veterans may be recuperating from war injuries, while others use their veteran benefits to treat an illness that developed during civilian life. Some of these hospitals have displays that easily identify them as a memorial. In the Audie Murphy Memorial Veterans' Administration Hospital at San Antonio, Texas, a room has been

2.2 World War I Soldiers and Sailors Memorial Hall, Kansas City, Kansas (Author's Collection)

set aside as a shrine to commemorate the heroic deeds of Lieutenant Audie Murphy. His medals, uniforms, and weapons are all displayed. The room is not merely a museum. It honors heroism and human sacrifice. It indirectly legitimizes the hospital's function to serve the sick and wounded of past wars. Society has an obligation to care for the wounds of those who defend it.

Buildings owned by veterans' organizations are also prominent forms of quasi-public memorials. Local posts of the American Legion and Veterans of Foreign Wars raise funds to build local facilities. In recent times, their buildings have tended to be modest in cost and design, with a sign or letters on the structure identifying the veterans' group and displaying the American flag. These posts are typically located where real estate costs are low since their membership is usually drawn from the common people. Although these organizations' buildings are typically modest, these facilities represent renewed memory of past wars. Membership in these organizations is replenished with every additional war or military conflict. New members keep the posts active, and new or renovated meeting halls keep alive the memory of service to the country without singling out any specific war.

Business Establishments

Private businesses are memorials when their merchandise and services are related to war. Like any other business, the motive of these enterprises is self-serving. There is generally no specific intent to evoke remembrance. Rather, they offer goods for sale that were coincidentally related to war efforts. Many people shop in Army and Navy surplus stores, for a variety of reasons. In past days many Boy Scouts bought their first backpack at such places, and children once supplemented their toy weapons with military paraphernalia from these stores. Some people still purchase soldier goods, but most of the actual goods used in war gradually disappear. When businesses cannot sell actual war goods, they provide substitutes to meet customer demands.

People have mixed feelings about such shops and about stores that offer war toys and games. Some parents feel that war is trivialized when children are allowed to play with combat toys. They think that G.I. Joe dolls and their accessories make war seem acceptable, and that toy planes, boats, and tanks legitimize war as a part of play in children's formative years. Other parents think that such toys are harmless, because they do not believe that children's play is connected with the reality of war and its consequences. Such families allow their children to play at war or have war-related hobbies. These toy stores offer items for older children as well, such as intricate models of weapons and board games like Battleship. Model shops offer teenagers and adults radio-controlled airplanes and boats to create more realistically battle scenes as a hobby. Home video games and video arcades allow them to play at being a fighter pilot or a submarine captain.

Parents often reinforce their own feelngs about war when they allow or disallow their children to buy war toys or to play war games.

The most sophisticated toys deal with war strategy and pseudo-realism. Specialty shops offer adult games of tactics, such as The Battle of Britain and The Battle of the Bulge. These games make war an intellectual battle much like chess. Plastic game pieces shaped like tanks and planes are equivalent to rooks and knights, and there is no death when one player defeats another. The ultimate toys of war are those which emulate real weapons. Some shops offer model gun kits that are exact replicas, except they do not fire. Such model making puts the hobbyist on the brink of having the real thing. In all these reconstructions of war, people convert war into play, and the horror of war is ignored. People want shops that specialize in war-related toys so they can create their own fantasies about war.

In some cities, there are shops which not only sell model warplanes and ships but also original medals and decorative weapons used during previous wars. Collectors of this type of war memorabilia call these items militaria, and these shops serve militaria collectors much like stores that specialize in coins or stamps. They also sell militaria books which describe the various artifacts, and shop owners are expected to be resident experts about war militaria. Customers depend upon the owner's knowledge to help them develop their collections. These shops typically offer militaria from both

2.3 The King's Crown, War Militaria Shop in Overland Park, Kansas (Author's Collection)

friend and foe, and some people do not understand how dealers and collectors willingly involve themselves in the buying and selling of enemy militaria, especially Nazi militaria. But buyers and collectors treat the historical origins of their goods much like stamp and coin collectors treat their materials. Militaria shops sustain the memory of past wars by enabling people to purchase artifacts, such as medals and edged weapons, that symbolize the military jewels of nations that once engaged in war.

Local souvenir shops can sell war-related objects without specializing in these goods. In the Ozark Mountains in Arkansas, it is common to see souvenir shops selling indigenous minerals and local craft goods, along with other commercial items associated with nearby recreation. Beach towels imprinted with a Confederate flag or a pot-bellied Confederate soldier saying "Forget Hell" make us aware of a regional allegiance to a bygone war. More acceptable to the public are bookstores that have sections dealing with military history. While many books are authentic accounts of history, most popular books about war are fictitious or are only picture books which give encyclopedic descriptions of weaponry and events. None of these items usually dominate a shop's merchandise, but they do remind us that people are interested in war and want to be able to buy these products.

Some businesses provide war-related entertainment. Theaters which periodically have war movies enable the public to see semi-true and fictional accounts of war. Billboard posters under glass are provided to attract customers, but war movie fans need no enticements. Movies enable people to experience war as an adventure without the threat of death.

Even restaurants may use war as a decorative theme. The 94th Aero Squadron Restaurant in Torrance, California, recreates a World War I pilot's quarters near the front. The restaurant is modeled after a French farmhouse which was supposedly used by an American squadron. Outside, there is a World War I biplane along with old wagons, a vintage truck, and a cannon. Its location near an airport further associates it with flying, and amid the roar of propellers customers can imagine that they have gone back in time. The farmhouse is rustic stone with a bunker-styled entrance way. Inside, old war memorabilia hang on the walls, and a fireplace with a mantle of mugs recreates the scene as it might have been. Vintage weapons decorate the bar to evoke the feeling of being near the battlefront. Photographs of actual war scenes can be seen, but the decor recreates superficially the daily life of fighter pilots. If people prefer to dine outdoors, diners can eat and drink on a patio delineated by a sandbag bunker wall and a barbed wire fence.[8] Places such as this treat war as fun, a night on the town. The filth of war is not part of these scenes since health codes and consumer expectations will not allow it. The pleasures of peace are intermingled with the images of war without distinguishing between them. War is misrepresented as a nostalgic spectacle.[9]

2.4 94th Aero Squadron Restaurant, Torrance, California (Author's Collection)

Like any other enterprise, businesses that use war in their goods and services operate on a demand basis. From time to time people seek the novelty of war as a distraction from everyday life. Some people may make it such a regular part of their lives that it becomes a fetish. But most people accept these businesses as curiosities or "theme" businesses. It is easy to criticize sellers of war goods and services, but it is the general public that makes them possible. People realize that such places are not involved in real war, and what is more revealing is that they typically enjoy the fantasy without the pain.

SIGNS

Public Signs

Signs guide us through the built landscape, and many signs convey messages about war. Public street signs can evoke past battles and heroes while business signs may use war to promote products and services. Most passersby take signs for granted, because they are connections to places rather than destinations. Yet, travelers are constantly confronted with signs which arouse latent memories. People are intent on where they are going, but the experience of seeing signs is part of remembering what was passed during the journey. The use of war references in signs gives an added dimension to travel, but it is an experience that is easy to overlook.[10]

Street names are labels of war history that people often take for granted. They are inconspicuous war memorials, but their territorial coverage is often greater than we imagine. It is ridiculous to think of a street-corner sign as a glorious war memorial. On the other hand, knowing that you are on Bunker Hill Avenue quietly reinforces the legitimacy of your nation. It certainly has a stronger message than Third Street. Among the many streets we pass, some remind us of warriors, battles, and regional allegiance. Grant Avenue and Lee Street herald soldiers regardless of allegiance. Valley Forge Lane and Ft. Sumter Drive never let us forget that soldiers died for us.

Streets dedicated to a war may be added as a city physically expands. Since Alexandria, Virginia, is a southern city, people might imagine that its major streets would be named mainly after soldiers and battles from the Civil War. Most of its downtown streets, however, are named after revolutionary heroes and even English royalty who lived before America's independence. Newer streets in Alexandria have commemorated the Civil War and match what we would expect to find. American cities have spread out over time, and newer streets in areas farther out are sometimes named after people and events of later wars.

Nearby conflicts often provide the inspiration for street names. In Texas it is common to find streets named Alamo, San Jacinto, Bowie, Houston, and Crockett, yet in Chicago such street names would be unusual. The city councils who name streets are not historians, but they often draw from well-known local history in naming public improvements.

Military installations embellish their traditions with streets named after famous soldiers and battles. While visitors know many of these names, there are some that will be unfamiliar. Military bases can specialize meaning for specific traditions. Fort Riley, Kansas, is a cavalry post, and many of its street names come from cavalry history. The use of particular warrior's names and battle names symbolically legitimizes the cavalry. These bases are infrequently visited and so these memorials may go unnoticed by the public,[11] but they do carry on tradition to the new generation of soldiers.

Highway dedications can be memorials. Signs that commemorate military organizations, such as Disabled American Veterans Memorial Highway and Blue Star Highway, are subtle reminders that Americans fought in our two world wars. The road dedication may seem nondescript and incidental, but it is an overlaid symbol. People may travel on a memorial highway only once or many times, and the lingering memory can seem unimportant but the subtle message is: We fought for our country. Remember us on your journey.

Rural communities often have a town sign to welcome visitors, and sometimes it includes official seals from veterans organizations. Welcome to our community signs often include an attached seal from the local chapter of the American Legion. Less often the seal of the Veterans of Foreign Wars may be displayed. The implied message is the same, that these groups are dedicated to the memory of U.S. soldiers and their efforts, and that they are part of the foundation of the community and its values. Obviously, these signs are small, unlike billboards which advertise products, but the message of community dignity is always present and most unlikely to change unless the sign becomes dilapidated.

Explicit war histories can be depicted in public signage, and history may be noted simply by a highway memorial plaque. A sign designating the Cherokee Trail of Tears can make one empathize with the Cherokees who suffered, and additional signs further encourage one to follow the path of their suffering. But such immediate emotions are those of the tourist and not of the resident. Passing the sign again and again makes the resident immune to the emotion of such remembrances. The sign loses its effectiveness and becomes just another message on the road amidst the many others.

Highway signs designating war-related historical events may be rituals in themselves. Anyone traveling on interstate highways has seen signs depicting local history at the rest stops. Many times the messages describe nearby battlefields or skirmishes. These signs are usually provided by the state, and the quality of design and construction imply that these signs are permanent and stalwart reminders of actual history versus promoted folklore.[12] Recognizing the implied importance of these signs, visitors pause to read them and to reflect for a moment on the heritage of their forefathers and how they fought to preserve the American way of life. These signs are often small lessons in American war history. Public support of signage creates a legitimate image of a war event unless popular understanding is to the contrary. When one highway sign and reading ritual follows another, we accept these messages as a matter of course, a linear one at that.

Business Signs

Businesses use war memory in their signs as a means to establish identity with their customers. Certain sections of the country are associated with particular wars and battles. As a result, area shops can attempt to capitalize on war memory to give their businesses a unique identity. An Alamo Motel in a Texas city is a more enticing name than Travelers Motel in attracting potential customers. Such practices enable businesses to demonstrate local pride in history.

Business signs keep alive memories of war by using historical language directly related to past conflicts. In the South, certain words have both regional. To many northerners the term evokes memory of the Civil War. Dixie depends on the viewer's place of origin. To many southerners, the word Dixie is another way to say "the South," but this meaning is largely regional. To many northerners the term evokes memory of the Civil War.

"Dixie" has developed more negative connotations than "the South"; it is meaner.[13] Labeling can be more specific, such as the Confederate Motel. History and value commitment is explicit in the label but there is no additional commentary presented to the visitor.

Sculpture can advertise a commercial scene. In northwest Arkansas there is a restaurant called The 1941 Cafe, named after the comical movie, *1941*, and its sign was built to look like the tail of a downed Japanese fighter plane. Unless one is familiar with the movie, a passerby may conclude that the sign is a form of prejudice against the Japanese. While intended to be only a satirical extension of the movie's theme to promote a cafe and bar, the sign evokes multiple and potentially contradictory messages which are not clear. About such signs, Lowenthal has said: "Instead of rescuing history from obscurity, such markers drown it in trivia."[14]

Commercial signs can be designated to establish a symbolic connection to existing war memorials. In Georgia, the Ft. Oglethorpe State Bank uses a symmetrical stack of cannonballs as its logo. Within the Chickamauga-Chatanooga Military Park, war memorials composed of cannonball stacks, known as mortuary markers, identify where Confederate and Union commanders were killed during the battle. The bank's logo is a subtle but sophisticated attempt to recognize local history without taking sides, South or North.

Promotional signs can be directly related to businesses that use war as part of their enterprise. Outside of Gettysburg, Pennsylvania, a billboard advertises a Civil War wax museum. The billboard's claim that it is the town's number one attraction ignores the legitimate importance of the battlefield that generates the museum's business. On the other hand, the billboard portrays the battle as an important event without partisan symbolism.

Sign messages are not always neutral. In the South, the war is subtly still fought. A billboard in Arkansas attempting to attract tourists says: Yankees Never Did Find Civil War Cave. Such a message conveys that some soldiers were not defeated, and some southerners may still wish to express some recognition of victory amidst defeat. Most people just bypass such enterprises, and the sign's message becomes the reality rather than the war site itself.

COMMUNITY OPEN SPACE

Public Greens

Parks, lawns to public buildings, boulevard strips, and traffic circles are often used as settings for war memorials. While people want these spaces as a relief from buildings and pavement, they also enjoy giving these places a

2.5 1941 Cafe Sign as a Satirical Image from the Second World War in Northwestern Arkansas (Author's Collection)

theme, and war memorials can fulfill that purpose. In some cases, townspeople search for a place to construct their monuments, and public greens offer common ground without territorial conflict. Public greens offer not only location but also public ownership of memorials, and the result is that townspeople can expect their monuments to be maintained. In the end public greens are convenient and preferred locations for war memorials.

Upon entering a public park, you may cross the threshold of a war memorial because of the park's name. Pershing Park tells us that this space is dedicated to a famous general, and in some instances, a statue or descriptive marker to that person may be present. A cannon may evoke memory of a past war. Naming a park can provide a simple, inexpensive memorial. Veterans Park is a generic name, but it is a constant, subtle reminder of the legitimacy of being a soldier, regardless of the legitimacy of any one war. Dedicating a park as a war memorial is a straightforward way to set aside place and time to commemorate the past, and monuments and weapons are embellishments to that purpose.

Many U.S. courthouses are surrounded by green space as well as being centrally located in downtown areas. In other cases courthouses are fronted by a formal public square that is treated as an extension of these local seats of government. A variety of war memorials can be found on courthouse lawns. In Cadiz, Kentucky, a drinking fountain commemorating the Confederate dead is available for public use, and in Tarboro, North Carolina, there is a Civil War memorial bell.[15] On the mall behind the public library in Cleveland, Ohio, a memorial flower garden is kept to remember those who served and those who died in past American wars. Such memorials are rare. Obelisks and cannons are more common, but the dominant form of memorial is the statue. In many northern communities, a statue of a Union soldier commemorates the local citizens who died in the Civil War. His counterpart, the Confederate soldier, is often found in southern towns. The general message is that we should remember these soldiers, and in the South one sometimes sees the inscription LEST WE FORGET.[16] Memorials to more recent wars can be found, and they seem to purport the same message. Courthouse lawn memorials are often large, but more importantly, they represent a significant financial contribution in one of the town's most conspicuous public areas. It may be the only significant art object in the community.

The notion of community commemoration in public greens, however, is not limited to a whole town or city, because communities exist within cities. For example, in Pittsburgh, Pennsylvania, parks in six of its political wards have monuments to commemorate local men and women who died in either World War I or II. At an even smaller scale, some neighborhood high schools and churches have memorials on their lawns to remember their own who fought and died.[17] Art is not exalted for the sake of art in these communities and neighborhoods, and war memorials provide the critical incentive for symbolic display of local identity. For better or worse, community support for building war memorial sculptures is not as prevalent as in the past. Memorial plaques are less expensive, and dedicated buildings fulfill practical needs. In more recent times, communities acknowledge a war sacrifice, but they are less able to afford a monument big enough to display on a public lawn.

Street boulevards often have landscaped median strips. These medians often contain sculpture, flower gardens, and memorials from various wars. There may be one monument or many within a boulevard's median. One of the better known boulevards is Monument Avenue in Richmond, Virginia. Monument Avenue is a symbolic parade of the most remembered men of the Confederacy, with big, elegant monuments to Matthew Maury, J. E. B. Stuart, Stonewall Jackson, Jefferson Davis, and Robert E. Lee.[18] The median can be a linear legacy of a past war or even a continuous tribute to a succession of wars.

In Washington, D.C., a number of traffic circles contain war memorials. Statues of generals Washington, Scott, Logan, Sheridan, and Thomas ride horseback above the traffic.[19] Although no longer popular as traffic separators, circles do provide a focal point and a geographic marker to passersby. These small but prominent greens are most often used for immortalizing significant soldiers and statesmen. While there is no apparent symbolic reason, there is a practical one. Portrayals of individuals are easier to assimilate in the rapid movement of a traffic circle than portrayals of, for example, an army division. Smaller towns, where traffic is light, may sometimes use these circles for a collective memorial. Traffic circles are no longer built as often as in the past, but those that still exist often provide a brief moment of remembrance for the traveler.

Cemeteries

Cemeteries are unavoidable public landscapes of death. Communities spatially isolate death from our daily lives by controlling the number of cemeteries that can be built. Inside the cemetery death becomes reality, and there is no sense of the normal life of the community. Large monuments reflect personal wealth, while the repetitious epitaphs and repeated gravestone designs marking a community's war dead evoke a collective identification and awareness of the community's sacrifice. The unavoidable visual counting of gravestones in the cemetery landscape makes it clear that death in war was transported to the community.

The collective power of the war dead is pervasive in a cemetery, because many veteran graves are interspersed with other dead. Walking about a cemetery, there are random encounters with military gravestones. Graves near one another are generally from the same time period, and in passing from one era to another the visitor is sure to see a marker for a soldier of

2.6 Robert E. Lee Memorial on Monument Avenue, Richmond, Virginia (Author's Collection)

that time. Other people may have been more or less important than the soldier, but their personal histories are unknown to the visitor. But a gravestone for a soldier from World War II has meaning even to the stranger. It even may be possible to imagine some of the hardships the soldier had to face.[20] What becomes clear when walking by war gravestones is the inability to escape their presence. They are everywhere, and it is easy to find them without even searching.

War memorials for specific wars can be found in cemeteries, and these ensembles of artifacts can have great collective power. Quite often soldiers are buried in some symmetrical fashion around a memorial, as if to say: "United we stood, united we rest. Remember what we did to preserve your way of life." Such ensembles can be small, but as the war graves are more numerous, the memorial arrangement becomes more powerful. Yet, as we forget a past war, the ensemble can become remembered as an interesting design in itself, placing little emphasis on its original meaning.

Cemetery plots may not be devoted to a single war but to wars in general. Such veteran plots within cemeteries are similar to one aspect of Arlington's Tomb of the Unknown Soldier. The buried are known, but as a new war passes new dead are interred to the designated hallowed ground. In this way, veterans who are perceived to have fought in an unjust war can be seen as honorable by being buried alongside others who fought in wars that were seen as just endeavors. In recent years veterans' groups have adopted the use of an eternal flame for their plots and memorials. The flame symbolizes a living memory for an honored past regardless of the war's legitimacy.

National cemeteries exist in or by some American communities. Their grounds are so immaculate that the lawns often appear to have been permanently purified against weeds. The design of these cemeteries is simple. Typically, there is a formal gate with an office nearby, and in some cases, a memorial chapel for funeral services has been built. The pervading impression, however, is the neat alignment of Christian crosses that are often interspersed with Star of David markers for Jewish dead. The uniform repetition of grave markers upon an immaculate turf creates a landscape in which "God and country" is made manifest. While some of the graves are immediate kin of veterans or war dead, visitors do not make this distinction. Rather, people feel that they are upon a sanctified field of honor which makes them pause to think: Because of their sacrifice, I am able to be a free American. Yet, the impression can be altered for some when they see the marker of a soldier who died in an unpopular war, such as Vietnam. Nonetheless, the unified visual message of a national cemetery can be forceful, and the message is patriotism.

The reification of war memories is likely to continue in community and national cemeteries, and the reason is practical rather than symbolic. The government offers to fund the gravestone of a war veteran. Without disrespect, relatives may feel the need to reduce funeral costs, and this is one way to do so. On the other hand, some veterans specifically wish to be identified with their war contribution.

The mark of veteranship is disproportionately displayed in our local and national cemeteries. Most people isolate cemeteries from their daily life, and such war memorials are those that people wish to avoid. A statue in a park represents patriotism, but a grave is a resounding reminder of the consequences of war, whether or not the buried soldier actually died in battle.

War Remains

When a war is over, the collective remains of weaponry and temporary military installations can be extensive. During the war, factories convert production to equipment, and temporary and permanent buildings are constructed to meet immediate needs. War is work in these places, and workers pull together in a singular effort to help gain a victory. When peace ultimately comes, many factories are converted into peace-time businesses, and military bases drastically reduce their activity or shut down altogether. Moreover, when the soldiers come home so does their weaponry, which is stored, scrapped, or sold, and war equipment may be stored on new sites not used during the war. The shift from war to peace often creates a shift in how war remains are used in the landscape.

For those people who fought or worked on the homefront, the remaining landscape of war at home is the visible remains of a chapter of their lives. War at home had a place, and passing by or visiting these sites stirs memories and provokes curiosity in those too young to remember the war. In time, however, these places slowly deteriorate or lose their war-related artifacts, and memory usually fades except for local accounts of historical interest.

Military storage yards provide one of the most dramatic scenes immediately following a war. After World War II, Rattlesnake Air Base at Pyote, Texas, was used as a holding place for B-29 bombers from the war in the Pacific. This collective air fleet was an imposing sight. Driving by the base, visitors could see row after row and column after column of B-29 air fortresses; it was a concentration of power. The bombers were in excellent shape and war markings for units, bombing runs, and bomber label art were still present. Yet, one knew that this magnificent sight represented the finality of the past rather than any portrayal of the future. It symbolized the disarmed potential for power, and in time, the bombers were scrapped or sold. The massive, dramatic scene of the bombers against the dry, serene landscape of west Texas is only made more ironic when one considers the destruction and loss of life it represented in a war that occurred thousands of miles away. Other such storage yards existed for less glamorous artifacts, such as tanks and jeeps, but the huge size of the bombers provided a significant presence, individually and collectively, which other weapons could not match. The Second World War was still a recent memory, and people felt a certain patriotic pride in these places and even sorrow that they must ultimately be dismantled. Nonetheless, these weaponscapes were nonsacred, because they only brought forth memories of war, not honor.

Weapon yards can be permanent institutions. On the outskirts of Tucson, Arizona, is the largest collection of used aircraft in the world, commonly known as the "boneyard."[21] David-Monthan Base contains thousands of retired aircraft of all vintages. Many of them were not used in war, but in

2.7 B-29 Bomber War Remains after World War II, Pyote, Texas (Courtesy of Ward County Historical Commission)

some sections, remains from the Vietnam War are still present. Some of the olive drab planes in the area containing B-52 bombers dropped tons of bombs in North Vietnam. Lined up symmetrically, they give visitors the feeling of an untended graveyard where the aircraft are both the dead and the grave marker. Located in Arizona because of its arid climate, the aircraft are embalmed with a vinyl coating for further protection.[22] Their parts have been salvaged for other aircraft in use, leaving the feeling that these graves have been systematically ransacked. Yet, such feelings are inauthentic. Planes are not people, and honor is not being defamed since commemoration is not part of the scene.

War remains for the U.S. Navy often reflect the means for war construction rather than the product of it. At the Charleston Navy Yard in Boston, Massachusetts, visitors mainly come to see historic ships that have been preserved, but nearby is a deserted manmade canyon. It is a drydock which was used to repair ships. Looking into its depths, one can imagine a huge ship being worked on by hundreds of workers. It symbolizes the labor of war without the threat of death. There is neither beauty nor sacredness here. Rather, visitors capture a sense of the enormous scale of production needed to engage in war.

Perhaps the most common remains are abandoned military bases. Old barracks and headquarters may remain, but what can be counted on are old foundations as well as runways at air bases. On current military bases, many barracks remain empty most of the year, but during World War II, the buildings and their exterior sites were spic and span and full of new recruits. Although these places were beehives of activity during the war, people now tend to overlook the importance of these sites. Such places convey a history of function rather than honor, although other parts of a base may contain monuments and even museums to reflect place history.

An often forgotten landscape is the remains of prisoner of war camps. Wire fences, building foundations, and remaining observation towers provide reminders of the war on the homefront. Little if any effort is made to preserve these sites, however. These camps were storage yards of people, and Americans who best remember these places associate them with German prisoners during the Second World War. Most of these sites were never expected to be permanent, and salvaging materials as well as time itself has reduced these camps to minimal reminders. Even when a camp was made of sturdy materials, neglect is still the status quo. Some camps are bitter reminders that Japanese-American citizens were unjustly interred as potential military threats. Their camp remains are not significantly different from those for former German camps, although some memorials have since been added. In the end, victors do not have an honorable image of prison sites, and they do not find it comfortable to remember them. While such places should be remembered, especially in cases of inhumanity, most U.S. prison sites mainly remain desolate landscapes of a forgotten past.

When war is over, many war remains are converted to other uses. Sometimes old barrack buildings were moved into communities and converted into school buildings or warehouses. Even weapons parts have been used. For a time, B-29 bombers' nose shells were used by some people as greenhouses or storage sheds in the poorer sections of town.[23] Not all war remains are stationary. In a rare instance, people can see a restored army jeep driving down the road or sitting in a used car lot. Some businesses even specialize in selling old military equipment, and it is still possible to see an equipment yard full of trucks, jeeps, and trailers from past wars. Yet, time takes its toll on mobile equipment, and car junkyards sometimes have an old war vehicle waiting for a restorer enthusiast to buy and rebuild it. Those who recognize all these types of war remains see how war objects are transformed into daily life, but this refitting of objects is usually apparent. These objects were designed to fit the specific needs of war, not the contextual character of a local townscape.

Public parks and playgrounds may not be named as war memorials, but they sometimes contain war artifacts. Many small American towns have a cannon from a previous war in the park, and some playgrounds in cities have war surplus aircraft which serve as jungle gyms. Many children find these old weapons irresistible. Sitting at a gun turret or in the cockpit of a B-25 bomber allows them to play at war. It is easy to imagine them proclaiming "a fighter at twelve o'clock high" or "bombs away." Playing with war weapons is one subtle way for children to shape their thinking about war.

Whether war remains are set temporarily or permanently in the landscape, they evoke an unjustified nostalgia. Planes, tanks, cannons, and other weapons have unique forms, and they may elicit feelings of excitement. What is missing, however, is the pain and death which surrounded these objects. War remains can survive wars, but their users often did not. We can imagine glory when seeing a B-25 bomber, but it is easy to forget that a crew member may have bled to death from bullet wounds, especially when the bullet holes on the plane's hull have been mended. War remains provide reminders and even unusual scenes in the landscape, but there is no sacredness in these artifacts. All war remains, weapons or not, are the dismantled means for conducting war.

MUSEUMS

Public War Museums

Some of the most identifiable buildings associated with war are public museums. War may be a museum's major focus or it may only be a minor part of the museum, but visitors expect public museums to present coordinated, accurate collections that record history, preserve objects, and further education.[24] People trust that museum exhibits will be legitimate portrayals of history, because the museum serves the public interest rather than itself.

The basic theme addressed by war museums involves recognition of those who fought in wars. Warriors are remembered for heroic deeds, and specific battles are portrayed chronologically. More often than not, weaponry and uniforms are displayed to account for war's material history. Displays are organized sequentially so visitors can follow a trail of exhibits that explains what they are seeing. Some institutions place more emphasis on honoring warriors, some are more concerned with weaponry and uniforms, and still others stress local historic battles. In general, though, museums tend to specialize so as not to duplicate exhibits at nearby institutions.

Public war museums must honor those who fought. Displays related to peace may be present, but humanitarian messages have more to do with future hope than with the historic realities of war. The ideal of honor, however, varies according to whom is being remembered and what is displayed. Honor is for people, not weapons, and as an ideal, it is distributed unevenly in war museum displays. Museums for warriors and battle events are expressions of honor while weapon and uniform museums can only allude to this ideal.

Warrior museums enable the public to come closer to people who had a role in history. Learning about the lives of military heroes or a military service branch helps visitors have a stronger grasp of who these people were. Hero museums focus even more sharply on individuals. A person's individual history is unique, and people are fascinated with heroes, especially if they have read many biographical histories. The most complete hero museums have been developed in recent history, and the best known are for General George Patton at Fort Knox, Kentucky; Admiral Chester Nimitz in Fredericksburg, Texas; General Douglas MacArthur's Memorial Museum in Newport News, Virginia; and Dwight D. Eisenhower's Presidential Museum in Abilene, Kansas.

While all these institutions vary in size and content, some common themes pervade all of them. Visitors watch a progressive story of the hero's life unfold through exhibits of boyhood possessions, uniforms and some weapons, pictorial portrayals of personal history, and image symbols. Personal artifacts are arranged in displays, and inscriptions describe the roles of these personal artifacts in the hero's life.

Boyhood possessions attempt to suggest cultural roots. At the George Patton museum, people can see the toy sword Patton made as a boy. A baby high chair, on the other hand, is a central artifact in describing the life of Nimitz. The Nimitz museum itself is the old Steamboat Hotel where he was raised. Most of MacArthur's childhood artifacts were destroyed or lost in Manila during World War II, but a silver baby cup remains to acknowledge his early life. Eisenhower's boyhood home has been restored, and people catch a glimpse of his humble midwestern beginnings. In the museum, visitors see his snow sled and high school mementos. These boyhood displays remind visitors that like most Americans of their era, these men had modest beginnings.

All of these museums exhibit uniforms and weaponry in varying amounts. For Patton and Eisenhower, West Point uniforms are displayed to illustrate the formative years of their military careers, while a Naval Academy uniform can be seen for Nimitz. The only memento for MacArthur is a West Point robe that he wore often but which only became his in 1965. Service uniforms are displayed for all of these men, especially those from the Second World War in which they gained their fame. Weapons are displayed to link the men's lives with war. Adjoining the honor gallery in the Patton museum are weapon exhibits containing historic tanks and armored vehicles from the United States, the Soviet Union, and Nazi Germany. Yet, the weapon displays from Patton's time in war are like exhibits in a natural history museum. The weaponry only gains significance when visitors realize that they are symbolically part of the Patton legacy. These weapons are extensions of Patton himself, the means to victory under his guidance. The Nimitz museum displays a hatch and porthole from the USS *Arizona* and a variety of small weapons from both American and Japanese forces. In comparison, the MacArthur Memorial Museum intentionally contains only his personal weapons and other symbolically important ones, such as the pistol General Tojo used in an attempted suicide. Rather than focusing on any one episode, such as World War II, this museum represents his career as a whole. Moreover, the museum is too small to devote itself to large objects of war. At the Eisenhower museum, a separate area is set aside below his honor gallery. Representative military vehicles and weapons that were used during his European command are displayed, and the juxtaposition of symbols of honor with weapons conveys the message that war is about weapons, not medals. The overriding message in all these weapon displays, modest or extensive, is that military honor is ultimately gained through war.

Pictorial portrayals of these generals are provided through paintings, murals, or photographs. Patton is portrayed only sparsely through these media. While photographs are used to depict his life, only a copy of a painted portrait is shown in the entranceway to his museum. Like the Patton museum, Nimitz is portrayed simply with a bronze bust and a portrait painting of him in full uniform. In comparison, MacArthur and Eisenhower are portrayed more vividly. Many of the gallery rooms in Mac-Arthur's museum contain paintings and murals that coincide with the period depicted by the artifacts displayed. Scenes from his command in World War I and the signing of the peace treaty with Japan depict him as a man with a mission. Eisenhower, however, is clearly presented as the greatest leader of the Second World War. Visitors who enter his museum are immediately confronted with large murals depicting his life and military career. At one end of the entrance hall a mural covers the entire wall and portrays his historical leadership in Europe, and the galleries that visitors eventually see are small echoes of the mural's message. In all these museums, photographs are refinements of unique events in these men's lives which are consistent with the generalized portrayals in paintings and murals. The messages are consistent and without the realities of conflict these men experienced in their rise to power.

In these halls of memory honor is made explicit through separate displays which exhibit the heroes' military decorations from home and abroad. For Patton and MacArthur, window cases are used, and miniature medals are displayed in a freestanding case in Nimitz's postwar gallery. For Eisenhower, a separate gallery has been constructed, and at its entrance, a small bust on a pedestal sits before a wall which has the inscription: DDE: A LEGACY OF HONOR. Many of the decorations are the same for all four military leaders. Befitting their relative fame and status, Nimitz has the fewest while Eisenhower has the most. Unit citations are provided for all four men. For Patton, a Third Army flag is decorated with division patches to signify his European command. In Eisenhower's honor gallery a similar banner illustrates the divisions under the American Expeditionary Force when he was Supreme Commander. Both MacArthur and Eisenhower have divisional flags displayed as symbolic honor bearers. For Nimitz, a U.S. Navy flag is encased with battle ribbons from the nation's naval conflicts.

Beyond these official symbols, personal gifts from military units are displayed as tokens of admiration. All these forms of honor have a double message. By honoring great men in history, the donors are honored as well.

Image symbols convey the individual character of the heroes. They were unique not only in what they did but also how they were thought to be. Such displays are not so much a history of these men but the image of them. At the Patton museum, visitors can see the infamous ivory-handled pistols and leather holsters he wore during the Second World War. It was part of his colorful image to fight any place at any time. Perhaps the most complete image of Patton is a lifelike mannequin showing the man in full uniform. Standing staunchly, wearing riding boots and holding his riding crop, the figure displays more than his service decorations, tenure stripes, and rank. It depicts an attitude, and it's easy for people to say to themselves: "There's old Blood and Guts." For MacArthur a small but purposively centered case is displayed. MacArthur's famous weathered general's hat, his sunglasses, and a corncob pipe are arranged as if he had just left them there. General Eisenhower's image is more subtle, for he is remembered for his management of war rather than for heroism in combat. The famous "Ike" jacket he popularized is displayed to illustrate his unique character. Of all these military leaders, Nimitz was the most modest, and his personal symbols reflect this. There are no popular symbols associated with him, but the Garden of Peace just outside of the museum exemplifies how people felt about the man. Donated by the Japanese government to honor Nimitz, the garden symbolizes Nimitz as a peaceful, kind man who tried to treat others with respect. Image symbols are selective history for all four of these heroes. These images are often how Americans wish to remember these men regardless of their specific histories.

With these presentations of artifacts, it is easy to question whether or not true history is being portrayed. These were intelligent and complex men. In his criticism of the MacArthur Memorial Museum, William Manchester wrote:

[I]nside is an immense collection of memorabilia. . . . It goes on and on. If these walls could talk, one feels, they would say something preposterous . . . the relics all seem curiously irrelevant. The spirit of the man is absent. . . . He was always elusive, but never more so than here.[25]

Museums can only go so far in portraying life, and for heroes, it is very difficult to capture the full essence of their lives. These men were not perfect, but their museums perfect them. They are made greater than life, and the American people often want such heroic images. The images become increasingly ornate and complex according to the status of those who are honored. Eisenhower's exhibits are extensive because he was a U.S. president, but he gained that office through his military accomplishments.

MacArthur and Nimitz are remembered more lavishly than Patton, because of their five-star officer rank and greater responsibility. Yet, all of them are distinguished from other leaders because they demonstrated an excellence beyond their fellow officers.

Collective groups are also honored as heroes. The West Point Museum partially portrays the academy's role in military history. Visitors can learn how its graduates have consistently fought with valor when the United States has gone to war. One of the most unique museums for collective honor is the Hall of Valor at the Virginia Military Institute in remembrance of cadets who fought for the Confederacy in the Battle of New Market. The museum attempts to convey the cadets' youthful courage, which is assumed to be a result of their training at V.M.I. Pictures, films, dioramas, artifacts, and figure displays depict their heroic fight. Yet, the portrayals do not only describe history. The museum is an embodiment of faith that the courage demonstrated at New Market is still being instilled at V.M.I. The honor is real, but the museum itself seems to be a self-promotion of the college. To honor war alumni is to honor these institutions, their past and present.

Weapon museums for past wars are among the most numerous types of museums portraying military history. Throughout the United States such museums are located at armed service bases to exhibit uniforms and weapons and to depict the history of that installation's branch of service.[26] Collective honor of people in particular branches of the armed services is present in these exhibits, but weaponry is the main attraction. At the Transportation Museum at Fort Eustis, Virginia, visitors see not only an array of military vehicles but also the unfolding history of the U.S. Army Transportation Corps. This museum focuses on the role of these historic vehicles in America's history, and secondarily honors the brave people who operated them. But trucks do not have the popular appeal of planes. The Air Force Museum at Wright-Patterson Air Force Base in Dayton, Ohio, is one of the most popular weapon museums in the United States. Aviation and war history are told through progressive exhibits in a large hangar structure. American as well as enemy planes enable visitors to sense the potential power of these weapons. The begging question is, where is the honor in this museum? Interspersed throughout the exhibits are display cases commemorating selected individuals who were famous leaders or pilots. There are displays for General Doolittle, pilot aces, minority people who were pioneers, and the role of women in aviation history. Outdoors, there is a walk lined with bronze plaques to commemorate air units that fought in past wars. Yet, honor is subliminal. Commemorating these people through displays, however, legitimizes the attraction and purpose of weaponry. Weapon museums enable people to explore their curiosities about machines, but such places do have a higher purpose. These museums attempt to demonstrate that weapons, popular or not, were important in serving the United States' war efforts.

Some weapon museums indirectly sanctify government. The War Memorial Museum in Newport News, Virginia, is a historical tribute to Virginians who have fought in past wars. Posters, uniforms, military decorations, and weaponry are used to portray past wars in much the same manner as museums at military installations. The museum's state theme enables it to be more than a comprehensive collection of artifacts from American wars. There are separate display cases for Virginians who distinguished themselves in combat, and these displays allow the museum to illustrate how Virginians have sacrificed their lives to preserve the American way of life. The state's traditional values are legitimized by honoring those who fought to uphold these beliefs.

The most visited weapon museum in the United States is the National Air and Space Museum in Washington, D.C., part of the Smithsonian Institution. The museum portrays America's aviation history and its role in war. Although mainly seen as a tourist attraction, the museum has an undertone of honor. Planes from the world wars comprise a large section of the museum, and several are suspended to give a feeling of action. Some of these air action scenes portray America working at war, and most visitors assume that Americans did an honorable job. There are no permanent exhibits to single out individual heroes, but temporary exhibits do depict the contributions of certain Americans. A temporary exhibit of the Black Eagles, the first aviation unit of black Americans, illustrated how their important contributions challenged racism during the Second World War.[27] While permanent and temporary displays have an undertone of honor, the National Air and Space Museum achieves sacredness not so much from its contents but from its location. The museum is in the symbolic heart of the nation's capital along the Mall between the Washington Monument and the Capitol. Some of this nation's most important monuments are located on or by the Washington Mall. The National Air and Space Museum prominently acts as a border to the Mall, and the museum becomes sacred by association with the Mall.

Hero and weapon museums can be removed from places of war, but museums for battle events cannot. A battle museum can make the nearby battlefield landscape more understandable. Today, preserved battlefields are maintained by state and federal governments, but the most prominent visitor museums are administered by the National Park Service. While each facility and battle is unique, all these museums use similar procedures for displays, and graphics provide a uniform message. Events leading up to a battle are explained, and visitors are told the battle's actual events. Finally, people learn the consequences. None of these museums attempts to be a large vault of artifacts. Rather, the intention is to educate visitors prior to their tour of the battlefield itself. Honor is conveyed through the descriptions of soldiers fighting for a purpose and the recognition of the courage displayed in their endeavor.

2.8 War Aircraft Display in the National Air and Space Museum, Washington, D.C. (Author's Collection)

These museums deliberately attempt to present a balanced view. Neither the American Indian nor the federal trooper is depicted as evil. The Confederacy's aims are not questioned, and neither is the Union made to appear righteous. The neutrality of these museums allows visitors to come to their own conclusions. People are left with a sense of honor for all, deserved or not.

Hero, weapon, and battle museums do have a common thread: the desire to portray the tumultuous side of American history. War is not questioned, and it is often treated as inevitable. By presenting the facts, museums avoid controversy about war, and conveying honor enables museums to legitimize their designed scenes of war.

Battlefields

When war is over, battlefields convert from landscapes of fear to landscapes of devastation. Because of the great loss of human life, it is easy to forget that the natural landscape has received at least as many wounds. It is scarred and made barren. Bombs have obliterated everything from new blades of grass to entire cities. In war, the landscape always suffers, and like wounded soldiers, it takes time for nature to heal the land. Slowly flowers and fauna return. The landscape's scars do not disappear, unless a society speeds the natural healing process by removing military debris and filling in the fox holes, trenches, and bomb craters.

These scars are badges of honor to the victors and blemishes of disgrace to the losers, and to remove them is to remove history. But putting the war in the past is a necessity, and societies attempt to return to normal life by rebuilding towns, and fields once again conform to the plow. Some chapters of war, however, are not easily forgotten, nor do people want to forget them.

In the postwar landscape, battle sites are often saved or restored to prewar conditions depending upon practical considerations and the importance of the conflict. When a battleground was in a city itself, it is too much to ask a whole community to remain in ruins as a memorial. A site may be set aside to commemorate a battle, although it may not be the one place where the most significant fighting occurred. A city's ongoing activities take precedence over the complete commemoration of a battle. It is simply too expensive. On the other hand, relatively undeveloped countryside is more amenable to landscape preservation. A battlefield can be physically embellished to display its importance. Minor skirmishes may be marked, but major battles are typically orchestrated in the landscape to commemorate a sequence of important events and people. The restoration of battlefields makes them landscaped museums.

Battlefields and their subsequent war memorials symbolically reorder the natural landscape as an expression of historical memory and change. In speaking of actual war, J. B. Jackson notes: "Armies do more than destroy, they create an order of their own. It was strange to observe how both sides superimposed a military landscape on the landscape of devastation."[28] Wars eventually pass, but for those who fought, return trips to battle sites after war evoke memories that tourists can never comprehend. It is the veteran's sense of an actual landscape combined with real experiences: "Even now, a generation later, some of them still discover that a certain smell, a certain taste, a certain kind of early morning overcast sky can bring back a mood, an event, a landscape from the past as if it had been yesterday."[29]

Veterans need no monuments to recall their experiences, but memorials enable those who did not fight to capture a small glimpse of the reality of battle. To enable visitors to comprehend battlefields as place, war memorials are often geographically located to link remembrance and place. Commemoration becomes authentic when it is connected to the actual historic site. Reconstructed memory, however, depends upon a battle's importance in history. Important battlefields on American soil are highly articulated landscapes while minor ones may only have a single monument or sign which gives a modest interpretation of events in place.

Battlefields such as Gettysburg and Vicksburg have been extensively and intricately memorialized, and the pattern that emerges tells visitors not only about the warring sides but also about the military units involved. Near the

2.9 American Redoubt and Cannons at Yorktown Battlefield, Virginia (Author's Collection)

battlefront there are monuments from states honoring their individual regiments. Behind these, states commemorate their own soldiers with grander monuments. Commanding generals and their headquarters were typically furthest from the battlefront, and their monuments depict their point of command. For the more famous commanders, equestrian statues are common, with less important officers having sizable but smaller monuments. These monuments often form a ring about the battlefield itself. Other battle sites demonstrate the sequence of places where the victors pushed back a defeated army.

Actual places of battle may or may not be symbolized with monuments. Few if any memorials are placed where hand to hand combat took place or where shells constantly fell to keep the enemy at a distance. On the other hand, the logistics of some battles demand remembrance of actual battle stands. At Custer Battlefield National Monument, the central point of focus is on the hill where Colonel Custer and his troops made their last stand. At Antietam Battlefield in Maryland, the Cornfield and Bloody Lane are known so well that surrounding memorials seem incidental. For those who know a battle's history, the natural landscape can be a more meaningful memorial than a monument.

Authentic cannons are often positioned at battlefront lines or near memorials to demonstrate the direction of battle. At critical points, historic markers describe the battle events as they developed, and people can attempt to assemble history and place as it happened. When alone, visitors can contemplate the scene and imagine the past, but it is difficult to reconstruct the scene. Passing cars, other visitors, singing birds, and even silence contradict the real noise of battle, and there is no foul stench or smell of gunpowder to indicate the horror of war. Although war cannot be experienced in these places, it can be contemplated, especially if visitors are knowledgeable about actual war events.

Historic battlefields are often given further meaning when war dead are buried nearby. Cemeteries communicate what battlefields cannot, the cost in human life. The visitor, in tallying the collective graves, can wonder if the battle was worth the price. On the other hand, cemeteries are visual understatements of war's price. Not all who died are buried at these cemeteries. Victors are interred, but the bodies of losers were often buried elsewhere. Even for victors, not all the bodies are recovered, and the remains of famous leaders were sometimes removed and buried at honorific sites. Visual images at cemeteries are even deceiving. Even, neat alignments of graves present death as a compact package, and the image of its symmetry can make visitors miscalculate the dead as if counting sardines in a tin. Nonetheless, battle cemeteries do enable visitors to recount a battlefield's history with the understanding that the common result of war is death. These cemeteries are comparable to small museums that are located by larger museums, and the larger museum setting is the battlefield.

While memorial battlefields are attempts to save the past, these valued landscapes alter the future by preserving land that might normally be developed.[30] Urban growth can surround battlefields, and their landscapes become time capsules of history. When the surrounding landscape is filled with the common repetition of city buildings and streets, the contrast makes these battlefields more valued as sacred sites. Their constant, explicit memory in place increases their separateness from daily life. As time passes and the memory of war fades, these sites can seem like unrealistic accounts of the past, a Disneyland of old cannons and strange monuments which are extraordinary in themselves. Honor as sacredness is present in these sites, but knowledge of history is necessary to make them meaningful places.

Museums as Commercial Tourism

Visitors to museums normally expect history to be presented accurately. But when museums are designed for entertainment, tourists not only accept but even anticipate a departure from strict historical truth. As Relph, a cultural geographer, says: "It seems for many people the purpose of travel is less to experience unique and different places than to collect those places."[31] Commercial museums can fulfill these expectations and can offer entertainment beyond that of tranquil public museums which convey and honor the past. People expect this entertainment, and ". . . the parapher-nalia of travel often becomes an object of fascination in itself."[32] History is often not enough, because tourists want an excitement of place which actual history may not deliver. These tourist museums can be " . . . absurd synthetic places made up of a surrealistic combination of history, myth, reality and fantasy."[33]

Even though commercial museums are inauthentic, they must have a legitimate appearance to attract customers. Such museums are typically located near historic sites not only to capture the attention of those who wish to visit an actual place associated with a war but also to attempt to legitimize their own existence. Commercial museums are parasites to authentic places.

War museums as commercial tourism have mainly developed near historic battlefields, In comparison, public museums which honor past wars need not depend upon historical authenticity of place since they have official means to obtain actual historical objects and professional curators with the knowledge to interpret them. Tourist museums, on the other hand, invest their efforts and funds into creating an impressive scene. They depend and thrive upon nearby public battlefield museums which offer honest scenes of actual history without the flair of entertainment.

Of all the American battle sites, Gettysburg, Pennsylvania, probably provides the greatest concentration of commercial tourist museums. The Battle at Gettysburg in 1863 is one of the nation's most famous battles. As part of the National Park Service, Gettysburg Battlefield is one of America's best-preserved battle sites as well as having some of its most mag-nificent war memorials. In the 1970s, the National Park Service recognized the necessity of coping with commercial intrusion.[34] Visitors recognize the commercialization at Gettysburg when they see the billboards just outside of town. One billboard says: Gettysburg's #1 Attraction, National Civil War Wax Museum.

Gettysburg's tourist museums are organized as a magnet market. Located on Baltimore Street and Steinwehr Avenue, the museums and adjacent souvenir shops are on a strip development near the national cemetery and the park's visitor center. Tourists who come to see the battlefield in Gettysburg National Military Park have little to do after the museum is closed and it is too dark to tour the battlefield. The commercial museums have a captive audience.

The architectural packaging of commercial museums is often designed to give the appearance of authenticity. The buildings often mimic the classical style and colonnades of legitimate museums and give visitors the feeling that they are about to enter an official monument. American and Confederate flags are mounted on the buildings as symbols of respect, and Civil War-type cannons sit outside to lend an air of authenticity. Competition among commercial museums necessitates the historical imagery, but sometimes the scene is blighted by nearby businesses and the museum itself. The Gettysburg Battle Theatre sign with an American eagle may pass as official, but the message below it, Cafeteria Parking in Rear, exposes the commercialism. When competition is not keen, such museums can be more flamboyant in their commercialism. The Confederama at Chattanooga, Tennessee, dramatizes the Battle of Chattanooga. Its building facade is not only crass but naive. Looking like a white castle with indented cornices, the Confederama in no way reflects the south's historical architecture. The huge letters and the Confederate flags painted on both square turrets promote the scene with no recognition that the Union fought in the battle, too. But this regionalism does identify the Confederama with its geographic clientele. While its style is recognized by most tourists as inauthentic, it does present the kind of image that attracts many customers.

Commercial advertising tells tourists what architectural imagery as a generalized illusion cannot. The National Civil War Wax Museum offers recreated scenes, such as Lincoln's Gettysburg Address and Pickett's Charge, and visitors are told in tourist pamphlets that they can "Relive the exciting moments of the Civil War. An educational and inspiring experience for all ages." At the Soldiers National Museum, handouts say: "the most beautiful exacting and exquisitely detailed battle Dioramas ever created of the Civil War. . . . A presentation of historic authenticity that will make your spine tingle." The Gettysburg Battle Theatre and Cafeteria tell visitors: "The exciting new process of Multi-media with Quadraphonic Sound and Moving Maps bring to life every major event of the decisive three day battle—in a manner everyone can understand."[35] All these messages attempt to tell the visitor that history can be made more truthful and exciting through contrived techniques.

Miniaturization is a technique used by tourist museums to convey authenticity. At the Battle Theatre, tourists can see: "25,000 hand-painted miniatures placed in positions held during battle." The Confederama in Tennessee, which portrays the Battle of Chattanooga much like the Battle Theatre portrays Gettysburg, colorfully says in its promotional literature: "More than 5,000 soldiers (made especially for Confederama in South Africa) show where armies moved as guns flash in battle and cannon puff real smoke, accompanied by a shot-by-shot explanation of these historic conflicts." In such scenes, tourists are expected to accept that the quality of toy soldiers is equivalent to authentic history.

After the show is over, commercial museums entice tourists to carry their experience with them through mementos. It is here that inauthenticity is clearest. The shops contain a variety of kitsch to suit the visitor. Union belt buckles and caps for northerners are for sale, and the same fare is offered with Confederate emblems for southerners. Additional goods, such as plates, brassware, and glassware are provided as gifts for friends back home. The visitor's excitement over the portrayal of war history is con-

2.10 Commercial War Museum in Gettysburg, Pennsylvania (Author's Collection)

verted into impulse buying, and remembering history is falsely translated into remembering friends and relatives.

The separation between private property and historic battlefields seems sufficient to keep the sacred apart from the nonsacred, but this is not always true. At Gettysburg, the commercial museums offer a package plan not only to see their museums but also to take bus tours that have taped narrations to see battle sites ''. . . which come alive through the magic of realistically taped narration and sound.'' Tourists can also rent prepared tapes and recorders so that they can '' . . . learn the history, geography and local legends that make you actually experience Gettysburg so it becomes a part of you. And you experience it in the comfort and privacy of your own car—at your own pace.'' These planned contrivances do give facts, but what is lost is self-reflection in the landscape. Tourists see an authentic landscape without an authentic, personal experience. Individual questioning and interpretation are lost to a contrived message.

Museums as commercial tourism are inauthentic experiences of war memory. Facts of battle may be told, but it is dramatized history without the intricacies of real events. These places develop and fine-tune their acts according to what the public will buy. They are parasites of authentic landscapes and have the atmosphere of a circus sideshow rather than a museum of authentic artifacts. Tourism, however, provides release from everyday life, and part of that release is escape from reality itself. Commercial museums provide a compromise that many tourists enjoy, a combination of history and fantasy that need not be authentic.

RITUAL SITES

Public Ceremonies

Rituals temporarily add definitions to place, and communities use them to reach beyond the experiences of daily life. In remembering war most people immediately think of patriotic ceremonies, such as Fourth of July parades, Memorial Day ceremonies, and veteran reunions. In former times Armistice Day was widely celebrated. Veterans and older people hope that these rituals will encourage younger people to continue past traditions of patriotism.

These events and others temporarily memorialize community space which then returns to normal use. Yi-Fu Tuan makes a pertinent comparison: "A ritual dance, while it lasts, converts a meadow into a sacred space, but as soon as the dance ends, the space reverts to a meadow."[36] Sacredness is expressed through the sharing of cherished values. We educate ourselves while being entertained. History is displayed with respect, while successfully carrying out the ritual can convey how we have improved in showing public affection.

Parades for American holidays are staged processionals which temporarily give patriotic meaning to main streets in our communities. The best example occurs on the Fourth of July. Before the parade, symbolic back-drops are often mounted to create a linear stage. Red, white, and blue bunting is sometimes used with a central blue drapery containing an American eagle with the word Welcome over its head. These manufactured banners are often used to celebrate other occasions, such as a rodeo or local fair. American flags on street posts are sometimes added. Finally, a reviewing stand, draped with red, white, and blue crepe paper may be added to judge local bands and parade floats. The parade and its sets create a temporary stage for patriotism.

The parade itself contains a number of components to celebrate Independence Day. It begins with a color guard from a local military unit displaying the American flag at high mast, and a state or military flag is set lower with both flag carriers bounded by soldiers carrying rifles. A local band then follows playing a traditional march, followed by the floats. Some may carry beauty queens, but the American Legion and the Veterans of Foreign Wars usually prepare floats with a patriotic message. Veterans may wear their old uniforms, displaying a transition of national faith from the First World War to Vietnam. Other organizations often do the same. Intermittently, a military unit may be marching, or a piece of army equipment may be driven down the street. Finally, everyone jokes about the city street sweepers as they clean up the horse manure left behind. The parade combines history, patriotism, and local culture to make it a meaningful event for townspeople.

Parades provide multiple symbolic interpretations of war memory. As patriotic displays pass, there is a consistent message which reminds us that our democratic society was born of war and that we must sometimes fight wars to preserve its freedoms. Soldiers are treated as heroes regardless of the fact that some may never have seen the battlefront. Some cynical observers may feel that no amount of patriotic display can justify our involvement in Vietnam, yet such contradictory beliefs are subdued. The parade as a temporary memorial immortalizes our past sacrifices in war. Except for a float exclaiming world peace in an inoffensive manner, antiwar messages are not part of the scene. J. B. Jackson, however, suggests that the parade as a political symbol is all but dead; it has become a popular form of theater with historical glamour but no history. It charms with entertainment that lacks commitment.[37] Nonetheless, patriotic parades enable townspeople to celebrate their identity as Americans. The history presented in these parades, simple or contradictory, reminds them that American war history should not be forgotten.

Firework displays glorify the battle for freedom. Most Americans have enjoyed an evening fireworks show after the traditional Fourth of July hot dogs, watermelon, and homemade ice cream. The whole event is an extension of Francis Scott Key's vivid portrayal of battle in the lyrics of his "Star-Spangled Banner." The fireworks negate the horror of battle. Onlookers see pretty bursts of light while temporarily shuddering to the noise of a loud rocket bomb. It is a portrayal of glory without the gore and blood of actual warfare. People add to and extend this drama by purchasing firecrackers and rockets at the local fireworks stand. People have come to realize the danger of handling fireworks, but the concern is safety, not the implication that these mini-explosives are weapons of war. There is an innocence here, but to some recent veterans, a rocket bomb may be too close to their war experiences. To them, it is the sound of death, not glory or freedom.

Memorial Day rituals are more somber occasions than holidays to victory. In past times, parades were staged to remember this day, but cemetery ceremonies are now more common. As in a Fourth of July parade, rites of preparation are made to sanctify the scene. The grounds are mowed, flowers are placed at gravestones, and American flags are appropriately placed. Attendants, often wearing the traditional red poppy, listen to speeches by local members of the American Legion or the Veterans of Foreign Wars. The essence of this ritual is that society cannot be permitted to forget the sacrifice of lives that these brave warriors made. The event reifies the hopes of those who attend. Samuel Bass Warner has said about Memorial Day:

For one day the cemeteries were a place for all the living and all the dead, and for this one day the bright-colored flowers and gaudy flags gave them almost a gay appearance. Death declared a holiday, not for itself but for the living, when together they could experience it and momentarily challenge its ultimate power.[38]

Remembrance on Memorial Day can be a challenge to the purpose of death in war itself. In angry comments about remembering the Vietnam dead on Memorial Day, a citizen from Stony Creek, Connecticut, once said:

2.11 American Flags as a Symbolic Scene Set for Memorial Day, Lawrence, Kansas (Author's Collection)

" . . . a great many others will be damned before we let the politicians do that to the young of our towns again."[39] The legitimacy of death is challenged, and mindless patriotism is cast aside without negating respect for the war dead.

While individuals may have private perceptions of Memorial Day, it has an officially sanctioned unified meaning. One curious manifestation of this official status is in Waterloo, New York. On a lawn in front of a public bulding, there is a memorial to Memorial Day which designates Waterloo as the birthplace of this ritual in 1866. Nearby is an official New York State cast-metal sign giving the history of Memorial Day at Waterloo and stating that Congress made Waterloo the official birthplace in 1966. A memorial to a war memorial is twice removed from the actual history of war, and this curious twist of logic can catch one's attention as much as the attempt to commemorate Memorial Day.

Veteran reunions enable those who fought to create their own sacred rituals. The best-known reunions commemorated two of the nation's most famous battles, and these ceremonies were held at Gettysburg, Pennsylvania, in 1913 and at Normandy, France, in 1984. Veterans responded similarly to both events. They searched for grave markers of friends who were killed and went to the very places where they fought to recapture their past. At Gettysburg, the Battle of Cemetery Ridge was symbolically retraced by the veterans themselves.[40] American soldiers who fought on Normandy's beaches roamed the sands to see where they scaled the defended line above.[41] Official ceremonies and memorial dedications occurred; President Wilson spoke at Gettysburg and President Reagan addressed selected veterans and foreign dignitaries at Normandy. Veterans used the reunions to recapture the importance of war events in their lives.

Amidst these memories of past glory and mourning, enemies became friends. Union and Confederate veterans ate and paraded together, and American and German soldiers shared their war experiences with friendship rather than malice. What permeated both these events and others like them was the mental presence of place. As Davis says: "The battlefield did more than merely keep alive their memories; it softened them and fostered the most pleasant."[42] Undoubtedly, this aura of common experience was the result of both age and maturity. Battle reunions usually occur long after war. Hate has largely faded, and knowing that they have only a few years to live, veterans realize that they must put aside their past prejudices. War made these veterans aware that battle may be necessary, but war must result in peace without acrimony.

Other veteran reunions are less sacred, but honoring the past is still one of their goals. Veteran units, such as an air force squadron or a submarine group, periodically gather to be with old friends. Even American Legion or Veterans of Foreign Wars conventions are gatherings to honor those who fought, although with less specific declarations of honor. While battle reunions typically occur on hallowed ground, these military unit reunions usually take place at hotels. A nearby public hall may be leased or a hotel convention room may be used. While such places may be nonsacred locations, sacredness is recreated through ceremony and a display of flags and all are honored, however briefly. Veteran conventions have developed a reputation as excuses for men to go out on the town, but for those select moments in their temporarily created halls of honor, veterans act as if they were attending church. Less known but unique reunions are veterans' honor powwows held by American Indians. Dances are dedicated to them, and traditional giveaways are held as honor rituals. Veterans distinguish themselves by wearing special shawls, half red and half blue, with military medals pinned on them like feather coups, traditional symbols of honor in the past. Such reunions reinforce Indian traditions that warriors are entitled to be honored for defending their people. All of these various reunions do stress remembrance, but there is a greater emphasis on fun and fellowship than at battle reunions.

Veteran reunions tend to be filled with a sense of self-renewal. Honoring those who died brings honor to those who remain and to the patriotic values that they hold. Moreover, those who fought and lived must be remembered for their willingness to serve under the threat of death. In some reunions, sacredness transcends the patriotic to evoke a feeling of world brotherhood.

Synthetic Dramas

While rituals are typically thought to be sacred, nonsacred events can ritualize places with inauthentic memories of war. Gun and memorabilia shows are temporary settings which often contain war artifacts for collectors. Battle reenactments as war dramas are attempts to replay actual war events although participants are more enamored with their roles than with actual history. Re-creationists can play at war with real uniforms and equipment and use the natural landscape as a gameboard. These rituals stress entertainment rather than history.

It is easy to imagine war as a synthetic ritual when going to see a war movie, but people create their own dramas with war. History can be part of the scene, but these activities are more about re-creation for self-interest than war itself.

Gun and memorabilia shows have become a permanent subculture in American life. At large shows, weapons of every type are available for sale, and many of them were used in past wars or are prototypes. M-1s, M-16s, samurai swords, bayonets, and other weapons are available. Combat gear is also popular, and camouflage fatigues, helmets, canteens, ammunition, and other goods can be bought. The crowd itself adds to the scene. Men in combat boots and fatigues can be seen with ammunition belts strapped over their shoulders. However, most men wear hunting gear or everyday dress. Some women attend, but the shows are clearly dominated by men.

Although weaponry is the main attraction, a few booths are strictly devoted to selling war decorations and edged weapons. The designs of these booths are quickly devised and appear crude compared to displays at war militaria shops. While display cases do exist, everything is displayed as if the occasion were a market bazaar. In many ways, these shows and displays are just that, but the customers they attract are usually curiosity seekers who wish to own some relic but lack the discerning taste of a knowledgeable collector.

Gun shows and their accompanying war memorabilia are distasteful to many people. They tend to be frequented more by the working-class man. Collectors can trade and also sell their goods. They are not concerned with the honor of war. Instead, they want to talk about combat, weapons, and other artifacts associated with war. The temporary character of these shows and the display skills of those who show their goods are often seen as crude, and this has given these shows and those who participate in them the image of being unsophisticated.

There are conflicts between people who display war relics at gun shows and those who participate in militaria shows. If outsiders believe that gun shows are in bad taste, serious collectors of militaria find them doubly offensive. They disdain what they see as the false connection between guns and the art of military decorations and of ornamental-edged weapons. War as memory for serious collectors involves aesthetics and military history. Not wanting to be associated with those who have lower quality goods and knowledge, these collectors have their own conventions. If gun shows convey the image of sloshing down beer, militaria shows have the atmosphere of wine and cheese. Those who attend wear a coat and tie or fashionable dress. Unlike the run-down discount store image of gun shows, hotel or convention hall rooms are chosen as more eloquent settings. Displays are immaculately set, as if the visitor were shopping in a fine department store. The separation between gun shows and militaria shows is one of low culture versus high culture.

War militaria shows recognize the role of these artifacts in war, but also separate them from war as objects of value. Collectors learn more about the items they collect, and during evening dinners at nearby restaurants, seminars ensue with agreements and arguments over particular items or classes of them. The exhibition of knowledge goes further. Writers of militaria books often attend these conventions and help collectors make new distinctions and discoveries about their collections. History is important at these militaria shows, but greater weight is placed upon the artifact's military history than its political history. American, British, Japanese, and Third Reich militaria carry equal weight in the sense that an artifact tends to be judged on its own aesthetic quality and rareness. Yet, even at these conventions, Nazi militaria are the most popular. Some collectors argue that there is more interest in collecting Third Reich objects because more care was taken in their design. Nevertheless, people who have displays at militaria shows often face the same criticism that they experience as collectors. Some outsiders feel that people who collect Third Reich militaria are insensitive to Nazi war crimes, and likewise, collectors feel that these charges are unjust.

Some people are not collectors of war items, but they may use these artifacts as props so that they can be role players of war history. Battle reenactments give participants the chance to play at war under the accepted auspices of patriotism. For many, it is an afternoon of fun which also offers the opportunity to replay history.

Battle reenactments of early American wars often take place on the actual historical site, which gives them a dimension of legitimacy. Battlefields from the American Revolution, the Civil War, and the American Indian wars are the most commonly used. Dressing up in realistic copies of historic uniforms is an essential aspect of these spectacles, and weapons may be collector's items or authentically detailed reproductions. Even cannons are used when available. Of course, no live ammunition fire is exchanged. Some reenactments are more sophisticated than others. While some organizers simply provide a show, others realistically attempt to portray troop movements as they actually occurred.

Although attempts are made to be authentic, battle reenactments are actually theatrical dramas. Feigned charges and the play action of death on the battlefield are ultimately satires of war. There is no genuine fear, and ceremonies and picnics afterwards do not redeem these battle dramas. Perhaps one of the clearest cases of exposing these inauthentic events is the Custer Re-Ride held in 1976 to commemorate the Battle of Little Big Horn. White men dressed as the Seventh Cavalry Unit, which fought and died in the battle. Riding horses on the route that Custer and his men took, they relived events as they were in 1876 except for one important fact. There was no battle. The American Indians who represented their victorious ancestors attended the public ceremony, but were not interested in the white man's game. In comparison, the reenactment group awarded themselves medals for their dramatization.[43] Battle reenactments tend to glorify war history more than to make people aware of its horror.

Battle reenactments of early American wars can capture some image of the past by using historic battlefields, but reenactments of later wars usually depend upon personal imagination. Experiences from the world wars have been reenacted by avid enthusiasts flying vintage aircraft. Not surprisingly, it is dominated by those who can afford to buy and to maintain these planes. Many of these organizations satirically refer to themselves as units of the Confederate Air Force, which obviously never existed. These groups play an active part in organizing air shows to display and fly their aircraft. The scene is sometimes made to appear more real. Pilots dress in period uniforms with full decorations, and when they fly, mock dogfights are stage. But unlike playing soldiers on a battlefield, they do not feign death by crashing their planes. Often these air shows gain a degree of credence through the appearance of authentic military aircraft and members of the U.S. Air Force flying current air weaponry.

Battle reenactments can be recreated and reduced in scale using models. In Ida Grove, Iowa, a wealthy model enthusiast has designed and built a battleground in his backyard so that he and his friends can play at war. Every year on an August weekend, as many as 28,000 people come to see the war games. The meticulous models of weapons, building structures, and the natural landscape provide a realistic game board. Model planes with wingspans from six to ten feet dive upon enemy installations, and bomb bursts appear with the aftermath of flames, smoke, and destruction. Near the end of the performance, a group of men reenact the historic World War II scene of U.S. Marines raising the American flag atop Mount Suribachi on Iwo Jima as the national anthem plays. Reviewing this spectacle, a newspaper reporter wrote: "The Wars of Ida Grove are fought every year. Cities are destroyed. Ships are sunk. Planes crash. Everybody loves it."[44] Modeled environments are a substitute for actual places where war occurred, and mock battles are only stereotypes of real events. The audience enjoys these dramas where destruction is limited to model airplanes, but one critical reality of war is missing—death. In battle reenactments with models, the spectacle of models performing in combat overshadows the historic reasons why wars were fought and the human costs involved. History becomes a lived fantasy without the political issues which were at stake. J. B. Jackson severely criticized these contrived fictions when he wrote:

[R]eenactments of historic episodes are gradually changing the new reconstructed environments into scenes of unreality, places where we can briefly relive the golden age and be purged of historic guilt. The past is brought back in all its richness. There is no lesson to learn, no covenant to honor; we are charmed into a state of innocence and become part of the environment. History ceases to exist.[45]

If battle reenactments lack history, war as a game totally ignores it. Private clubs have organized to play war on the weekend. Weekend excursions have even been organized as a mini-vacation for those who only want to have a one-time experience. Members tramp through the woods and shoot one another with paint pistols. A splotch of paint on the opponent's chest symbolizes death. Historical garb is unnecessary, and war is enjoyed as an event unto itself.

Not all war games are innocent. Commando schools exist to train people to be like commandos, and the more serious students train to be soldiers of fortune. War becomes technique and practical expertise. All these advanced game players are supplemented with magazines and places to shop for weapons and accessories. They do not buy toys, and companies offer them "assault systems" of real weapons. The more these commando schools treat their version of war as real, the more the real historical purposes behind war are lost.

All these various forms of synthetic rituals are inauthentic experiences of war. Some are more serious detachments than others, especially when war is treated as a game. Shows for collectors are less alarming since artifacts are kept to be seen rather than used, but even here, history can be falsely separated from the political history and horror of war. All rituals which deviate from war as political history, modest or extreme, become synthetic in meaning.

MEMORY AND LANDSCAPE

War memorials ultimately juxtapose our failures and successes in realizing human values in the designed landscape. Remembering the past cannot be separated from the values that communities wish to embrace, but are their ideals served in the present or in the past? David Lowenthal has said that communities often idealize the past as a sanctuary from an awful present.[46] Do war memorials provide sanctuaries from an awful present by idealizing the past? A community's landscape may in fact be improved, but these memorials also represent failure, the failure to prevent war. Sacred memorials recognize the awful cost of war as well as the ideal of peace, temporary though it may be. Are sacred memorials sanctuaries? Yes, if we see the local landscape as chaos; no, if we see war memorials as an expression of the inability to prevent war. War memorials can provide contradictory messages within the designed landscape.

It is a mistake to think that sacred war memorials are only polite gestures in the landscape. The desire of local people to remember the war dead is done through a variety of means which are readily available. These sacred war memorials, large or small, could have been dedicated to other people or events. But a war memorial is a way both to be patriotic and to remember the tragedy of losing local loved ones. Patriotism becomes authentic by being physically manifested in sacred memorials and by the intimate experience of those memorials.[47] Loyalty is no longer merely a word or feeling; it has local place.[48]

Nonsacred memorials cannot be reduced to oddities in the landscape. Most of them demonstrate the role of free enterprise in American society. If there is a way to make a dollar on an idea, someone will. War is an idea grounded in history, and many people find war history exciting. They are willing to pay for artifacts or participate in events that fulfill their curiosities about war. In contrast, war remains are often public property, and the lack of interest surrounding these remains is that government can only create legitimate memory upon places and artifacts that are declared sacred. War surplus is something that government wishes to discard, not cherish. Nonsacred memorials are not common. They are often crowded out by other, more powerful experiences. Nonetheless, they do persist as part of the landscape.

War memory in the landscape becomes active through rituals, sacred or nonsacred. What is important is that rituals enable people to use war as an ongoing event in their lives. Rituals transform the landscape and memory associated with it, even if only for a short time. These events can become enhanced and made more intricate to portray war history, or they can fade away if people no longer consider the events or war history itself to be important. All rituals depend upon self-renewal among their players to validate the ritual scene, sacred or not. Rituals enable people to focus on war memory, and their performances temporarily renew those memories in the landscape.

The social purposes of war memorials—identity, service, honor, and humanitarianism—only partially fulfill shared human values in the designed landscape. Sacred memorials legitimize these human values, but no one expects memorials to express the full range of desirable human values. Nonsacred memorials can idealize the past, but they do little to help realize human values. History and human values are used selectively. People can identify with past wars through personal collections of militaria and some services which use war as a business. But in the end, nonsacred memorials cannot better the concerns for honor and humanitarianism which appeal to a higher sense of self and responsibility.

Relating social purposes to war memorials depends upon perceiving the need for both. It can be argued that human values must inevitably be expressed somewhere in the designed landscape. The placement of human values is spatially uneven, and the means to give place meaning vary. The relationships, however, are strategic. What society values and what it wants to remember about war is reflected in the variety of social and physical settings for sacred and nonsacred memorials that exist. War memorials not only evoke war history, but more importantly, they evoke the history that people want to remember.

CHAPTER THREE

MONUMENTS TO VICTORY
AS JUSTICE

ALL PEOPLE WANT TO EXPERIENCE a sense of victory in their lives and
want a way to remember that feeling. Meeting a challenge, correcting a
wrong, or a combination of both of these allow us to increase our self-
esteem. An award or a ritual of honor can help to sanction those who died
in these endeavors.

War memorials to victory are trophies that not only keep us mindful of
who won, but also assure us that the war was honorable. God was on the
side of the victors, and therefore their cause was righteous. This victory
equals glory theory also applies to victory memorials. Whatever misdeeds a
regiment may have committed are forgotten in the victory memorials which
commemorate them.

Memorials to victory are associated with a sense of dignity; this con-
tributes to their sanctity. Sculptures or cenotaphs of war events are usually
made of fine materials. Granite, marble, and bronze have a long life, since
they keep their shape and deteriorate slowly. Since symbolic messages must
be steadfast and solid, good materials are practical expressions of permanence. Design quality is usually the best that can be afforded. Eminent
sculptors or designers are sought to create works that incorporate accepted
notions of beauty. More often than not, the viewer must look up to see the
memorial. This design technique works as a metaphor, since we look "up"
to people we respect. Although soldiers may be portrayed in tattered clothes
or in poses of suffering, there is a stable sense of onwardness. Inscriptions,

simple or lengthy, are well conceived and are sometimes written by poets to embellish the emotional impact of the scene.

The American Revolution and both world wars are commonly believed to be wars to preserve justice and freedom. Most Americans accept these wars as honorable battles for life, liberty, and the pursuit of happiness. While each of the three wars is unique, they have been memoralized in similar ways.

THE AMERICAN REVOLUTION

The American Revolution is at the core of American tradition. Even though other components of American life may be rejected, Americans are generally unified in the belief that the Revolution was a just and righteous war.[1] Revolutionary times are seen by many Americans to be the most vivid and meaningful part of their national history.[2]

A nation cannot deny its beginnings, because to do so is to deny the values that legitimized the country's formation. Americans embrace their national roots, and many war memorials of the American Revolution are ultimately icons for the worship of America, that is, a form of civil religion. Yet, as in a church, some symbols are more important than others, and they present many different messages. Revolutionary war memorials tend to reflect stages of historical development. We have memorialized defiance, revolt, independence, endurance, and—finally—victory.

The first stage, defiance, actually began before the Revolution. John Adams once wrote to Thomas Jefferson: "The Revolution was in the Minds of the People fifteen years before a drop of blood was drawn at Lexington."[3] This was the time of defiance, and two events stand out as most memorable—the Boston Massacre and the Boston Tea Party.

On the evening of March 5, 1770, in Boston, British soldiers shot into a hostile crowd and five Americans were killed in what is now called the Boston Massacre.[4] In front of Boston's Old State House, there is a traffic triangle, and within it is a circular pattern of stones with a star in the middle. This marker identifies where the massacre occurred. Except for a general map on the City Hall plaza, there are no other specific signs announcing what the stone marker is. It is said that as a gesture of respect no one who knows the marker's history will walk on the stone circle. A clue to the full meaning of this memorial is on the cornice atop the Old State House. To the upper left is a lion, and on the right is a unicorn. These national symbols of Great Britain still preside over the circle.[5] The historic preservation of the Old State House and of the circle of stones perpetuates a subtle, political statement. The presence of the lion and unicorn on American soil symbolizes colonialism. The circle of stone marks the spot where Americans first openly rebelled against this political control. While many Bostonians are aware of this historic spot and its meaning, most outsiders are unfamiliar with it. Americans are vaguely aware that the Boston Massacre occurred, but they have no image of exactly where it happened or how it has been commemorated.

The second defiant event was the Boston Tea Party. On December 6, 1773, a band of colonists boarded three ships laden with tea at Griffin's wharf and threw the valuable cargo overboard in rebellion against tax sanctions. The actual site is now on dry land.[6] While a plaque commemorates the site—now on Atlantic Avenue—tourists prefer to associate the Boston Tea Party with Boston Harbor and the old sailing ships and other reminders of life in Revolutionary times found there.

Boston has obliged tourists by opening a replica ship, the *Brig Beaver II*, and a small museum and shop alongside the Congress Street Bridge. Visitors who enter this small complex see a sign saying: The single most important event leading to the American Revolution. The museum contains information about the history of tea and the events leading to the Tea Party. Visitors can board the *Brig Beaver II*, where they can see stage-set tea crates floating in the harbor. It is the sort of tactic we would expect at Disneyland, not at a serious historical site. Before leaving, visitors are offered a free cup of tea and a visit to the Tea Party Store where little crates of tea are for sale. While a city plaque designates this small complex as the official Tea Party Site and part of a 1976 bicentennial project, it is really synthetic history combined with good intentions and some old-fashioned free enterprise. The new official Boston Tea Party site is so festive in atmosphere that its political history cannot be taken seriously. American tourists are offered a patriotic good time without the seriousness of the 1773 rebellion. On the other hand, it is the type of place that many Americans enjoy as vacation entertainment, and when they arrive home, they can proudly say: "We were there." The new Boston Tea Party site provides an official historical place with patriotic scenery, but this setting obscures the political issues surrounding the 1773 rebellion.

The defiance of the Boston Tea Party led inevitably to outright revolt. Americans responded by taking arms against the British in three significant confrontations—Lexington, Concord, and Bunker Hill.

On the morning of April 19, 1775, eight American militiamen were killed on the Lexington Green by British troops who were on their way to seize ammunitions at Concord. No one knows whether an American or a British soldier fired the first shot, but with that shot the American revolt had begun.[7]

Lexington Green is considered to be the most symbolic American green.[8] Located near the town's center, the triangular lawn is punctuated at one corner by the well-known Minuteman statue. It faces oncoming traffic and "stands with a spirited, careless accuracy (much) as aviators or paratroopers in olive drab."[9] Near the green's center stands an American flag. On a boulder are inscribed the infamous words of John Parker, who called out to his minutemen: "STAND YOUR GROUND. DON'T FIRE UNLESS YOU ARE

3.1 The Minuteman Statue at Lexington Green, Lexington, Massachusetts (Author's Collection)

FIRED UPON, BUT IF THEY WANT A WAR, LET IT BEGIN HERE.''[10] Beyond some small markers on a small rise rests perhaps one of this country's oldest war memorials. Built in 1799, it is a square column topped by an obelisk. On one side is inscribed a dedication to the minutemen who died there on April 19, 1775. This monument, which was built by those who were there, is not what most people remember about Lexington. Instead, what they remember is the Minuteman statue created by a sculptor who drank up his sculptor's fee and had to be hounded by local citizens to finish the project.[11] While tourists may prefer to view either the statue or the obelisk, it is the Green and the American flag in its center which truly remind them: It started here.[12] Naive tourists who walk about the Green can easily reduce their visit here to a snapshot of Americana. More informed people provide an overlay of meaning that they have acquired through the study of American history. Naive and informed visitors, however, are joined in their feelings about the Green in one way. The Lexington Green is the preservation of a political ideal—Americans are willing to fight for their rights.

Traveling along Battle Road, tourists then come to the other place that makes April 19, 1775, a famous date in history, the Old North Bridge at Concord. When the British troops left Lexington Green, they marched toward Concord. At the bridge they were met by waiting minutemen who had heard the news of the shooting on Lexington Green. Unlike Lexington, there was no doubt who fired first. The British shot volleys first, but it was the Americans who fired last, since the British broke ranks and fled.[13]

Most Americans learn about Concord in public school, and people who travel there are perhaps drawn by the lure of the phrase associated with Concord, ''The shot heard round the world.'' A visit allows tourists to join phrase to place. Ultimately, the Old North Bridge is Concord's main attraction. Having been replaced and even redesigned numerous times over the years, the bridge is more important as a symbol of revolt than as an historical artifact in itself. On the east side of the Concord River, a simple obelisk erected in 1836 marks the place where the British met the Americans in battle. When Americans experienced a resurgence of patriotism after the Civil War, the citizens of Massachusetts built the Soldier Monument on the bridge's west side, and Ralph Waldo Emerson orated at its dedication in 1867.[14] Tourists who have not previously visited this monument can quickly appreciate its symbolic connection to the bridge. Facing the bridge with a determined look, a soldier holds a rifle with a wheelbarrow at his side, and the statue conveys the thought: We shall defend our land. The site of the obelisk, bridge, and statue is more than a commemoration to the Battle of Concord. It is a political comment which echoes the message of Lexington Green—Americans are willing to fight for their political rights. At Concord, visitors get one other message. They can win the fight.

The remaining Concord portion of the Minuteman National Park is not what one would imagine as a site for a nation's glorious beginning. Visitors

3.2 The Old North Bridge as a Symbol of Revolt, Concord, Massachusetts (Author's Collection)

can take trails and imagine that they are on a primitive country walk. The grounds are not highly manicured as they are in other national parks. From time to time, visitors walk past the remains of the foundations of houses which belonged to minutemen who fought at the bridge. The Concord landscape is probably an honest statement of what it was like in those times. It is peaceful and undisturbed by lawnmowers and shrub trimmers. The bridge and the main two monuments do not dominate this quiet setting. Visitors can imagine this American landscape as it really was in 1775 and experience a simple sense of patriotism without being either cynical or bloated with pride. Reflecting upon grade school history, the visitor understands that it was common people who fought, not for a glorious cause which had been intellectualized, but for basic human decency. The sanctity of this landscape becomes more apparent to visitors when they leave. The suburban homes and commercial development along the road bring the tourist back to the present. The site of the Battle of Concord and its surrounding landscape have been preserved in the same manner as the Old Faithful geyser in Yellowstone National Park. If either place was allowed to be altered, the history of place would be defiled. Old Faithful represents humankind's respect for nature. The Concord landscape represents the preservation of America's most basic political purpose—freedom.

The American revolt crystallized with the Battle of Bunker Hill. In June 1775, American troops were ordered to defend Bunker Hill, across the Charles River from Boston. The rebels constructed a defensive redoubt on Breed's Hill, a lower flank of Bunker Hill. The fighting was fierce, and the Americans lost the battle. However, the British paid a heavy price in casualties, and their officers were never again as aggressive. The battle also gave the Continental Congress hope, since American troops had proved they had the will to fight.[15] Bunker Hill became famous for the gutsy fighting order issued to the American troops: "Don't fire until you see the whites of their eyes." Against this rebel perseverance, the British who fought at Bunker Hill realized they had won a battle but were psychologically losing the war.

Dedicated in 1842, the Bunker Hill Monument stands 220 feet high and is visible from many points in Boston. Its obelisk design is similar to many other nineteenth-century war memorials, and its location in a city neighborhood square rather than a large public park underplays its political importance. Walking up the steps, visitors see the typical brown National Park Service sign identifying the monument. Along the rail, however, is a stone tablet provided by the State of Massachusetts. It says: "THIS HAND OPPOSED TO TYRANTS SEARCHES WITH A SWORD FOR PEACEFUL CONDITIONS UNDER LIBERTY." At the top of the stairs is a statue of Colonel Prescott, a commander at Bunker Hill, whose statuesque pose explains the Massachusetts inscription. He holds his sword casually as if calmly prepared for battle, and Prescott's pose and sword symbolize American independence from British tyranny. Behind the statue and monument is a small classical building that serves as an entranceway to the monument's interior stairs and to the museum. While the museum offers little to clarify the battle's history, it does have a small diorama that shows American soldiers on the hill looking toward the front, prepared to fight.[16] A primary attraction of a visit to the monument's top is its view of Boston. Except for the hill, there is no authentic landscape remaining. The Bunker Hill Monument is a symbolic replacement for a battlefield which is now covered with urban development. The actual spots where Americans lost their lives in defense of their cause are now paved over or covered by someone's living room floor. The monument geographically limits the political memory of the Battle of Bunker Hill to the national park grounds. While the battle's history has not been explicitly preserved at the site, Bostonians can stand at numerous points in the city and say to visitors: "That monument on the hill across the river is where Americans fought the British." The Bunker Hill Monument announces loudly that American revolt was justified.

Below the hill by the historic Charleston Navy Yard is the Bunker Hill

Pavilion, which is run by a nonprofit corporation. Unlike the monument on the hill, the pavilion actively caters to tourists. The main attraction is a media show. A promotional pamphlet tells the visitor:

"Whites of Their Eyes" gives you a whole new perspective on the American Revolution. . . . You're there as America first proves its military mettle. . . . All this is brought to you in-the-round with more than a thousand color slides, 14 screens, 22 life-size customed figures and seven channels of sound. Don't miss the experience of seeing the "Whites of Their Eyes."

Although the pavilion is tastefully done, it does give the visitor the feeling of "rooting for the home team." The American kitsch for sale in the lobby is much like that available at a college football game. The pavilion does give visitors an opportunity to learn history, but the media show is a fast-moving drama more than a thoughtful analysis of historic political events. Bunker Hill Pavilion is packaged entertainment with a patriotic message.

Urban growth in the Boston region has made it difficult for people to recapture the American Revolutionary spirit when they visit these memorials to defiance and revolt. The urban memorials have been subjected to change more than the rural ones. Nonetheless, all of these memorials are spatial capsules which geographically keep intact the historic foundation. Regardless of future growth, most Americans will continue to identify Boston and its environs as the place where the nation's political consciousness was first converted into action against British colonialism.

While the Boston region is the site of defiance and revolt, Philadelphia —the birthplace of the Declaration of Independence—is the heartland of American independence. The Independence National Historic Park was created in 1948 to restore and preserve the places in old Philadelphia associated with the American Revolution.[17] The national park is a mecca for vacationing Americans who are curious about their country's origins. Most visitors visit Independence Hall and the Liberty Bell Pavilion, and they may take a side trip to see the Betsy Ross House.

At Independence Hall, visitors see the Assembly Room where the Declaration of Independence was argued over and finally adopted on July 4, 1776. The Assembly Room is simple and stark, and there are no decorative ornaments to evoke an air of nationalism. Visitors get the true impression that this was a room where a group of men got down to the practical business of making a nation. The remainder of the national park is a historic stage set which supports the political importance of what was done in the Assembly Room.

In contrast to the straightforward approach to history in Independence Hall, the Liberty Bell Pavilion symbolizes nationalistic fervor. Built on Independence Mall and on a central axis with the hall, the pavilion is designed solely to display the bell. This axial arrangement is a subtle site design technique which encourages visitors to associate the hall with the pavilion. Visitors stand in line for tours through the pavilion, and during as well as after a park ranger's presentation, people are constantly trying to reach, touch, and photograph the bell. They seem to bestow it with magical powers, as if patriotic forces emanate from it. While the bell itself was originally part of Independence Hall, it is the bell that seems to stir people. It is easy to think of it ringing in liberty, to recognize it as a symbol for the celebration of national independence.

Two blocks east of Independence Mall and outside of the national park is the Betsy Ross House, which is maintained by a nonprofit organization. Betsy Ross is remembered for having designed and sewn the American flag. When walking east from the mall on Arch Street to visit Betsy Ross's House, tourists realize that they are on the right trail when they pass Betsy's Place, a small gift shop with an American flag hanging from the building. From a distance, one might mistake it for the real thing, except for the We Sell Kodak Film sign which reveals its true nature. Visitors identify the real Betsy Ross House when they see a large copy of the first American flag in front of the building. A garden runs alongside the house, and the rooms inside are furnished in eighteenth-century style. In one room, visitors can see a mannequin posed as Betsy Ross making an American flag. One easily imagines that this is where our nation's first flag was made. After the tour is finished, visitors may notice a discreet, mannerly sign that says: This Great American Home is protected by Sears Paint as part of an ongoing effort to help preserve American Heritage. The sign is not convincing, because what is being preserved is more than a house exterior. The American flag and the Betsy Ross House are symbols of independence and the public interest. Private enterprise, however, does not always serve or protect that interest. What is good for Sears Paint is not necessarily good for the nation. Tourists may enjoy their visit to the Betsy Ross House as a way to understand better the American past, but they may also question the commercial advertisement at a public place of honor.

A lesser known monument perhaps captures the essence of independence in Philadelphia's historic area. *The Signer* is a statue of a citizen with a feather quill in one hand. In his other hand a rolled scroll is raised above his head. While respectfully classical, *The Signer* has a more basic message, the celebration of a hard-won victory. Independence National Historic Park and other nearby historic sites preserve this same spirit of celebration of the nation's official political birth as expressed in the Declaration of Independence.

After the Declaration of Independence, the American Revolution became a war of endurance. While battles at Ticonderoga, Saratoga, Bennington, and others are remembered, the most memorable symbol to endurance is not a battle but a camp, Valley Forge. In the winter of 1777, General George Washington's troops settled about 20 miles outside Philadelphia to stand in readiness near the British, just far enough away to consolidate the army. As the tourist pamphlet says: "Valley Forge is the story of an army's epic struggle to survive against terrible odds, against hunger, disease and the unrelenting forces of nature." In spite of adverse conditions, that time was used to transform a collection of men into a unified fighting force. Valley Forge was a victory not of weapons but of will, an ordeal that enabled Americans to endure the war for the next five years.

Valley Forge is more a shrine than a national park. The only profane space is the large parking lot by the visitors' center, a necessary concession to tourism. When visitors begin their tour on the outer line road, they first encounter reconstructed redoubts with cannons and huts that were used by a variety of army brigades. The huts are constructed of logs, mud, and shingled roofs, and with their quaint building style, it is hard to imagine the miseries that soldiers suffered within their shelter. Although national park officials have good intentions, the manicured landscape surrounding the huts "museumifies" the landscape and makes it into a patriotic display rather than a historic reconstruction.[18] The huts, trees, and grass are so well kept that it is difficult to imagine that soldiers suffered from cold and misery. The intent in preserving Valley Forge was to remember this suffering. Visitors cannot appreciate the meaning of the huts and their surroundings unless they are already aware of the hardships that took place here. A visit to the museum in the visitors' center can better prepare them to interpret this well-kept landscape. Without this understanding, the sacred nature of the natural features and the buildings is lost.

Visitors soon see the National Memorial Arch. This is the main symbol of Valley Forge, but it further represents the rite of passage of the Revolutionary army from confused volunteers to a united military force. The arch's keystone is emblematically ornamented with an American eagle—the symbol of the spirit of Valley Forge soldiers who endured. The arch's inscription describes it vividly:

NAKED AND STARVING AS THEY ARE
WE CANNOT ENOUGH ADMIRE
THE INCOMPARABLE PATIENCE AND FIDELITY
OF THE SOLDIER

The tour continues past equestrian figures and small memorials. General Anthony Wayne's statue stands on a mound on the edge of the outer defense line in a pose of preparedness. Looking downhill, visitors can no longer imagine what General Wayne was prepared to defend when they see a modern Maginot line, U.S. Interstate 76, which is the Pennsylvania Turnpike. Other small memorials are in less conspicuous places and commemorate other groups who fought. Many memorials were dedicated by the Daughters of the American Revolution. Although many generals are remembered through memorials, one individual is honored above the rest.

3.3 Valley Forge Memorial Arch, Valley Forge, Pennsylvania (Author's Collection)

Americans associate Valley Forge almost immediately with the camp's commanding general, George Washington. Tourists first encounter Washington's headquarters on the driving route. It is a restored stone house marked by a general's flag. Visitors can tour the house and try to imagine how he lived in those times.

Farther along the road is the most intricate memorial at Valley Forge, the Washington Memorial Chapel and Carillon. The chapel, officially named the National Shrine at Valley Forge, is steeped in symbolism. Inside the sanctuary, each choir stall commemorates a separate brigade through different carvings of uniformed soldiers. Flags above the choir stalls represent

Army, Navy, and French participation in the Revolution. Stained glass windows intentionally include red and blue to represent the nation's colors. The ceiling is decorated with the seals from all 50 states, physically arranged in the order in which they joined the Union. The pews are called the Pews of the Patriots, since they each commemorate a patriot or group of patriots. Over the main entrance door is the George Washington window which depicts various periods in his life. Walking from the entrance toward the Door of the Allies, one can see a tablet of the Declaration of Independence above the door. To the door's left is a statue of Washington showing " . . . him bearing the burdens of war—anxiety in his face, determination in the grip of the sword, confidence and hope in the pose of the whole figure."[19] The chapel is easily interpreted as a political expression of the concept of God and country. The architectural message is that the United States was the righteous result of obeying God's will under the leadership of George Washington.

The Washington Memorial National Carillon is connected to the chapel by the Porch of the Allies. The porch itself has separate symbolic bays for foreign notables in the Revolution, such as Von Steuben and Lafayette. While Christian symbolism dominates the chapel, the carillon is filled with symbols of patriotism. There is a bell for each state, territory, and the District of Columbia, and a special one was dedicated as the National Birthday Bell.[20] In a niche of the carillon's exterior turret tower, a statue of George Washington stands in military dress in a pose of preparedness. Not surprisingly, the carillon is topped with an American flag. The Washington Chapel, Porch of the Allies, and the carillon are symbolic attempts to show the purpose behind Valley Forge. Their message is that America was founded upon human rights informed by Christian principles, and when these principles were challenged by the British, American colonists and concerned foreigners defended these ideals in the American Revolution. The political meaning of these architectural messages, however, evolved from European political thought. The philosophical seeds of democracy started in Europe, and at the same time, European culture was fully committed to Christianity. Colonial settlers brought both of these beliefs to America, and these beliefs are expressed in the carillon and chapel. The Porch of the Allies, which connects these two structures, reinforces the historic fact that Europe first jointly embraced these two beliefs, and foreigners such as Lafayette and Von Steuben are testaments to these political roots. These three architectural monuments speak to European history as well as American history.

While none of the Revolutionary battlefields captures the sense of endurance as well as Valley Forge, they are still popular with tourists. At Bennington, Vermont, an obelisk and a statue of Colonel Seth Warner commemorate the Battle of Bennington. Ironically, the battle was actually fought in the state of New York. When visitors drive from Bennington to the battlefield, they can stand atop a hill and orient themselves to the battlefield using a bronze terrain map which is the memorial for the actual battle. At Saratoga, one can see a manicured battlefield, a Gothic-style obelisk (the main monument), cannons, and other typical memorials. There is one atypical memorial. General Benedict Arnold, later infamous as a traitor, was shot in the second battle of Saratoga, and a memorial was built to commemorate his injury. Upon a tombstone-shaped marker, a cannon is carved and overlapped with an officer's boot, epaulet, and a partial wreath. This memorial to Arnold honors his defense of Saratoga, but it is probably viewed skeptically by patriotic American visitors. Arnold served honorably, but he was also a traitor. The memorial's existence is in worthy recognition of his great victory, but the monument's small size also recognizes Arnold's treachery. Other memorials to Revolutionary battles are often more nondescript than those at Bennington and Saratoga. Numerous road markers identify small battles and nearby events. Some signs were made locally while others are generic state markers that commemorate all historical events in a similar fashion. Nearby communities use these signs to associate themselves with a proud segment of American history. However modest, historical battle markers enable tourists to recognize that this was where part of the American Revolution was won, and local communities want part of that glory. Well known or obscure, Revolutionary battlefields are remembered as events on the road to American victory.

America's final victory over the British was at the Battle of Yorktown in Virginia, and the battlefield is now a national monument. Upon entering the visitors' center at Yorktown Battlefield, tourists quickly get the historic message. An official seal above the main entrance reads: Yorktown 1781—The Final Winning of American Independence. Inside, they learn the battle's history and even see a section of the British frigate *Charon* which was sunk during the American siege on Cornwallis. On the battlefield, visitors can explore American, French, and British redoubts to grasp a sense of the battle. For children, these earthern defense bunkers make an unusual playground. Running up and down embankment tops and pretending to fire the cannons are not experiences that children get in the typical city park. The adults may have a clearer understanding of the site's historic importance, but they too are surrounded by an unfamiliar landscape with few informative markers. There are no substantial monuments to make one pause and pay respect for what the American victory meant. The battlefield is more like a preserved game board than a memorial to those who fought.

Not far from the visitors' center is a delightful pedestrian bridge which leads to the Yorktown Memorial. This memorial to America's ultimate victory is surprisingly somber. An angel of victory stands atop a Corinthian column with an eagle adorning its capital. Instead of an upreached arm hailing victory, the angel's hands reach out. This reaching out of hands is reproduced below at the base with British and American shields set side by

3.4 Monument to the Victory at Yorktown, Virginia (Author's Collection)

side. These two design elements are attempts to emblematize peace, but the one at the base has a subtle political message. The American shield ever so slightly overlaps the British shield, and below these shields, American and French troops are commemorated. Great Britain is politely but discreetly treated as the loser. In the end, the Yorktown Memorial is a solemn experience, and its understatement signifies how Americans have come to remember the battle. Yorktown was an important victory, but the cherished memories of the American Revolution are not here.

Regardless of the battle, the remembrance of victory is inseparable from honor for those soldiers who died. For other wars, most Americans identify the Tomb of the Unknown Soldier at Arlington National Cemetery with this sacrifice. There is a similar commemoration for the American Revolution in Philadelphia's Washington Square, and it is called the Tomb of the Unknown Soldier of the American Revolution.

Beyond similar names and the presence of human remains, the memorials at Arlington and Philadelphia have little in common. There is no 24-hour honor guard at Philadelphia as there is at Arlington. While the purpose is to remember an anonymous Revolutionary soldier, a statue of George Washington stands over the tomb. If passersby do not come close enough to read the inscription, they can easily mistake it for a memorial to Washington. Like Arlington, the tomb is separated from the public by a chain barrier, but in Philadelphia, the barrier and the immediate environs are treated profanely. People sometimes use the chain as a bench where they can gather, talk, and drink. In recent times an eternal flame has been added, but the flame holder and its protective screen are coated with a carbon residue. Like the eternal flame holder, the statue and cenotaph have not been cleaned for a good while. In comparison, the Arlington tomb and its surroundings are immaculate.

While aging memorials are fondly thought to develop a graceful patina, the cleanliness of the Arlington tomb demonstrates vigilance in remembrance. The Tomb of the Unknown Soldier of the American Revolution has received no such attention. Perhaps we no longer care. Or perhaps the Philadelphia tomb is the victim of a much deeper problem, its location on the fringe of an economically depressed area near the edge of Independence Mall. In referring to Independence National Historic Park, Sternlieb, a city planner, says: "If you go to Philadelphia, you see possibly one of the most charming urban environments in the world. You step two or three blocks out of the charmed zone and you are in the middle of a jungle."[21] While the tomb is modestly maintained in recognition of its sacredness, it is on the edge of a profane urban environment. The men who fought for life, liberty, and the pursuit of happiness are ironically commemorated in an area which has become known for killing, segregation, and a dead-end life of poverty. The unknown soldier is matched by the no-name people of the ghettos. Remembering those who fought in the American Revolution and acknowledging the realities of poverty are both valid, but the hope of the political ideal expressed in remembering the unknown soldier is contradicted by present political realities in Philadelphia.

Beyond commemorating the common soldier, many American cities dedicated memorials to Revolutionary heroes. These monuments were built primarily in the eastern United States, and they honored those men who have popularly become known as the founding fathers. Among all of them, General George Washington was the favorite. In New York City, Union Square is dominated by an equestrian statue of Washington with the Liberty Pole Memorial to independence behind him. While the city's Washington Arch commemorates the centennial of his inauguration as president, one statue on the arch honors him as a general. Other cities, such as Pittsburgh, Baltimore, and Chicago, have monuments for Washington. In some cities, special monuments have been dedicated to local heroes in the American Revolution. Boston has honored Paul Revere, while Philadelphia has commemorated Benjamin Franklin. The sprinkling of these heroic monuments in American cities gives a legitimacy to urban places, but the noble purpose expressed in these statues is not always matched by the surroundings. A Washington statue can make townspeople and visitors proud, but when its location in the city is unsafe and unclean, the stronger feeling may be one of forlorn patriotism. George Washington may be a sacred symbol of the nation, but American cities are not hallowed ground. The continued respect for Revolutionary heroes is often measured by how well cities clean the stain and graffiti from their statues. The social problems of American cities make it difficult for them to match the political ideals that are represented in their memorials to Revolutionary heroes.

Not all heroes are memorialized in cities. Beneath the chapel at the Naval Academy in Annapolis, Maryland, the body of John Paul Jones is entombed. Some of his personal belongings are displayed in wall cases in the circular room. Jones is remembered as the nation's first naval hero. Memorials to him connect American naval history to the Revolution and the founding of the nation.

Washington, D.C., has become the most hallowed ground upon which to build memorials for heroes of the American Revolution. Memorials to Revolutionary heroes are in many squares and parks. Seeing one monument after another, visitors are able to consider subtly that these heroes helped in making the nation a reality. On the other hand, there is often confusion about what is being honored, Revolutionary heroes or government leaders. Many Americans choose the Washington Monument when thinking of a national memorial, but what is being remembered is not clear—George Washington as a general or as a U.S. president? Some people may say both, but symbolic meaning is equivocal here as it is for a few other dual-purpose monuments such as the Alexander Hamilton monument and the Jefferson memorial. Perhaps one of the nation's most unusual and elegant memorials to America's first heroes are the Revolutionary War doors to the House of Representatives and to the Senate in the U.S. Capitol. Made of bronze panels, the doors depict the history of the Revolution.[22] The deeper symbolism, however, is in their placement rather than in the meticulous design details. As holistic symbols, the doors give the political message that the democracy practiced inside was assured by the heroic sacrifices of the nation's founding fathers. Washington's memorials for heroes of the American Revolution have a common thread. They serve as permanent statements that it took brave soldiers to provide the opportunity for good government. The hero monuments help ritualize the nation's political beginnings, and they legitimize—correctly or not—current political authority and national decisions. Viewing these memorials, visitors may falsely assume that the kind of morals and bravery exhibited in the American Revolution are always being practiced in the Congress, the White House, and the federal bureaucracy.

City monuments and national memorials in Washington were built primarily during the nation's rise as an industrial power in the late nineteenth and early twentieth centuries. During this time, Americans wanted to beautify their cities. At the same time they sought ways to express pride in their country. Building war memorials to the founding fathers enabled Americans to legitimize their national identity and pride. Using the economic wealth created by the industrial revolution, American cities were able to implement these memorial projects, and the federal government had a reliable financial source to beautify the nation's capital.

When considering all the memorials that have been built to commemorate the American Revolution, it is independence that Americans cherish the most. The defiance of the Boston Tea Party and the revolt of the "shot heard round the world" at Concord are important, and Americans have not forgotten the endurance shown at Valley Forge; but the victory at Yorktown is typically overlooked. America's bicentennial celebration was not for 1781, the year that the Revolutionaries defeated the British. It was for 1776, the year that the Declaration of Independence was signed.

The bicentennial in 1976 demonstrated not only that the Revolution was one of America's favorite wars but also that its citizens could create remembrance in all aspects of American life. Operation Sail brought over 200 old sailing vessels into New York's harbor as 6 million watched the event. A 76-hour vigil was held by thousands of visitors at the site of the Declaration of Independence in the National Archives at Washington, D.C.[23] In contrast to these cultural events, there were more popular activities such as parades, national birthday parties, and dedication of local bicentennial projects which often also commemorated local history.

As with any event, the bicentennial was a chance for American free enterprise to make a dollar. The bicentennial year wallowed in kitsch. There was a dazzling array of bicentennial mugs, ash trays, door mats, toilet seats, beer cans, and other profane objects. The most obscene bicentennial event occurred when San Francisco prostitutes offered a hustler's special for $17.76.[24] Many business people saw the bicentennial only as a money-making venture. Their spirit was capitalistic, not patriotic.

Americans were not naive. They neither asked for this bicentennial kitsch nor took responsibility for it, and most importantly, nobody was taken in.[25] Michael Kammen, an American historian, emphasizes American's combination of love and hatred for bicentennial kitsch by introducing his book, *A Season of Youth*, with a quote from Ann Landers's column:[26]

DEAR ANN LANDERS: I am just as enthusiastic about the Bicentennial as the next person, but the lunatics who live across the street have made our neighborhood the laughing stock of the town. People come from miles around just to look.

They painted their house red, white and blue. Five flagpoles in the front yard fly Old Glory from dawn till dusk. Last week they put up three huge paper mache figures: Betsy Ross sewing a flag; George Washington crossing the Delaware; and John Hancock signing the Declaration of Independence.

There are two enormous neon lights on the front porch that flash off and on all night long. The message is "Happy Birthday, U.S.A." We can't get to sleep because the lights shine in our bedroom window.

The worst is the music. A public-address system blasts the "Battle Hymn of the Republic," the National Anthem and "God Bless America" from 6:00 P.M. until midnight.

Yesterday the nut who owns the house was out mowing the grass in an Uncle Sam costume—fake beard, hat and all.

The traffic jam in front of our place was unbelievable. Our lawn is a mess. What can we do about this?—WE LOVE AMERICA, TOO, BUT. . .

DEAR LOVE: You can notify the police. Mr. Superpatriot is infringing on your inalienable right to the pursuit of happiness. He is also disturbing the peace and creating a public nuisance. Get going.

The bicentennial was a joyful but superficial celebration. Lester H. Fishel, an American historian, has called the bicentennial an event that allowed the nation's past to invade the present.[27] Profound remembrance of the American Revolution is best understood when the parades are over and the souvenir sellers are forgotten. Americans fondly remember the Revolution, because they see it as the mechanism which made the American way of life possible. It is seen as a just war which enabled a free society to develop. The Revolution's permanent memorials, such as Lexington Green or Independence Hall, are cherished as roots of liberty. Many foreigners think of the Statue of Liberty as this country's most eminent symbol, and it is not accidental that the tablet she holds has imprinted in Roman numerals: July 4, 1776. The American Revolution is a continuous source of national identity that cannot be captured in any single event or memorial.

WORLD WAR I

World War I is often called the Great War or the War to End All Wars. Never before in history had so many nations been involved in one conflict. New technologies brought new horrors to battle. The days of the horse cavalry were gone forever. Instead, gas warfare, tanks, powerful bombs, and submarines made it possible to kill thousands of the enemy without seeing a single enemy soldier's face. Even though air battles had some of the qualities of medieval jousting, war was no longer an exercise in individual bravery, nor was it the triumph of a collective will. World War I demonstrated to the world the viciousness of mechanical warfare. Many Americans believed that war on such a scale could never happen again; the human costs were too great. They innocently believed that the horror of war would finally bring peace.

Memorials to commemorate this war continued many past traditions, but there were significant innovations. Tradition was maintained through statues and style. For example, in many towns the Doughboy statue was used as a monument prototype, just as the soldier statue had been used for Union and Confederate monuments commemorating the Civil War.[28] Weapons and soldiers were still used in designs, although angels were used less frequently. More importantly, the classical style was not only continued, but was employed in an even grander manner.[29] World War I memorials performed three functions not previously fulfilled in U.S. history: the utilization of war memorials as focal points in city design; the intensified memorialization of the nation's capital; and the creation of memorials on foreign soil. Tradition and innovation in American war memorials of this period represented two different but related purposes. Americans wanted a steadfast, national image, but they had to adapt to new circumstances which provided the opportunity to enhance that image. Americans thought that memorials for World War I dead were necessary tributes, and they also found these monuments to be good ways to express their nationalistic pride.

While many classical monuments continued past traditions, the most dramatic sculptural composition commissioned for World War I was *Wars of America* located in the Newark, New Jersey Military Park. *Wars of America* is comprised of 42 figures and 2 horses standing on a granite base. The monument was of "a much greater size and complexity than had yet been done in the United States."[30] Fighting men from the American Revolution to World War I are intermingled in a forward thrusting movement as if to say collectively: "We served and fought to continue the American way of life." Surrounded by a fence of overlapping bronze swords, *Wars of America* symbolically legitimizes all the nation's wars between 1776 and 1918 by including representations of them between the depiction of these two "just" wars, the American Revolution and the World War. More simply, even if some past actions were not acceptable, World War I demonstrated that the United States was nonetheless on the right course, the path of justice. *Wars of America* was large for its time, but larger and even more innovative memorials were still to be built.

The Columbian Exposition of 1893 in Chicago aroused citizen interest in what is now called the City Beautiful movement. For the most part, American cities were haphazard arrangements, the results of rapid expansion during the industrial age. The exposition's "Great White City" in the classical style generated much excitement about how cities could change their image. Daniel Burnham, the best-known city planner of that day, said: "Make no little plans, they have no magic to stir men's blood. Make big plans."[31] Many cities attempted to do just that. New street arrangements, parks, and building improvements were the main elements of these plans. Victory in the Spanish-American War and new-found recognition as a power in the world community made the nation optimistic about what it could do and become.[32] As Mel Scott, a city planning historian, has said: "Americans needed something more soul-satisfying than trunk sewers. . . . They also needed, for their spirits, . . . civic centers, decorative monuments, . . . and all of the street furnishings—fountains, ornamental benches, statues, and memorials—common in European cities."[33] Many town squares and public buildings at the turn of the century were the result of the City Beautiful movement. Many plans were never implemented, and the movement began to lose favor because it was based mainly on aesthetics rather than on solving social problems. Yet, many civic leaders still clung to the goal of beautifying their cities. The desire to commemorate World War I enabled some remaining support for the City Beautiful movement to be rekindled and realized in war memorials. Two cities in particular excelled the others in combining the goals of the City Beautiful movement and the commemoration of the war—Indianapolis and Kansas City.

Indianapolis, Indiana, clearly stands out from all other cities in its use of World War I memorials as a means to implement the City Beautiful movement. Five downtown blocks were cleared to make room for a Memorial Plaza, the Memorial Shrine, the national headquarters of the American Legion, and the offices of other auxiliary patriotic groups.[34] Many Indianapolis citizens felt that too many landmarks were destroyed,[35] and the money could be better spent for local social programs.[36] In the face of these objections, why did such a huge commemoration occur in Indianapolis? Beyond the desire to improve the downtown area was the guaranteed method of payment. The War Memorial Plaza and the Memorial Shrine itself were funded by the state of Indiana in lieu of paying a bonus to World War I veterans, although many veterans were not particularly happy with the state's decision.[37] Nonetheless, Indiana veterans were ultimately honored more than their fellow soldiers. The Memorial Plaza is the largest war memorial project ever built in the United States.

3.5 Wars of America Monument, Newark, New Jersey (Photograph by Glen Frieson)

The Indiana War Memorial Plaza has three major memorials—Cenotaph Square, the Memorial Shrine, and Obelisk Square. At the north end of the mall in a sunken garden alongside the national headquarters of the American Legion is Cenotaph Square. The Cenotaph is a symbolic, rather than an actual, tomb in remembrance of the first soldier from Indiana who died in the Great War. The Cenotaph is small and unassuming in itself, but it contains this florid inscription: "A TRIBUTE BY INDIANA TO THE HALLOWED MEMORY OF THE GLORIOUS DEAD WHO SERVED IN THE WORLD WAR." The square gains its formal power not from the cenotaph but from its stone-paved square. A column surrounded by trimmed shrubbery stands at each corner of the square. The four columns are topped with eagles whose wings are aimed vertically as they face inwardly toward the cenotaph. If visitors visually string the eagle's wing tips from one corner to the next around the square, they can imagine a reenactment of the cenotaph as a volume of space. The cenotaph is a sacred space within a sacred space, but more importantly, the larger sacred space bounded by eagles symbolizes the steadfast guarding of the honor of a symbolic tomb. Beside the Cenotaph Square stands a flagpole topped with an eagle of the same style. Waving above the double sacred space square, the flag plays the role of head honor guard. the eagles facing toward the cenotaph visually express vigilance in remembering the dead. The entire design of the square and cenotaph, however, represents continued nationalism. The cenotaph represents death in a particular war, but the eagles and the American flag are perpetual images that Americans interpret as defining the "good nation."

Toward the south end of the mall is the World War I Memorial Shrine. It was built at a cost of $11 million and was dedicated on Armistice Day in 1933. The immediate response to viewing the Memorial Shrine is that it is a huge fortress, and there is no other World War I monument to match its size in the United States.

Once one grasps the massive scale of the steps and building bulk, numerous details come into focus. On the southern steps is the statue, *Pro Patria* (for country), which is " . . . a gallant inspiring youth enfolded by the American Flag, suggesting the love of beauty, love of liberty and the spirit of sacrifice for the preservation of our ideals must not die but must carry on as the guiding motives of our National life."[38] Behind the statue are stone lions sitting at the ends of a stone balustrade. Under each lion's chin is a Union shield. The symbolic message is one of protection. Above the symbolic doors to the Memorial, visitors read: "TO VINDICATE THE PRINCIPLES OF PEACE AND JUSTICE IN THE WORLD." Even higher is an Ionic colonnade, and on top of it on each of the four facades, there are six figures that represent the values of the memorial. They are courage, memory, peace, victory, liberty, and patriotism.[39] Most visitors are unaware of all the intricate symbolism employed in the memorial, and of the enormous

3.6 Cenotaph Square on the War Memorial Plaza, Indianapolis, Indiana (Author's Collection)

expense involved in its construction. They are more likely to note the straightforward inscription just above the colonnade: "INDIANA WORLD WAR MEMORIAL." Externally, it is a big memorial for a big war, and all it needs is a label. The political message behind this monument, however, is that it took a world power to help win a world war, and the memorial shrine is a proclamation of that nationalism.

Inside the memorial, visitors begin a ritual journey to remember those who died. First, in the lobby people can see a small memorial altar honoring Indianans who have received the Congressional Medal of Honor. To reach the shrine room, visitors must climb a long flight of stairs. On both walls are multitudes of framed plaques listing the names of those who died. Halfway up the visitor is encouraged to stop, rest, and read an inscription honoring the dead. Before reaching the shrine room, visitors have been thoroughly made aware of the Indianans who died in World War I, and they anticipate that their final destination is a special place in which to give homage to those who died.

At the shrine room's entrance, visitors pass between large red marble columns. In the center of this four-story room is the Memorial Cenotaph. On its top is a Union shield in red, white, and blue, surrounded by a wreath. The cenotaph is set apart by a one-step platform with ornamental fire urns at its corners, and this arrangement is at the very center of the room. The pedestal urns are silent guards to enforce respect in the presence of the Memorial Cenotaph.

The display surrounding the cenotaph is dramatic, even slightly mysterious. The windows behind the exterior Ionic colonnade provide a dark natural blue-green light. Above, the ceiling is lit with a matrix of small lights of the same color. In the middle of the ceiling hangs a geometric chandelier known as the Star of Destiny which shines white light directly upon the cenotaph. Lighted portraits of military leaders from the various Allied countries hang along the walls. There are Allied flags in the corners, and above door level an art deco style frieze, which portrays scenes from the war, rings the room. All of this rich decoration is in an eerie light, and this atmosphere is strangely but pleasantly enhanced by the aroma of fresh floor wax. The aroma itself makes one aware of the "spit and polish" care which is given to this remembrance of the honored dead. The cenotaph in the shrine room can easily be interpreted as a Tomb to an Unknown Indiana Soldier, but it is actually an encasement containing mechanical equipment. It seems incongruous that the ultimate center of this sacred and patriotic space is filled with cogs and wheels. The cynic will view the shrine room as a stage set of political propaganda designed to evoke patriotic feelings. But for visitors who lost family members during the war, the shrine room's decor is a proper setting, like a chapel, in which to pay homage to Americans who died for their country. Among American war memorials, there is no equivalent to the shrine room. The craftsmanship and grand opulence of its interior has not been surpassed, and it is unlikely that a more grandiose memorial will be built in the near future. Patriot or cynic, all visitors can agree that the shrine room is a display that supports the righteousness of the United States as a nation.

In contrast to Cenotaph Square and the Memorial Shrine, Obelisk Square is simple. At the center is an obelisk with bronze reliefs on each side symbolizing religion, science, education, and law. Henry Hering, the sculptor, chose these themes because: "Upon these four fundamentals are built the foundation of our nation, without any one of which, it could not long survive."[40] None of the reliefs are military, and the square is now a quiet retreat with a fountain and flags from all 50 states flying nearby. At one time the square was paved, and captured German field artillery pieces were placed at each corner. With these artifacts of war removed, Obelisk Square is now a memorial to a past war which carries a meaning beyond its original intent. While not as elegant as the other two war memorials on the plaza, it has timeless quality that these other monuments, tied as they are to a specific war, lack.

The entire War Memorial Plaza is gradually becoming resymbolized. World War I is still remembered, but more recent wars distance the plaza's grand remembrance to the Great War. Gradually, the War Memorial Plaza

3.7 Obelisk Square and the Memorial Shrine on War Memorial Plaza, Indianapolis, Indiana (Author's Collection)

and Shrine have become to Indianapolis what the Eiffel Tower is to Paris, a city symbol more than a commemoration.[41] The political interpretation is increasingly one of civic pride instead of fervent nationalism. Yet, the War Memorial Plaza offers the best historical example of incorporating the City Beautiful movement into war memorials.

If Indianapolis was the grandest attempt to implement the City Beautiful in the construction of World War I memorials, then Kansas City, Missouri, was clearly second in importance. Kansas City's beautification plan had largely been ignored, but the completion of Liberty Memorial in 1926 was the implementation of an altered form of that plan.[42] Unlike the War Memorial Plaza in Indianapolis, the Liberty Memorial was built not in the downtown but on its edge, near the Union Railroad Station. The site offers a magnificent view of the city, and its 33-acre site adjoins a 173-acre park which gives an even grander scale to the memorial's image.[43] It rises like a midwestern Acropolis. Unlike the Indianapolis project, Kansas City's monument was strictly a local financial effort, which explains to a great extent its smaller scale. Nonetheless, the Liberty Memorial was a civic project which gave Kansas City some national recognition and helped it to shed its cow-town image.

The Liberty Memorial was intended not only to remember those who died in the war but also to serve as a symbol of peace. The memorial's elements consist of a tower and court, memorial halls, and a commemorative frieze. While the different elements in the memorial vary in the manner in which World War I is commemorated, patriotic service and peace are repeatedly stressed.

The tower and court are the first architectural features that captivate the visitor's attention. While the tower is the most dominant structure, visitors are more immediately confronted with two colossal sphinxes that serve as an entrance to the court. Both figures shroud their faces, symbolizing Memory and the Future. As the memorial's architect, H. Van Buren Magonigle, said: "Memory faces east toward Flanders Fields and the seat of war, the Future faces west where the course of Empire takes its way, and is veiled as the Future is veiled."[44] After walking between the sphinxes, visitors stand directly in front of the tower, known as the Torch of Liberty. Its huge size is overpowering. At the tower's top are four winged figures which symbolize the four guardians of peace—Honor, Courage, Patriotism, and Sacrifice.[45] Most people do not have the faintest notion of the tower's intended symbolism. For a small fee visitors can ride to the tower's top and take an "Eiffel Tower" view of Kansas City. While the tower's symbolism may be veiled, and the most affecting elements of the memorial are its size and its magnificent view, still visitors realize the solemn purpose when they read the inscription on the tower's shaft:

IN HONOR OF THOSE WHO SERVED IN THE WORLD WAR
IN DEFENSE OF LIBERTY AND OUR COUNTRY

Although the tower and sphinxes are abstract in their meaning, the memorial halls have more explicit messages. The World War One Museum is the only museum in the United States which is strictly devoted to the Great War. The museum was originally designed and used as a flag shrine which displayed banners of the Allies, a few artifacts, and some posters. Today, the museum is packed with well-designed display cases and exhibits to capture a sense of the war's unique character. The assembled artifacts clearly express war history, while the flags represent those Allied countries who fought. Peace is directly expressed through biblical inscriptions over the entrance inside such as: "THEY SHALL BEAT THEIR SWORDS INTO PLOW-SHARES AND THEIR SPEARS INTO PRUNING HOOKS" and "NATION SHALL NOT LIFT UP SWORD AGAINST NATION NEITHER SHALL THEY LEARN WAR ANY MORE." The combined message of the artifacts, flags, and inscriptions is clear: This is how we had to fight this war, and we don't want to do it again. At the same time, the museum's well-designed interior reflects national pride.

Memory Hall is more solemn in meaning than the museum. Under the inscription "WE ARE THE DEAD," bronze tablets list the names of soldiers

3.8 Liberty Memorial Tower and Memory Hall, Kansas City, Missouri (Author's Collection)

from Kansas City who were killed. Encircling the lower walls are decorative maps of the Army and Navy campaigns. The most dominating features of Memory Hall, however, are its huge painting and murals. On the left upper wall is the painting, *Pantheon de la Guerre*, which is a classically styled panorama of Allied leaders celebrating victory. On the right side, a trio of murals is entitled *Women in War*. The center mural is dedicated to all women who served at the battlefield. The two flanking murals commemorate women on the homefront who lost loved ones in World War I. The mural on the end wall is dominated by the seated figure of Victory, flanked by crosses marking soldiers' graves; directly behind her is a furling American flag. In the far background extending the full width of the mural, troops march before a cathedral in a shadowy mist. The mural's message is that while the Americans were ultimately victorious over the destructive forces of war, the sacrifice in lives was great. The mural says visually: "An American victory ultimately dominated over war's destruction but at the sacrifice of those who served." This message is echoed by a mural at the other end of Memory Hall above the room's entrance. The mural portrays the major military Allied leaders—Jacques, Diaz, Foch, Pershing, and Beatty—and more than 100 Kansas City residents who attended the original dedication of the Liberty Memorial. At the bottom center of the mural two Boy Scouts hold a scroll which is inscribed: "THE DEAD WE HONOR HERE MADE THE NOBLE SACRIFICE FOR A CAUSE THAT WOULD NOT BE FORGOTTEN." Memory Hall explores the meaning of death in World War I, not the means. The dead are named and the places where they fought are shown, thus making the war explicit. On the other hand, the murals commemorate victory with grand scale and classicism. The physical means to fight war and the realities of combat are displayed in the museum while the painting and murals in Memory Hall portray both the glory and the human costs of achieving victory. The museum and Memory Hall balance one another in their political messages. The realities of war must be interpreted beyond its mere physical artifacts. Ideals must be expressed. On the other hand, these ideals are facetious if they are not grounded in the ugly realities of war.

While the tower, court, and memorial hall explicitly commemorate World War I, the Liberty Frieze on the north wall is more philosophical in meaning. Eighteen feet in height, 148 feet long, and bounded by Union shields, the frieze depicts the progress of nations from war to peace. The progression of symbolism includes: destruction; reactive patriotism; war as futility, with the Four Horsemen of the Apocalypse; permanently injured people; the grief-stricken family; the armistice; a welcoming group of peace; morality and sanctity of the home protected by justice; bulls representing societal confidence in the future; an agricultural group representing the fullness of nature; and the figure of industry representing future construction.[46] Below the frieze are fountains which surround the visitor with peaceful white noise. While carved inscriptions hint at the frieze's philosophical meaning, few people grasp its totality unless they read the frieze's inscriptions and study the reliefs thoroughly.

Unlike the War Memorial Plaza and its structures in Indianapolis, the Liberty Memorial is more purely a shrine. There are no administrative buildings on its site, and visitors see the Liberty Memorial and its landscape more as a sacred space than as a city park or urban plaza. Yet, the intent of the City Beautiful movement was to emphasize urban life amidst a well-designed city. In some respects, the Liberty Memorial epitomizes what was wrong with most City Beautiful movement projects. Elegant structures were often built which had little to do with the early life of the city. Nonetheless, the Liberty Memorial did contribute to Kansas City's image as a progressive community.

World War I memorials gave communities an opportunity to renew their hopes for the City Beautiful movement. While not saved by these memorials, the movement did allow communities both to improve their downtowns and to remember the war. In many cities, public buildings were common commemorations used to beautify the downtown. San Francisco's City Beautiful project, the Civic Center, is particularly noteworthy for its use of war memorials. As one part of the complex, the Veteran's Building and the Opera House are joined by a landscaped court, and all three elements form the World War I Memorial of San Francisco.[47] In Nashville, the Tennessee Memorial Building, located by an urban square, was a central element in its small City Beautiful effort.[48] Other cities simply built civic auditoriums, which were commonly called the Soldiers and Sailors Memorial Hall. As the automobile placed greater pressure on urban areas, bridges as memorials were considered to be useful commemorations as well as civic design improvements, and a few cities took this alternative.[49] Some civic leaders saw memorials as a means to build city facilities that citizens might not approve if the projects were not called war memorials. Other city politicians thought public projects as memorials were economically more practical than huge, expensive shrines. Most city leaders did feel a responsibility to commemorate World War I, but they also saw the chance to use public support for memorials to further their City Beautiful plans.

This practical approach, however, had its critics among those who designed memorials. H. Van Buren Magonigle, architect for the Liberty Memorial, said: " . . . the movement toward community buildings as war memorials throughout the country has been a little over enthusiastic, a little misguided . . . the purpose for which a utilitarian building was originally built is almost invariably lost sight of, but one never forgets the purpose for which a beautiful monument was erected."[50] Egerton Swarthout, another architect, was more emphatic: " . . . no memorial, if it is to be a real memorial, can serve any useful purpose . . . no structure can serve two purposes."[51] Whittick, an architectural historian, later commented that utilitarian memorials are "pseudo-memorial(s) . . . calling them memorials will not make them so."[52] Critics of utilitarian war memorials were obviously purists. They wanted to sustain pure ideals, such as honor and sacrifice. They saw clarity of purpose as the way to achieve clarity in design. In contrast to these positions, multipurpose facilities lacked sanctity as well as clarity of purpose. Soldier and sailor memorial halls were used for entertainment and public events that had no direct relationship to those who fought and died. A memorial bridge is a structure that people drive over to get to work, not one which encourages them to pause in memory. Critics challenged the lack of ritual in utilitarian memorials. They did not see how it was possible to express and uphold ideals without ritual. Shrines are purposely designed to ritualize ideals, and critics were unwilling to compromise their desires for clarity of purpose, ritual, and design.

World War I memorials as civic improvements represent the largest local monuments to war in American cities. They would not have been possible without the City Beautiful ideology, but they also had local support. Approximately 150,000 Kansas City residents attended the dedication of the Liberty Memorial in 1926.[53] The utilitarian character of many World War I memorials engendered support from a vital group, the veterans.[54] At the time, museums and auditoriums were still accepted and appreciated by veterans, but many veterans felt that practical memorials served their experience better than earlier memorials. They had seen a new, techno-logical kind of war that no urban cosmetics could glorify.

Architectural critics may have been displeased with the emerging utilitar-ianism, but in Washington, D.C., their views were prevailing. In the 1920s, the nation's capital already had some memorials to our founding fathers, such as the Washington Monument and the forthcoming Lincoln Memorial. There were also memorials to many figures from the Civil War, and the Spanish-American War had been remembered with remnants from the bat-tleship *Maine* in Arlington National Cemetery. Nevertheless, recognition of the various armed services had not yet been done. Most service memorials were dedicated in the 1930s, and they filled this void.

The Army's First and Second divisions both have prominent memorials at the Ellipse in Washington, D.C. Both monuments glorify victory. The First Division monument is an 80-foot column surmounted by a gilded bronze figure of Victory on a sphere. Her wings suggest the perfection of body and soul. She has a flag in her right hand, and her left hand is extended to bless the dead. At the base is a general commemoration to those who died in "The" World War, and nearby are bronze plates inscribed with the names of the 5,599 who died serving the "Big Red One."[55] In the spring, red flowers form a red number one in front of the memorial as a grand entry to the monument. The Second Division memorial is a gateway protected by a blazing sword with the division's insignia, the head of an Indian chief on a star, on the sword's hilt.[56] At the base, it is simply marked "TO OUR DEAD." Symbolically, the sword can be seen as the successful protector of the portal to what our nation values. These two memorials of this period represent some of the earliest major attempts to commemorate Americans who died in battle on foreign soil. In the past, service memorials were built upon battlefields, because the battles were fought on American soil. Soldiers who died in Belgium and France would be remembered there, but the division memorials were a way to express victory and to remember the dead on home soil. The U.S. Army played a big role in World War I, and the First and Second Divisions memorials' sites and design reflect that effort.

The Navy-Marine Memorial, dedicated in 1934, is considered by many critics to be one of the most beautiful war memorials in this country, but it is largely unknown. The monument's tumultuous waves symbolize conflict while hovering gulls symbolize servicemen "who have gone down to the sea in ships, and have done business in the great waters."[57] The memorial is not as elaborate as was initially intended. Plaques depicting Navy and Marine history were to be included, but private funding was insufficient.[58] Located in a rather inaccessible spot, the visitor usually sees the memorial while crossing the Potomac River on Route 95 or driving along the George Washington Memorial Parkway. Unless one knows what it is, the Navy-Marine Memorial has an unclear meaning since the monument does not use typical symbols of weaponry or sailors for symbols. It can be easily misinterpreted as being something other than a war memorial, although its location in Washington hints at its national importance. The U.S. Navy's role in World War I was seen as important, but most Americans primarily remember the conflict as a land war. Visitors may be pleased that the Navy-Marine Memorial is located near the waters of the Potomac River, since those it commemorates often lost their lives at sea. Nonetheless, its remote location and ambiguous design underplay the role of the U.S. Navy and Marines while the division memorials on the Ellipse emphasize the Army's role.

Memorials for auxiliary services commemorate World War I but less emphatically than those for the major armed services. The Jane A. Delano monument in the garden of the Red Cross Headquarters remembers nurses who died in the war.[59] A veiled woman without a uniform and with extended hands symbolizes universal service. A similar monument for Delano was dedicated in 1938 at Arlington National Cemetery in memory of her distinguished service as head of the Army Nursing Corps.[60] In 1966 the National Guard symbolized this war, along with others, by placing a plaque depicting warfare on the facade of its headquarters. Memorials for these auxiliary service groups demonstrate a pluralism in memory. While these groups had fewer people than the regular armed services, they still wanted to recognize their efforts and sacrifice in the war. A visitor to Washington, D.C., will not readily notice that these less well-known groups have been

3.9 World War I Portion of the U.S. Army's Second Division Memorial, Washington, D.C. (Author's Collection)

3.10 The Navy-Marine Memorial for the First World War, Washington, D.C. (Author's Collection)

commemorated, because their monuments are geographically scattered about the capital. The auxiliary service memorials are less glamorous, fewer in number, and less noticeable than the regular armed service memorials.

A memorial to all who served in World War I from the District of Columbia was built on the south side of the Mall between the Washington Monument and the Lincoln Memorial. It is a dome supported by a colonnade and is inscribed on its cornice to those who died in "The" World War. While simple in structure and statement, its circular shape and protective canopy can symbolize unity and protection of this country's principles. Oddly enough, it is rather inconspicuous. Drivers may see it while passing it on Independence Avenue, and pedestrians may catch a glimpse of it as they walk on the Mall. Because it is hidden by trees, passersby may not bother to investigate unless they happen to pause at the nearby public restrooms. There is a peculiar predicament about this monument. The people who lived in the nation's capital wanted to remember its contribution to the war, but in the capital, national monuments are more important than local ones. Other American cities were able to provide prime locations for their memorials. Citizens in the District of Columbia, however, did not have that alternative. From a distance, this local monument can easily be misperceived to be a national war memorial or a monument for some other purpose.

The most recent commemoration for the First World War is the American Expeditionary Forces Memorial. Official action began in 1956, and Pershing Square was completed in 1982. It is dedicated to all Americans who fought in Europe during World War I, and on a granite wall maps of the major battle campaigns are displayed. Nonetheless, it is General Pershing who is singularly honored. His statue stands before another granite wall which reads simply: "JOHN J. PERSHING." As the leading military figure for World War I, he is symbolically portrayed as the spokesman for those who died. On the other side of the wall on which his name is inscribed, General Pershing's tribute to those who fought is the memorial's inscription:

> IN THEIR DEVOTION, THEIR VALOR, AND IN THE LOYAL FULFILLMENT
> OF THEIR OBLIGATIONS, THE OFFICERS AND MEN OF THE AMERICAN
> EXPEDITIONARY FORCES HAVE LEFT A HERITAGE OF WHICH
> THOSE WHO FOLLOW MAY EVER BE PROUD.

The American Expeditionary Forces Memorial consolidates the best-known memories of World War I. In principle, the memorial commemorates all of those who fought. The campaign maps single out the U.S. Army for special commemoration, and finally, General Pershing is the one person who is most identified with the war. This square with its fountain and monument is one of the most pleasant places in Washington, and Pershing Square may be the last dedication to World War I in the city, but it is surely the most delineated. The AEF Memorial, however, is not the most important monument for the First World War.

The most significant sanctification of ground in the capital for World War I was Arlington National Cemetery. Arlington was originally a cemetery for the Union dead of the American Civil War, but commemorating the World War I dead proved conclusively that it was the national cemetery of the United States.[61] Hundreds of soldiers from this war were buried there, including notables such as General John J. Pershing. The tomb of the Unknown Soldier is the most significant memorial from the First World War. On Memorial Day in 1921 the body of an unknown soldier who fought in France's Marne Valley was selected. The ship *Olympia* delivered the body to the Washington Naval Yard on November 9 where it was received amidst military ceremonies. On November 11, Armistice Day, the unknown soldier was placed in the tomb as President Warren Harding and hundreds of dignitaries from Allied nations watched. During the ceremonies, the president posthumously conferred the Congressional Medal of Honor, the nation's highest honor. In time, foreign countries repeated this citation by bestowing their highest decoration upon this U.S. soldier who symbolized all American soldiers.[62] The Memorial Hall behind the tomb houses these honors for public display. The tomb itself is the crux of it all. The inscription says simply: "HERE RESTS IN HONORED GLORY AN

AMERICAN SOLDIER KNOWN BUT TO GOD.'' The tomb enbodies the idealism
to faith in the common man,[63] regardless of background, and it ties that
idealism to God. While World War I may have been regrettable, sacrificed
American soldiers are made sacred not only by fellow countrymen but also
in the sight of God. The U.S. cause was thus justified and made holy. Since
its dedication, the tomb has been guarded 24 hours a day by select members
of the U.S. Army's Old Guard. What is guarded is more than an unknown
soldier; it is the very symbol of national sacrifice.

The Tomb of the Unknown Soldier, the inclusion of war dead in Arlington National Cemetery, and the armed services memorials were all World
War I commemorations which finally fixed the nation's capital as the
ultimate sacred place for war memorials. It was an obvious and logical
choice, but the sanctification had finally been made.

The last significant development in patterns of national memorials to
result from World War I was the building of memorials on foreign soil,
primarily in France. These monuments were seen as a necessity because over
30,000 American soldiers were buried in cemeteries near the battlefront. In

3.11 Tomb of the Unknown Soldier, Arlington National Cemetery, Arlington,
Virginia (Author's Collection)

response to this, the American Battle Monuments Commission was created by an act of Congress in 1923 to select qualified architects.[64]

These architects rejected modernism and designed their memorials mainly in the neoclassicist style, a strong architectural movement at the time. As one of the more prominent memorial architects, Paul Cret, said: " . . . our knowledge of the architecture of antiquity has come down to us through its finest forms . . . a work of commemorative architecture which has little chance of enduring is hardly worthy of its name."[65]

American designers selectively employed elements of classicism and history. For example, the Oise-Aisne American Memorial has decorative medallions in which "the modern soldier is contrasted with the medieval crusader."[66] Above the portal of the Aisne-Marne Memorial, a crusader in armor is flanked by shields of the United States and France.[67] At Château-Thierry two Greek classical figures, one with a sword, stand with hands joined to symbolize the tie between American and French troops.[68] American symbolism was often displayed by using a sculpture of the American bald eagle with the Union shield on its breast. Classical symbolism gave architects the historical remembrance and notions of valor that they wished to depict, but in so doing it virtually ignored the reality of modern technological warfare. The memorials often portray warfare as it was three centuries before, adding only the symbol of the American eagle. Some exceptions exist. For example, the Somme Chapel has bas-reliefs of artillery, rifles, and a tank, and at Oise-Aisne, capitals for the memorial's colonnade are carved with grenades, hand weapons, propellers, and army division seals. Yet these modern symbols were exceptions rather than the rule. In contrast, many French memorials realistically portrayed the modern soldier, new weapons, and collective suffering, although a number of French memorials were classical in style. The French had experienced the horrors of modern warfare on their own doorstep, and the war itself offered ample symbolism. Most of the American architects had decided that the best memorial was in the neoclassical style with no design compromises. In that decision, they compromised history. Modern warfare was the result of a technological age. The Classical Age had past, and the symbols of that age insufficiently explained the memories of modern warfare and the suffering of those who fought it.

American memorial sites did not emphasize the preservation of battlefield sites. In contrast, Canada restored its trenches as well as those of the German front line at Vimy Ridge, France. Nearby tunnels still contain battlefield debris.[69] At the Somme battlefield, Great Britain has maintained British and German trenches without restoring them.[70] Finally, France has done likewise by leaving remaining ruins of fortresses, trenches, and bomb craters.[71] In contrast, American memorials were largely limited to cemeteries, chapels, and monuments. American cemeteries were located where U.S. troops had fought, but the historical landscape of the war itself was ignored.

3.12 Château-Thierry Monument, France (Author's Collection)

There were some consistent spatial patterns in the design of these American memorials. Many sites had cemeteries with individual grave markers, with a collective battlefield memorial strategically placed near the cemetery.[72] De Busscher, a French journalist, depicts the American tradition of cemeteries as democratic, because each soldier's grave is identified, and as orderly and severe because of their simple geometric lines.[73] The clearest design feature of major U.S. memorials was the grandness of scale. Given the American architects' adoption of the neoclassicist style, hugeness was rather inevitable. As De Busscher comments:

Neo-classical, America's commemorative monuments are in proportion to the U.S.A.'s wide open spaces, immense and colossal, and sometimes even of a quasi-(Albert) Speerian order . . . a characteristic which is accentuated even more by the permanent figuration of the American Eagle which is always sculpted in gigantic proportions.[74]

The United States was not the only nation to erect grandiose memorials. Many Allied countries had large memorials which indirectly symbolized the number of soldiers committed at particular battlefronts. While valor is often portrayed in these monuments, sheer size depicts the incredible loss of life which was partially due to modern warfare. To some, the scale may portray the absurdity of the Great War and its costs and serve as a severe warning for the future.[75] Size denotes power, and the monuments' inscriptions often speak of how Allied power achieved an ultimate good. The

3.13 Chapel Interior at the Aisne-Marne American Cemetery, Belleau Wood, France (Courtesy of the American Battle Monuments Commission)

modern visitor may see negative symbolism in this glorification of power, but before World War II, the belief that the Great War was an act of finality meant that a memorial's size as a metaphor for power carried a positive meaning.

Unlike World War I memorials in the United States, American memorials in Europe were strictly shrines. They were mostly in open countryside rather than in cities. Few constraints existed, and there were no reasons to make them utilitarian. These European memorials are considered by critics to be some of America's finest monuments.[76] The use of site planning to make symbolic connections between the cemeteries and the monuments commemorating those who died is seen as an American hallmark.[77] These memorials set the precedent for how American overseas memorials would be designed in the future.

Memorials for the First World War commemorated not only those who sacrificed their lives, but also the deep belief that there would be no more "great wars." But in the 1930s, even as these memorials were being embellished and new ones begun, this belief was challenged by the rise of Imperial Japan and Nazi Germany. America's involvement in World War II nullified this symbolism, leaving these memorials without any clarity of meaning.[78]

WORLD WAR II

Americans eagerly volunteered for military service during World War II, and their righteous valor for God and country was strong but less naive than in 1917. World War I taught the American people that even in a just war the age of chivalry, if it ever existed, was now past. Yet the Second World War was seen as just. Nazism had to be stopped, and Japan could not expect to go unchallenged after its unprovoked attack on U.S. territory. Seeing the American cause in balanced retrospect, Paul Fussell, a literary critic, has commented:

If we locked away and humiliated Japanese Americans, we gassed no Jews, Gypsies, or homosexuals, and we hanged no partisans. If we bombed Dresden, it was someone else who exterminated the Polish officer corps in the Katyn Forest. We did not starve or work our prisoners to death in Siberia or Manchuria, nor hack off the heads of enemy airmen brought down. We did, to be sure, our share of soldierly looting and raping, but in context these are peccadilloes.[79]

Fighting for this just cause exacted a heavy cost in lives. The United States entered the war after the bombing of Pearl Harbor in 1941, and American casualties were far greater than in World War I. The reason is simple. The U.S. armed forces fought about twice as long and in greater numbers than they did in World War I. Over 390,000 American servicemen were killed in battle in the Atlantic and Pacific campaigns, and over 1 million Americans eventually died from the war.

With so many Americans killed, remembering the sacrifice through war memorials was indeed a large task, and three overall patterns emerged. First, the number of war memorials on foreign soil was significantly increased. In these memorials, some design schemes were continued from the past and some new innovations were introduced. Second, new memorials in Washington, D.C., basically articulated past design efforts rather than diverging or creating new patterns. Finally, the American people generally changed their attitudes about what war memorials should be.

While building memorials and cemeteries for World War I provided the basic framework, the American Battle Monuments Commission also learned from what they saw as past mistakes. There were particular problems with memorials voluntarily provided by military units. Troop memorials " . . . in the past unfortunately had all too often been found to be poorly designed, poorly constructed, and lacking provision for maintenance."[80] The commission discouraged military groups from building memorials as they had done after World War I.

The major change by the American Battle Monuments Commission was in the coordination of memorial efforts. In World War I, some of the major memorials were not located near cemeteries, while others were nearby but not part of the cemetery's design. The commission stopped such separate site locations. To make design efforts more consistent, each cemetery was required to have a small devotional chapel, to inscribe names of those missing in the area, and to have a permanent graphic record of fighting actions by troops in nearby battles. The commission also decided that consistency in design quality was needed as well and chose architects who were thought to be outstanding. At the same time, each architect usually collaborated with a landscape architect, a sculptor, and a muralist or painter. The entire design team was composed of Americans. Yet no architect or artist was allowed to work on more than one project.[81] While the commission wanted efforts to be organized and consistent, it purposely attempted to avoid duplication in memorial designs.

The task of preparing the cemeteries was large, but completion was relatively quick. Designers were selected in 1947, and the American Battle Monuments Commission began to construct and maintain the selected cemetery sites in 1949. After World War I, eight cemeteries had been built with 30,920 graves. The commission supervised the construction of 14 cemeteries containing 93,235 graves from World War II.[82] Although the task of providing graves and memorial facilities was massive, deriving design solutions was expedient since the architects knew the number of service people to be buried. The commission decided that there would be no further burials in these cemeteries unless remains were found in battlefields. The graves "with their memorials constitute inviolable shrines."[83]

The American Battle Monuments Commission had wanted consistency in memorial design and essentially got those results. Yet, design consistency was not a rubber stamp duplication of World War I memorials. Many design transformations took place between the First and Second World Wars, and these were incorporated in overseas memorials for World War II.

Site planning was on an enormous scale, but it was also more intricate than before. The greater number of war dead from World War II meant that cemeteries had to be much larger, and the landscape scale made many cemeteries from the Great War seem small. These earlier cemeteries were typically laid out in rectilinear schemes, such as Saint Mihiel, which contains over 4,000 graves. In comparison, the Lorraine American Cemetery from the Second World War has over 10,000 graves, but less regimented site planning. At Lorraine a curvilinear pattern known as parterre, borrowed from French landscaping, was used to break up the overall pattern and prevent it from being a simple mass.[84] While curvilinear plot segments could be unusual in form, all segments combined to form an overall design in the parterre. While most World War II cemeteries were not as intricate as Lorraine, the principle of curvilinear patterns for grave areas was the most common approach. Symbolically, World War I cemeteries with rectilinear plotting provide an almost militant feeling. Their straightforward shapes give a visual unity which speaks to a social unity: "Our cause was just. United we rest in the belief that our efforts were justified." In contrast, the curvilinear layouts in World War II cemeteries portray a more tranquil feeling as if to say: "Our cause was just, but more importantly we are now at peace." The need to break up large grave sections for design purposes unavoidably provided new symbolic interpretations of the cemetery landscape.

When visiting cemeteries from either World War I or II, American visitors immediately sense that they are on an isolated bit of American ground amidst the land of another country. Most of these national cemeteries are completely enclosed by walls of trees and exclude any potential outside visual disturbance. After leaving the parking lot to enter the main grounds, visitors often see a sign stating Silence and Respect. In a few cemeteries, there are international-style markers, a red circle with a slash painted over a dog, used to keep out pets. It is a polite reminder that these grounds should not be defiled. Visitors, American or not, are visually prepared to enter a sanctified landscape.

The American cemeteries are immaculate. The grass is neatly mowed and edged. Leaves are immediately raked, and trees and shrubbery are neatly trimmed. Crosses are constantly scrubbed to clean bird droppings and all of them are kept perfectly vertical. The memorial chapels and museums have an unused look, and it is hard to imagine that they were not built recently. This tremendous upkeep gives these memorial cemeteries a timeless character, and the political message is that the United States is vigilant in its remembrance of the past.

While curvilinear patterns and a manicured landscape may provide a

3.14 Rectilinear Site Plan of the Meuse-Argonne American Cemetery and Memorial for World War I, France (Courtesy of the American Battle Monuments Commission)

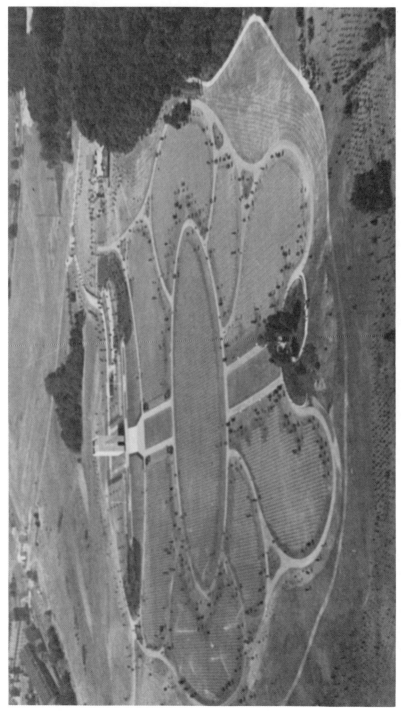

3.15 Curvilinear Site Plan of the Lorraine American Cemetery and Memorial, France (Courtesy of the American Battle Monuments Commission)

relaxed atmosphere, the visitor cannot escape the sheer number of graves. It is not just cross after cross. It is row after row and then section after section. Only when visitors focus on a single cross can they escape this field of graves. Yet, such enormity must be visually organized and accessible. Like memorials from World War I, the cemeteries from the Second World War often contain a central mall as a spine to access graves and maintain visual organization. Such malls are typically longer, because the graves are more numerous. The designed patterns and well-kept landscape reduce the harshness of so many graves. Yet, visitors visually realize the cost of human life in the Second World War. Death in these memorial cemeteries becomes more than a number in a history book.

At Normandy American Cemetery, the long walk between its memorial and the chapel accentuates the great number of deaths. The feeling becomes more real as the visitor looks seaward and imagines the fighting that took place on the nearby beaches. The many columns of graves along the mall almost evoke the feeling of soldiers landing at the beach. The visual explicitness of the graves demonstrates that the cost in human life was immense.

The site planning at the Normandy American Cemetery is unlike any other American memorial in Europe because it goes outside its walls. Beyond the western wall and below are the beaches where U.S. troops landed. At a vista point there is a memorial map which tells where events happened. The more adventurous visitors can walk down the slope and see an old German defense bunker, and some people go down to the beach itself. Looking back, one can capture a sense of the difficult task American soldiers had in capturing the shoreline and moving inland. After trodding up the slope where so many died, visitors can appreciate even more the hardship and sacrifice of the men buried in the cemetery.

The conceptual plans for chapels in these cemeteries were much like those for World War I. Typically a chapel is on high ground with steps leading to its entrance. On such a plateau the visitor often sees a broad field of graves below. Inside the chapel there is usually an altar with a cross and candles at the far end. The visitor normally sees the American flag and military banners about the altar. Natural as well as artificial lighting make the altar a focal point. Inscriptions often go beyond mere commemoration of the war dead, frequently stressing both God and country. For example, at the Rhone American Cemetery Chapel, the visitor can read:

O LORD SUPPORT US ALL THE DAY LONG UNTIL OUR WORK IS DONE.
THEN IN THY MERCY GRANT US A HOLY REST AND PEACE AT THE LAST.

THIS CHAPEL HAS BEEN ERECTED BY THE UNITED STATES OF AMERICA
AS A SACRED RENDEZVOUS OF A GRATEFUL PEOPLE
WITH ITS IMMORTAL DEAD.[85]

This theme is reinforced by the artwork inside and outside the chapel. Sculpture, bas-reliefs, mosaics, and stained glass windows use a variety of

3.16 Normandy American Cemetery and Memorial, France (Courtesy of the American Battle Monuments Commission)

symbolic combinations. If religious figures or a cross are not behind the altar, stained glass windows with an American eagle or service symbols will be present.[86] The same is true for exterior motifs. Yet, religious symbols tend to dominate. God before country, that is, religious freedom before nationalism, has been a tradition of American life. Thus American values are not only reinforced but also exalted. There is also the unavoidable reality that the visitor who enters a chapel can briefly escape the magnitude of death which is ever-present outside the chapel walls. If the visitor does not feel redemption within the chapel, at least there is sanctuary from death, the reprieve of God and country over the sadness and horror of death.

Possibly the most significant innovation introduced in World War II overseas memorials was the wall of the missing. World War I memorials included walls of the missing, but they were interior chapel walls. In comparison, walls of the missing for World War II memorials were exterior design features. More often than not, there was simply not enough wall space inside the chapels to include the names of all those missing. The names of those who died in nearby conflicts were also carved in stone. As a design concept, the wall of the missing enabled memorial architects to make a visual connection between the soldiers buried in the cemetery and their missing comrades.

3.17 Wall of the Missing at Lorraine American Cemetery and Memorial, near St. Avold, France (Courtesy of the American Battle Monuments Commission)

Compared to the cemetery fields, a wall of the missing intensifies the reality of sacrifice. The density and proximity of names on these walls has a powerful impact. On these walls, names do not merely fill all the available space, they also easily permit manipulation for symbolic purposes. The most intricate examples of a design for a wall of the missing are the national cemeteries at Honolulu and Manila. At Honolulu, the courts of the missing are used as hierarchical elements along an axis of steps leading to the Memorial Chapel. The metaphorical statement is: Our deaths were steps to victory for God and country. In Manila, visitors can walk along a mall toward the chapel. At the mall's end, people must walk up steps and then walk to the chapel under one of two hemicycles. The roof of each hemicycle is supported by a colonnade, and each fin wall in the colonnades is completely inscribed with the names of the missing. Wall after wall is thus inscribed, and even in a casual walk visitors must pass name after name. This has the effect at first of personalizing the sacrifice, giving death a name. Finally the accumulation of names is so great that it is easy to become numbed by it. The only way to recapture the intensity of the names is to back away and view the hemicycle structures. In these memorials, death surrounds visitors horizontally as do the cemetery fields, but in addition, the walls of the missing spatially define death vertically. When visitors see both the walls and the grave fields, they are encapsulated three-dimensionally with the memory of sacrifice.

While other walls of the missing are not as elaborate as these two, they are commonly used as a ritual space for moving from one symbolic area to another, such as from a mall to a chapel or from museum to chapel. Along this short journey, landscaping, pools, and warm-feeling building materials typically create an air of serenity. The atmosphere is a symbolic dialectic, an environment of peace juxtaposed against the constant notation of violent death.

Near the chapel there is usually a museum. As specified by the American Battle Monuments Commission, its purpose is to depict through artwork the historic battles that occurred near the memorial. Battle maps are made with glass mosaics, enamel appliques, or engravings on marble, and they portray the general and specific campaigns that were fought by land, air, and sea. On some maps, angels of war are depicted as fighting for the righteous cause of the Allies. More often than not, these are factual, neutral commentaries which describe historical events. The artwork and architectural space is quite orderly and the portrayal of information is not a symbolic attempt to praise God and country. The museum's purpose is to describe historical accounts, not to be evocative.

While architects for World War II overseas memorials rejected the more

3.18 Honolulu Memorial National Cemetery of the Pacific, Honolulu, Hawaii (Courtesy of the American Battle Monuments Commission)

traditional chapel and museum designs used in World War I, neither did they fully embrace modernism. Most of the chapel designs employed either austere classicism from the 1930s, art deco, or (in a few cases) modest modernism. Although the architects were sensitive to site planning and co-ordinated symbolism, they did not attempt to follow the modern stylists of their day, such as Frank Lloyd Wright or Mies Van der Rohe. There were some exceptions. The Cambridge and Henri Chapelle American Cemetery Chapels were modern in style. In contrast, the Brittany American Cemetery Chapel was not noticeably different from most of the World War I chapels. The variety of styles is a reflection not so much of the design values considered to be important in war memorials but of the values which were vying for prominence in the architectural profession. Architecture was undergoing a transformation from neoclassicism to art deco to modernism, and World War II memorials reflected that transformation to some extent.

Artwork tended to follow the same pattern as the architecture since the architects set forth the design agenda. Religious and classical figures were commonly chosen as they had been for World War I memorials, but sculpture figures of the common soldier were not often used. At one extreme, Brittany American Cemetery has a sculpture of a classical youth fighting a dragon of evil. At the other extreme, the *Brothers in Arms* statue at the Sicily-Rome Cemetery depicts two bare-breasted soldiers who are wearing their dog tags and walking arm in arm. The most realistic portrayal of warriors is at the Cambridge Cemetery where soldiers stand in combat dress by the wall of the missing. The sculpture in these cemeteries is typical of sculpture used with American architecture in the 1930s, although due to the purpose of the memorials the symbolism used had more sacred overtones. Like the American architecture of the 1930s, the cemetery sculpture for World War II overseas memorials was less classical than World War I overseas memorials, but the use of traditional symbols continued.

The placement of sculpture works always had a symbolic purpose. They were often focal points which incorporated the many values that made up the particular commemorative message. Whether encircled by inscriptions or at the end of an axis within the cemetery or chapel, these sculptures give symbolic expression to concepts that are not easily verbalized, such as peace, justice, sacrifice, the human spirit, God, country, bravery, memory, honor, brotherhood, and freedom.[87]

The new policy of placing both the chapel and the memorial in the cemetery in World War II overseas memorials allowed virtuous symbols, classical or modern, to provide a stronger counterbalance to the sea of graves. Symbolically, horrific death is subdued to realize honor in death. Even though classic symbols, such as St. George symbolizing the young American warrior on the Manila Chapel, are unknown to most Americans, such portrayals clearly convey respect. Symbolism in the sculpture and the chapel architecture are given immediate legitimacy and meaning by the presence of the grave markers nearby. This is in contrast to many World War I memorials which were physically separated from cemeteries. The Great War memorials, such as Château-Thierry, exalt classic virtues of honor and remembrance without the realization of death which only grave markers in a cemetery can bring. Such memorials are one-half of a dialectic without the presence of the other half. No synthesis can occur. World War II overseas memorial designs have been lauded for the synthesis they permit between the memorial elements and the cemetery.[88]

In addition to the national cemeteries, some overseas memorials were built to remember military units and organizations. For example, the First Army Division used a pylon-shaped memorial listing those who died at numerous battle sites in Europe. At Omaha Beach, the National Guard has built a memorial atop a German bunker to commemorate its members. It is a simple U-shaped wall with inscriptions, but its victory position atop the bunker is somewhat reminiscent of Marines upon Mount Suribachi at Iwo Jima. In some cases, other countries have provided memorials for Americans. At Omaha Beach, the French have built a wedge-shaped memorial symbolizing the Allied thrust on June 6, 1944. At Normandy, homemade local memorials carry such inscriptions as "IN HONOR OF OUR USA LIBERATORS." All of these specialized memorials commemorate specific small moments in the war. In contrast, the large American cemeteries and memorials are cathedrals of coordinated remembrance.

Within the continental United States, the East and West Coast memorials located in New York and San Francisco echo some of the elements of the overseas memorials. These commemorations are dedicated to those members of the U.S. armed services who lost their lives during the Second World War in Atlantic and Pacific waters. While there could be no cemeteries for these people, the American Battle Monuments Commission required that a list of the missing be included as part of these memorials. As a result, both coastal memorials have walls of the missing which are reminiscent of the design solutions used in overseas memorials.

While the basic elements for the coastal memorials are the same, their designs are substantially different. The West Coast memorial is serene. A statue of Columbia stands calmly by to honor the dead listed on the gently curving wall of the missing. The only warlike symbols are a small bas-relief of the mythical horse Pegasus rising from the sea and a bas-relief of an American eagle at the wall's end. In contrast, the East Coast memorial is more militant. It is composed of two colonnades of walls, which lead to a diving American eagle fashioned in black marble. The eagle is carrying a wreath in its talons and is flying just above a sea wave. The inscription for both East and West Coast memorials is the same, except for the identification "Pacific" or "Atlantic."[89] While any regional comparison is questionable, the vibrancy of symbolism in each memorial is in keeping with its setting. The East Coast memorial is on Manhattan Island in New York

City's Battery Park whereas the West Coast memorial is situated on a rather quiet promontory site near the Presidio at San Francisco. While these memorials may reflect their settings, the wall of the missing binds them both to other national memorials for World War II.

Another quite different coastal monument is clearly significant, the USS *Arizona* Memorial at Honolulu, Hawaii. Its simple design represents the passage of time. According to the architect, Alfred Preis, "The form, wherein the structure sags in the center but stands strong and vigorous at the ends expresses initial defeat and ultimate victory."[90] The memorial is anchored to the USS *Arizona*'s remains. Visitors travel by shuttle boats to the memorial. Once inside, visitors see the ship's recovered bell. Symbolically, this end of the memorial can be seen as American strength before the war, and the ship's bell can recall the Liberty Bell in Philadelphia. At the center, where the upper structure sags and both the top and sides are open, the sunken remains of the USS *Arizona* can be seen. To those who remember, this vividly recalls December 7, 1941. On that day the U.S. Pacific naval fleet of battleships and cruisers was essentially destroyed, and 2,400 Americans lost their lives.[91] In the words of President Franklin Roosevelt, it was a day of infamy. While this defeat is remembered, it is contradicted by the American flag which flies from a flagpole mounted to the ship's hull, suggesting victory rising from defeat. Moving away from the memorial's center, visitors enter the shrine room which is lighted by stained glass windows on both its side walls. Upon the back wall is the explicit memorial, the names of those servicemen who died on the USS *Arizona*. The wall is as tall as the opposite end, thus finalizing the memorial's time symbolism—from strength to defeat and then to ultimate victory.

The USS *Arizona* Memorial was designed with a unified symbolism, but it has been overlaid with numerous others. Some politicians wanted it to " . . . stand as a national memorial to eternal vigilance against the dangers of surprise attack."[92] Others wanted the memorial to carry the more strident symbolism of preparedness against Godless communism.[93] Still others wanted " . . . to pay full homage to all of the people who died during the attack, including shore-based personnel and civilians."[94] Another view was that the memorial should emphasize the need for peace, much like the Japanese Peace Park Memorial at Hiroshima.[95] Ultimately, the memorial honors those who died on the USS *Arizona*, without rejecting other possible interpretations.[96] The architect's symbolism is not readily understood, and given the many contradictory views over what should be remembered, the USS *Arizona* Memorial will continue to have multiple political and symbolic meanings.

Many of the World War II memorials built in Washington, D.C., added to the essential pattern of remembrance set forth after World War I. Some memorials were updated. For example, new inscriptions and actual physical additions were made to the First and Second Army Division monuments to

3.19 USS *Arizona* Memorial, Honolulu, Hawaii (Courtesy of the Department Defense Still Media Records Center, Washington, D.C.)

extend the tribute from World War I. Elsewhere in the city, the American Institute of Architects dedicated a memorial by its Octagon House to those in their profession who died in battle. When the American Legion built a new national headquarters in 1947, a World War II GI sculpture was mounted on the facade.[97] On Massachusetts Avenue, a memorial to Sir Winston Churchill was erected. The uninformed passerby might consider this monument to be only a statue of a past statesman, but a close look shows that two fingers of the statue's uplifted right hand are flashing the "V" for victory sign which Churchill made famous during the Second World War. In nearby Falls Church, Virginia, the Four Chaplains Memorial Fountain was dedicated to the chaplains of the United States armed forces. The sculpture portrays the dove of peace and the hull of the *Dorchester*, the ship on which four chaplains sacrificed their lives to save others onboard. By the side of a pool, the four chaplains are represented by four sand-cast panels with religious symbolism conveying the interdenominational aspects of religious faith.[98] These updated and new monuments repeated efforts for commemoration begun after World War I with auxiliary service memorials. New memorials honored groups not commemorated before, and old groups were recognized once again. These new monuments and embellished old ones thoroughly established war memorials as one facet of the capital's image as the home of American democracy.

Memorials within Arlington National Cemetery continued to embellish past monumental practices, and small as well as large additions were made. The cemetery had Grant, Sheridan, and Sherman drives for the Civil War; Roosevelt Drive for the Spanish-American War; and Pershing Drive for World War I. Now there was Patton Drive in memory of General George S. Patton, commander of the Third Army in Europe, as well as streets for General Douglas MacArthur and Admiral Chester Nimitz. Along the entrance drive to the cemetery the 101 Airborne Division Memorial was added. No general monument for the Second World War was erected, but old memorials were updated. The Argonne Cross monument from World War I was updated with a dedication to the Second World War. Most importantly, The Tomb of the Unknown Soldier was symbolically renewed with the addition of a new unknown serviceman in 1958.[99] The small number of new monuments and the renewal of many older ones allowed Arlington National Cemetery to become simultaneously renewed and strengthened as the nation's primary war memorial.

While most World War II memorials followed tradition, the Netherlands Carillon and the Marine Corps Memorial were substantial innovations in comparison to past war memorials. In gratitude for the United States' efforts in liberating the Netherlands from Nazi Germany, the Dutch people raised funds to donate a carillon. This memorial of bells was symbolic of their liberation, because the Dutch rang cathedral bells in their cities on May 5, 1945, the day that the Netherlands was liberated. Fifteen years later it was dedicated to the American people. Unlike other war memorials of its time in Washington, it is extremely modern, devoid of ornament and not immediately understood as a war memorial. At the plaza entrance to the Netherlands Carillon, two abstract bronze cat figures, sometimes called the panthers, act as symbolic guards. In the carillon itself, the 49 bells have coats of arms as symbols identifying all the Dutch areas which contributed.[100] The stark, modern carillon is the only bell tower in Washington which is a war memorial.

A short walk from the carillon is the Marine Corps War Memorial, now one of the best-known monuments for any American war. It was inspired by a photograph by Joe Rosenthal which shows a small detachment of American Marines implanting the American flag atop Mount Suribachi during the bloody battle of Iwo Jima.[101] As Paul Fussell has said about the flag-raising scene at Iwo Jima: "The image is that of committee, soiled and exhausted, to be sure, but nevertheless acting 'as one man' in a rare, and thus precious moment of unanimity . . . an emblem of the common will triumphant."[102] The memorial does not merely replicate the photographic image; it magnifies it. It is huge and realistically alive. The monument has a black marble base, and upon it, six bronze statues are standing on a mound of granite stones holding a flagpole which is flying the American flag. Granite was used for the sculpture's base to simulate the volcanic rock at Mount Suribachi. The figure's action positions in raising the flag symbolize a thrusting determination to defeat Japan. Most important, an American flag flies continuously as a symbol of vigilance. Yet, visitors soon become aware that it is not just a memorial to a single war. When walking around the black marble base, visitors see the names of all the various wars in which Marines have fought since Tripoli. Yet, the Iwo Jima image popularly identifies the monument with the Second World War, and it has passed so completely into the common experience that photos of it are often used as background for the national anthem on nightly television sign offs. The Marine Corps Memorial is probably the best-known American war memorial that Americans associate with victory and justice.

While the U.S. government had continued and even improved war memorial efforts in Washington and overseas, local communities were less interested in building monuments to remember World War II. Skepticism and practicality led to a new tradition of commemoration. Many communities already had a Civil War monument, then a Spanish-American War monument, and finally one for the Great War, and another monument seemed to be senseless repetition. A memorial needed to be useful. After World War I, several utilitarian memorials were built, such as soldiers and sailors auditoriums and other public buildings at civic centers, state grounds, and universities. Americans wanted to be even more practical and democratic in commemorating World War II. The war had come on the heels of the Great Depression, and as a result there was a backlog of practical public projects still to be built. To many townspeople, even old and new veterans, statues did not make much sense. Many communities built parks, swimming pools, recreation centers, hospitals, and schools as memorials. In Blytheville, Arkansas, community folk chose to build a house for a mother whose son was killed in action.[103] If World War II needed to be remembered and the town needed a new public facility, it was cheaper to dedicate a building as a memorial than to pay for a statue to put in front of it. The nation's recent history of war and economic depression made local Americans less romantic but not less patriotic. It was better to put patriotism to work than to stare at a shrine.

There was a substantive criticism about shrines which went beyond practicality. Immediately after the war, Joseph Hudnut, dean of architecture at Harvard University, said in support of utilitarian memorials:

If our soldiers remain anonymous in our useful buildings, that is because they are already anonymous, being inseparable from the nation out of which they sprang. How then can one give them added life except in the life of that nation? The monument recites names, dates, events, and our own piety, but never the spirit. That also the monument does not remember.[104]

Some communities did build monuments, but these memorials were often inspired by traditional ideas rather than the new utilitarian motives of

3.20 Marine Corps War Memorial, Arlington, Virginia (Author's Collection)

modernism. A good example is the War Memorial Fountain in Cleveland, Ohio. Started as a community project in 1946, it was completed 18 years later after many delays. By 1964, the Korean War had also been fought, and separate plaques for World War II and the Korean War were discreetly placed. Entitled *Peace Rising from the Flames of War*, the memorial is literal enough to interpret its meaning. It is an art deco-style sculpture of a youth reaching skyward away from flames which emanate from a globe which symbolizes a world made up of superstition and fear.[105] As with many overseas memorials, the Cleveland memorial design addresses the need to strive for the good in the human spirit, but like so many overseas memorials, its style was essentially dead, an art form from the recent but clearly bygone day of the 1930s. Art deco was the last architectural style that used classical symbols to represent patriotism, justice, and other classical themes. The language of classical symbolism used in past memorials was dying, because modernism was becoming the dominant architectural style. The lack of ornament in modernism paralleled utilitarian notions about war memorials. Modernism reduced everything to bare essentials. With the rise of this new utilitarian approach to war memorials, few communities built monuments as shrines.

Overall, memorials for World War II represent a nation's historical completion of a schema for commemoration. Overseas memorial schemes refined the general process and plan begun after World War I. A few new alternatives for monuments, such as the Netherlands Carillon, were built in Washington, D.C., but more importantly, for the first time older memorials were symbolically reified, such as the Tomb of the Unknown Soldier. With local communities having built statues and formal civic memorials in the past, they decided to memorialize more basic functions of life, such as schools and parks. A collective view emerged. National memorials, domestic and overseas, still needed to be shrines, but local memorials should provide a useful way for townspeople to remember their friends who fought and died in the Second World War.

SYMBOLS OF JUSTICE

While historical circumstances dominate what is commemorated, memorials for these wars represent the nation's development of spatial ritual for its honored values. National sacred places, such as Concord Bridge, were first established to commemorate events in the American Revolution. Later, the world wars legitimized procedures and places for war memorials, such as Arlington National Cemetery and memorials on foreign soil. These commemorative patterns might have evolved from other wars, but it is doubtful. War memorial development in the United States was not so much an evolutionary historical process as it was an immediate response to the nation's deeds of justice. These righteous wars embodied the nation's values more than any other wars before or since, and as a result the memorials for them have become national symbols, which cumulatively add to the desired American image of a strong but just nation.

CHAPTER FOUR
MONUMENTS TO VICTORY
AS MANIFEST DESTINY

Wʜᴇɴ ᴀ ᴄᴏᴜɴᴛʀʏ ᴡɪɴs ᴀ ᴡᴀʀ, its people can easily conclude that their victory was justified, but victories are often won by aggressors rather than defenders. Nationalism is often used to conceal the true motives of power and greed. An aggressor country can proclaim that it must defend its integrity, territory, and citizens, but behind the flag-waving the nation's government may be waiting for an excuse to begin a fight. When conflict ultimately comes, there can be the appearance of a just war where none exists. When the war is over, a country can celebrate its victory as just while purposely underplaying real political gains, such as power and territory. While these wars are promoted as good wars, some people will begin to question the appearance of justice versus the political gains. These wars may come to be seen as unjust or less than just.

There is a common thread running through U.S. wars of questionable victory. These wars were politically justified through Manifest Destiny. It was the American belief that the nation had the God-given right to expand its territories. As a result of this policy, wars on the American continent were inevitable. The War of 1812, American Indian wars, the Mexican wars, and the Spanish-American War were all conflicts that the United States ultimately won. However, the nation's motives in these wars have been questioned. These wars enabled the United States to expand westward to the Pacific and gain control of critical territories and waterways beyond the continent. America's power increased after these wars regardless of whether or not the victories could be justified.

Memorials for Manifest Destiny wars are often less visible than those for America's unquestionably just wars—the American Revolution and the world wars. While these wars are remembered, individual battles and heroes are often commemorated more than the fact that a war was won. War memorials commemorate victory, but monuments for these wars often contain symbolic messages which have contradictory meanings. People can question whether past events are worthy of being commemorated. War memorials give respectability to historical acts, but not all of America's victorious actions were respectable in the wars of Manifest Destiny.

THE WAR OF 1812

The War of 1812 has often been called a tie. While American " . . . war aims had not been gained, nothing had been lost."[1] In the short run this view was true, but from the perspective of history, the war was a resounding victory for the United States. The War of 1812 stimulated the development of national pride. More pragmatically it proved to Americans that they could defend themselves against the British and keep them out. As a result, the alliance between the American Indians and the British against the United States was broken, and the Indians had to defend themselves in future wars. Great Britain ensured American expansionism in the West with the British Treaty Line of 1818, which is now the Canadian border. Spain, a declining world power, realized that it could not defend its American territories when a stronger Great Britain was unable to overcome the Americans. Rather than engaging in an inevitable war, Spain ceded Florida to the United States in 1819 with a settlement of outstanding monetary claims.[2] The War of 1812 was not merely a tie. It was a warning to other nations which held territories on the continent that the United States intended to move them out.

As the United States began its period of expansionism, people wanted to express a national identity with symbols. Part of this symbolism was eventually orchestrated through war memorials for the American Revolution and the War of 1812. In remembering the War of 1812, two basic patterns emerged. Battle sites in the Great Lakes, the Chesapeake Bay, and New Orleans were commemorated, and certain artifacts from these battles have been transformed into national symbols and enhanced by well-known patriotic slogans.

The most important monument in the Great Lakes is Perry's Victory and International Peace Memorial. In the Battle of Lake Erie on September 10, 1813, Captain Oliver Hazard Perry successfully led his two ships, the *Lawrence* and the *Niagara*, to victory over the British. Perry made the battle famous with his words: "We have met the enemy and they are ours."

Over a hundred years later, the memorial was constructed by Put-in-Bay on Bass Island. Its symbolic purpose is not only to remember Perry's victory but also to celebrate a lasting peace between Canada and the United States. The memorial is not only one of the nation's largest war monuments but also one of the simplest. The massive Doric column with a pedestaled fire urn on its top resembles a victory column or perhaps a symbolic torch. Its enormous size makes the monument a spectacle as vast as peering into the Grand Canyon. When it is artificially lit at night, the memorial is quite spectacular. It can be seen for miles. It acts as a light tower and, for some, as a metaphorical "beacon of hope."

The plaza and the memorial's interior hall more clearly convey what is being remembered. Two stone urns are placed on each side of the steps leading up to the memorial plaza as a symbolic gateway of remembrance. The left urn commemorates the USS *Lawrence* while the one on the right is dedicated to the USS *Niagara*. Inside the memorial hall the walls are engraved with the names of those American sailors who died in the Battle of Lake Erie. On the floor is a stone informing the visitor that three Americans and three British officers lie in a crypt beneath the floor. The joint internment of these war dead is a simple way of honoring friend and foe together in a gesture of peace. On the other hand, the names of the American dead on the walls of honor make it clear that the emphasis is on remembering the Americans. Some U.S. presidents have made commemorative statements about the memorial's peaceful purpose. Bronze plaques display the words of presidents Taft, Wilson, and Kennedy asking for remembrance and peace in the future. All these individual commemorations on the plaza and in the memorial hall allow the Battle of Lake Erie to be remembered more specifically than by the victory column alone.

On closer inspection, there is confusing symbolism in the Perry monument. Although the monument appears to be unified in its various levels of symbolism, a trip to the top of the monument reveals decorative lions' heads beneath the urn and atop the pedestals. Americans might expect eagles to represent an American victory, not lions, which symbolize Great Britain. It is ironic that the enemy's national symbol graces the pinnacle of this monument. The memorial's architect, however, never gave any symbolic explanation for these lions. Visitors may expect the lions to have symbolic meaning, but there is none.

On the memorial's grounds there are less dramatic but still important symbolic messages. The most prevalent is the joint flying of American and Canadian flags at the same height to symbolize an equal peace. The monument is also a place for enjoyment. The National Park Service provides evening programs, such as "Nineteenth-Century Medicine and Death," to teach history and entertain visitors. These symbolic messages say that now there is peace, and while time goes on, people should remember that wars lead into other histories that they need to understand.

4.1 Perry's Victory and International Peace Memorial, Lake Erie (Author's Collection)

While Perry's Victory and International Peace Memorial is the most dominant commemoration of the War of 1812 in the Great Lakes area, military forts are next in importance. A number of small forts no longer exist, and all that remains are earth embankments on farms with a state marker on a nearby road. Visitors can stop to read why these military posts were important in American history, but they can only imagine what once existed. Some forts, however, have been restored.

Immediately south of Toledo, Ohio, is Fort Meigs, which was built in 1813 under the command of General William H. Harrison, later president of the United States.[3] Fort Meigs is typical of the wooden stockade forts of its time. Being administered locally rather than by the National Park Service, this historic fort lacks the meticulous maintenance of a national monument, although the caretakers do try to emulate the National Park Service. There are few visitors, and it is possible to walk about the grounds totally undisturbed. Along the north wall are gun emplacements which face the Maunee River. An American flag waves alongside on a simple staff made of lashed wooden poles. It was here that American troops shot at British troops across the river and successfully defended themselves against a siege.[4] On the grounds within the walls, there are a few markers with pictorial descriptions, a few cannons, some earth redoubts, and a simple cabin which once served as a storehouse. The most prominent object is the obelisk memorial which commemorates the building of Fort Meigs. A brief inscription is dedicated to the fort's history. Along the wall are block houses open to the public. While all these elements exist, the visitor's main impression is of a huge lawn surrounded by a wooden fence. Fort life is not intensely captured, although the small number of employees dress in traditional attire. The actual importance of Fort Meigs is perhaps captured neither by its monument nor its remains but by what is not there. Immediately outside the fort's entrance is a stone pedestal base dedicated to Pennsylvania soldiers who fought there in 1813, but there is no statue atop the pedestal. Even for fellow Pennsylvanians, Fort Meigs is symbolically important, but not important enough to pay for a statue. The site represents history for local people to promote, but compared to Perry's Battle of Lake Erie, most Americans are unaware of Ft. Meigs.

Of all the American forts involved in the War of 1812, Fort Niagara is the best known and most visited in the Great Lakes region. Visitors to nearby Niagara Falls can easily catch another attraction in a one-day visit. Fort Niagara is not solely a memorial to the War of 1812. Established in the sixteenth century, it has a colorful history, first being occupied by the French, then the British, and finally the Americans. Fort Niagara's military history is somewhat embarrassing to America. The fort became American property with the signing of the Treaty of Paris in 1783. Because the U.S. government owed money to Loyalists, however, the British refused to leave. With the Jay Treaty of 1796, U.S. troops finally occupied Fort Niagara for the first time.[5] When the War of 1812 broke out, the British quickly recaptured the fort and held it for the remainder of the war. Americans occupied the fort once and for all after the Treaty of Ghent in 1814.

Fort Niagara is mainly associated with the War of 1812, because its active military history ends with that war. While visitors may be aware of the fort's connection to the War of 1812, for most it is simply an interesting old fort. Fort Niagara is entertaining, and it has a latent amusement park character. Before entering, visitors see highly manicured earth embankments, and they cross a wooden bridge into a gatehouse with a royal seal above the door. While the fort is obviously a military one, one is reminded of entering the fantasy castle at Disneyland. Once inside, visitors can learn the fort's history by taking guided tours to see various buildings, gun emplacements, and particular points on the grounds. Summer tourists are able to see archeologists at work systematically digging for artifacts. Near the center are the flags of France, Great Britain, and the United States. A decorative cannon is nearby. On the lakeside, fort employees in traditional British military dress simulate a cannon firing for everyone's enjoyment. Visitors enjoy the little show, and no one seems to mind that the cannon crew is symbolically shooting at Americans. Moreover, while American symbolism is present, such as the American flag, there is a British royal seal over the block house entrance. It reminds the visitor that this is one historic site in the United States that Americans never dominated in battle.

Fort Niagara's most specific memorial to the War of 1812 is an indirect commemoration. On the lakeside wall is the Rush-Bagot Memorial which is dedicated to an 1817 treaty between the U.S. and Great Britain for naval disarmament in the Great Lakes. The memorial is starkly simply. The entrance walls honor the American and British diplomats who negotiated

4.2 Fort Niagara State Historical Park, New York (Author's Collection)

the 1817 treaty. At the end of the left entrance wall is a bas-relief of America's Rush, and on the right is a similar relief for Britain's Bagot. At the top of the steps is an altar on which rests a bronze plaque. Bounded between wreaths of peace, the seal of the United States on the left, and Great Britain's seal on the right, the plaque is fully covered with an inscription that quotes the terms of the 1817 treaty. The treaty inscription physically ties American symbolism to British symbolism in a political bond. While not as grand in scale as Perry's Victory and International Peace Memorial on Lake Erie, the Rush-Bagot Memorial serves the same purpose of commemorating peace for Lake Ontario.

Some War of 1812 memorials commemorate war heroes and battles rather than peace. Often these serve to provide communities with a local identity. The Commodore Oliver Hazard Perry Monument, now standing in Perrysburg, Ohio, was first placed and dedicated in Cleveland in 1860 as the first public monument in the state of Ohio.[6] The statue of Perry, who is in a position of readiness, stands in a city park at the end of the main street. Its most important function is to provide a civic identity by memorializing the city's namesake. Erie, Pennsylvania, has a Perry Monument located on the Presque Isle Peninsula. It is a victory column with an urn supported by a pedestal on its top. The island is mainly devoted to outdoor recreation, and the memorial provides an attraction for visitors. Near Erie's downtown area, tourists can go aboard the restored *Niagara* to see the weapon that made Perry's success possible.[7] All of these memorials serve as a way for communities to establish local identity, but they teach little about the War of 1812 itself.

Although Lake Erie and then Lake Ontario are associated most with the War of 1812, Commodore Thomas MacDonough's victory over the British on Lake Champlain has also been commemorated. The MacDonough Memorial, which stands in Plattsburgh, New York, is a large obelisk with a spread-winged eagle perching at its top. Above the base cornice the names of MacDonough's small fleet of ships—*Saratoga*, *Ticonderoga*, *Preble*, and *Eagle*—are inscribed. Beneath the cornice is a stone relief which bands around the obelisk. The sculpted relief intertwines images of naval weaponry and classical armor, with the American eagle embellishing the design at key points. While the symbols in this bas-relief are many, they convey the feeling of decoration rather than any orchestrated meaning. The obelisk and the perched eagle, easily conceived as symbols of victory, convey the primary message, but visitors must read the monument's inscription to identify it as a War of 1812 memorial.[8] Like many obelisks, the MacDonough Memorial "marks the spot" without explaining the historical importance.

The primary messages conveyed by 1812 memorials on the Great Lakes are first victory, and then peace. Americans visiting these major memorials for the War of 1812 learn little about what was at stake.[9] Americans sought not only to defeat the British, but also to expand their territories into Canada. Their failure to do so stirred the beginnings of Canadian patriotism. Moreover, U.S. aggression has been symbolically covered by commemorating peace. It is necessary to visit memorials on the Canadian side to realize that Americans were the aggressors in this conflict.

The defense of the Chesapeake Bay area, while ultimately successful, was a difficult and somewhat embarrassing episode for the Americans. The British defeated the Americans at Blandenburg, Maryland. This opened the door for the attack on Washington, D.C., itself. The Capitol, the White House, and other major buildings were burned on August 24, 1814. The British then tried to take Baltimore, but the British army and naval forces were repelled, most notably at Fort McHenry.[10]

The memorials commemorating the Chesapeake Bay campaign celebrate the victorious defense of Baltimore; the humiliating defeat in Washington, D.C., is simply ignored. The insult to the young nation of being defeated in its own capital goes unmarked. The Capitol and the White House were rebuilt, but without any explicit symbolism expressing their phoenixlike resurrection.

In Baltimore, "The Monument City," the reverse is true. Baltimore has the highest density of War of 1812 memorials in the country. Commemoration centers on Fort McHenry, with most of the other memorials playing supporting roles.

Fort McHenry is known as the birthplace of "The Star-Spangled Banner." Francis Scott Key wrote America's national anthem after watching the nightlong bombardment of Fort McHenry and seeing the flag illuminated in the battle light. Fort McHenry's defense was not only the decisive victory in the Chesapeake Bay campaign, but also the sacred ground of a nation's patriotism. When singing the national anthem, Americans typically imagine Fort McHenry in the night: "O say can you see . . . that our flag was still there."

At the Fort McHenry National Monument and Historic Shrine visitors can watch a patriotic movie depicting the War of 1812, Fort McHenry's role in the Battle of Baltimore, and the legacy of Francis Scott Key's "The Star-Spangled Bannner." For the grand finale, the curtains are drawn to reveal, through the glass wall, Fort McHenry itself. This historical background makes it easier for visitors to appreciate the statue of Major George Armistead, the U.S. commander of Fort McHenry, which stands at the outside entrance to the visitors' center. It enhances the visitors' enthusiasm and understanding of the other memorials at Fort McHenry as well.

The fort structure is star-shaped with five bastions, and outside of its walls are earth redoubts with strategically placed cannons. Soldiers' quarters, Armistead's headquarters, guardhouses, and underground rooms which were used for a prison during the Civil War are open to the public. For children, the fort is a playground for "pretend" wars, in spite of signs beneath each cannon which read Stay Off Cannon. From these cannon positions, the visitor has a view of Baltimore's port and can imagine where the battle was fought after reading a nearby descriptive plaque on a podium. Learning history, seeing where it happened, and taking positions beside a cannon enable visitors to use their imagination to reenact the battle of Fort McHenry.

In the afternoons, a volunteer group dressed in U.S. military uniforms of the 1812 era perform a flag ceremony for visitors on the fort's parade ground. After squad drills and a roll from the drummer the massive American flag is replaced by another with an appropriate gun salute. The American flag is the symbolic heart of Fort McHenry. If not for "The Star-Spangled Banner," this shrine would only be another old fort which might have been destroyed. At Fort McHenry, Americans can try to experience more closely what the national anthem creates in the poetic landscape of its lyrics.

With so much emphasis on the heritage of the national anthem, it was inevitable that its author, Francis Scott Key, would be commemorated. On the park's grounds a statue of Orpheus, a mythological Greek hero of music and poetry, was dedicated in memory of Francis Scott Key and the soldiers and sailors who fought in the battles surrounding Baltimore.[11] Although the monument is dedicated to those who fought, the memorial's theme is overwhelmingly related to Key's contribution. The birth of an American symbol, "The Star-Spangled Banner," is memorialized much more strongly than those who fought. The American flag flies over Fort McHenry both night and day, and together the fort and flag symbolize national vigilance. The statue of Orpheus is emblematic of the man who put this symbolism into lyrics.

The city of Baltimore has some memorials for the War of 1812 which continue the Star-Spangled Banner theme, such as the Star-Spangled Banner Flag House and Museum to honor Mary Pickersgill, who made the famous flag.[12] The Francis Scott Key Monument further embellishes the national anthem theme. A bronze statue of Key sits in a stone boat offering the manuscript of "The Star-Spangled Banner" to a bronze Columbia who stands on a marble pedestal and symbolizes the American spirit.[13] The entire ensemble can be interpreted as the furtherance and enhancement of American patriotism. In this case, the War of 1812 is a means to a more important end, nationalism. Moreover, the flag's history is recounted in symbols with the Star-Spangled Banner Monument, dedicated in 1914 as a centennial remembrance. In the memorial, two children holding a scroll remind Americans not only that the national anthem was written in Baltimore but also that we should learn about its patriotic purpose.[14] These memorials enable the city of Baltimore to embellish the American flag's symbolism and to share in the glory made possible by the fighting at Fort McHenry.

The most important memorial of historical importance is the Battle Monument which commemorates the Battle of Baltimore. Perhaps its greatest claim to fame is that the Battle Monument is considered to be "The first substantial war memorial built in the United States."[15] While passersby might think that the Battle Monument is just an ornamental structure, the memorial's symbolism is actually quite complex. Atop is a statue that represents Baltimore as she holds up a crown of glory. A rudder held in the other hand represents navigation as guidance. At her side is an eagle symbolizing the United States. The monument's column is a carved Roman fasus, staves symmetrically bound to symbolize the Union. Atop the column is a laurel wreath connoting glory, and just below it a cypress wreath represents mourning. At the column's base is an inscription commemorating the Battle of North Point, and beside the inscription are the bodies of griffins, each with an eagle's head, combining symbols of immortality and nationalism. The cornice of the pedestal base is decorated with a winged globe in an Egyptian style as a symbol of eternity and the flight of time. The base itself is constructed of rustic stone to represent strength, and the black doors for the base symbolize the entrance to a cenotaph which symbolically holds those who fought and died in the Battle of Baltimore.[16] The Battle Monument's symbolism is highly organized, and more importantly, it is the first significant example of the European tradition of war memorials being used in the United States.

While local people may proudly point to the Battle Monument as one of the first war memorials in the United States, its symbolism may easily escape most people. They see a classical-style monument now surrounded by large buildings. The Battle Monument requires a knowledge of classical symbolism in order to understand it. Seeing eagles and a statue with a raised arm conveys an obvious message to most people, that of national victory. With the passing of classicism, Americans are less familiar with the monument's vocabulary. The Battle Monument is more elegant than Fort McHenry, but lacks its clarity of purpose.

In remembrance of all the battles of the Chesapeake Bay campaign, the pattern has been to convert victory into patriotism. While memorials to the War of 1812 do exist in Washington, D.C., there are none for the actual events that occurred there. Many Americans are unaware of the burning of Washington and, outside of history books, only guided tours through the Capitol and the White House point it out. In contrast, the Battle of Baltimore has been converted into a national symbol with Fort McHenry and the writing of "The Star-Spangled Banner." This symbolism is so strong that America's war aims of Manifest Destiny can easily be overlooked, along with the national disgrace of Washington being burned.

If victory and defeat are mixed in the Chesapeake Bay campaign, there is no such confusion regarding the Battle of New Orleans in the southwestern campaign. In January 1815, General Andrew Jackson and his American

4.3 The Battle Monument for the War of 1812, Baltimore, Maryland
(Author's Collection)

troops were victorious over the attacking British forces on the Chalmette plantation. Although the Treaty of Ghent had been signed to end the war in December 1814, the Battle of New Orleans in January 1815 provided a spark to American patriotism and immediately made Andrew Jackson a national hero.

The Chalmette National Historical Park commemorates Jackson's victory. Like many national park battlefields, actual events are reconstructed in the landscape. Earth embankments supported with wooden planks demarcate the American battle line, with old cannons strategically placed to reinforce the image. In the visitor center, an electric map program and a slide show depict battle events. A small museum houses artifacts as well as a diorama to further understanding. The main memorial to the Battle of New Orleans is the Chalmette Victory Monument which is located on the American side of the battle line. Similar in design to many obelisk war memorials built in the nineteenth century, it merely marks the spot where the battle was won. Except for its Egyptian-style doorways, the Chalmette Monument is void of ornament, but its form is carried over to the adjacent national cemetery. Some grave markers are miniatures of the Chalmette Monument, even though the markers were not made for those Americans who died at Chalmette. Nonetheless, the miniatures are a way of affirming the continuity of purpose of those who died at the Battle of New Orleans. In total, there is little symbolism at Chalmette, and what there is, is simplistic.[17] The primary meaning is that the United States defeated the British in their last confrontation.

Probably the most familiar memorial associated with the Battle of New Orleans is the equestrian statue of General Andrew Jackson on Jackson Square in New Orleans' French Quarter. With Jackson raising his officer's hat, and his horse rearing up, the Jackson memorial portrays an air of confidence and forwardness. On the pedestal base is the inscription: "THE UNION MUST AND SHALL BE PRESERVED." Many visitors might assume that this statement pertains to the War of 1812, but this is not the case. U.S. General Benjamin Butler loosely paraphrased a Jackson quote and had the translation inscribed immediately after the Civil War when Union troops occupied New Orleans. Oddly enough, the inscription is quite appropriate to Jackson's purposes for fighting the British at Chalmette, although the memorial has conflicting meanings for many citizens of New Orleans.[18] Nonetheless, the Jackson memorial is a point of local pride and symbol of an American victory.

While Andrew Jackson's victory at the Battle of New Orleans is glorified, few Americans are aware of his other exploits in the southwestern campaign. Andrew Jackson sought not only to defeat the British, but also to gain territory from the Creek Indians and Spain. While these conflicts were smaller and less well known than the Battle of New Orleans, they had far-reaching consequences. The defeat of the Creeks moved the Indians west of the Mississippi River, and the capture of Pensacola discouraged Spain in its efforts to retain Florida.[19] Behind the glory of New Orleans was the quiet but steady force of Manifest Destiny.

Being less well known, the Creek and Spanish conflicts have few memorial dedicated to them. The Horseshoe Bend National Military Park is the most significant memorial to Andrew Jackson's southwestern campaign other than his fight at Chalmette, but it is still unknown. Most people can easily confuse Horseshoe Bend with a Civil War battle since Alabama is primarily remembered for its home defense of the Confederacy. At the park, the memorial commemorating Jackson's victory over the Creeks is starkly simple. Known as the Congressional Monument, it is a polished stone monolith which simply says: "HERE ON THE HORSESHOE BATTLEGROUND GENERAL ANDREW JACKSON AND HIS BRAVE MEN BROKE THE POWER OF THE CREEK INDIANS UNDER CHIEF MANUWA." While it was suggested that the Creek Indians should be commemorated on the monument, it has not been done.[20] At Fort Toulouse, there is a simple rough stone obelisk with an inscription on a bronze plaque commemorating the surrender of the Creeks to General Jackson.[21] If the southwestern campaign itself is barely remembered, Jackson's invasion of Fort Barrancas at Pensacola has been forgotten. There is no monument, not even a typical state historical marker noting Jackson's attack.[22] War memorials for Jackson's conquests outside of New Orleans are not only few but also lacking in symbolism which might provide some hint of U.S. aggression.

In retrospect, the Battle of New Orleans has overshadowed the political importance of other battles in the southwestern campaign, and war memorials in this region reflect this attitude. Unlike the other battle campaigns for the War of 1812, crucial victories are forgotten. Yet of all the battles fought, Jackson's victories over the Creek nation and the potential threat to the Spanish created by the taking of Pensacola eventually reaped the greatest territorial rewards. Manifest Destiny is not explicitly acknowledged, while American victory and honor are celebrated at Chalmette National Historical Park and Jackson Square in New Orleans.

While the Great Lakes, Chesapeake, and southwestern campaigns were commemorated differently, the War of 1812 was significant in the emergence of national symbols. Each of these campaigns contributed to this symbolism, and the most central gathering point of national memory is Washington, D.C., and nearby sites. Foremost among these symbols is "The Star-Spangled Banner." Fort McHenry is the place that people associate with the national anthem, although the actual flag which flew "through the perilous fight" now resides in the Museum of American History of the Smithsonian Institution. Tattered with age, bedraggled, and with fragments missing due to souvenir hunters, the Star-Spangled Banner is the ultimate war memorial for the War of 1812. The war's purpose and its territorial consequences seem to be forgotten.[23]

The other major commemoration for the War of 1812 is in the nation's capital behind the White House. Lafayette Park initially appears to be a remembrance to the American Revolution. Monuments at the square's corners depict foreign military leaders Von Steuben, Kosciusko, de Rochambeau, and Lafayette, but in the center is an equestrian statue of General Andrew Jackson, replicas of which exist in Nashville and New Orleans's Jackson Square. Moreover, Lafayette Square is bounded to the east by Madison Place, which honors Madison, president during the War of 1812. On the west side is Jackson Place. All these places were named after famous men who fought against Great Britain. Symbolically, the entire square is a statement of defiance, both domestic and foreign, against Great Britain. Still, there is a hint of Manifest Destiny. General Jackson proudly faces west, symbolic of American territorial gains due to his southwestern campaign. More to the point are the four cannons which are symmetrically grouped around the statue's base. Taken by Jackson in his capture of Pensacola, Florida, these Spanish cannons symbolize Jackson's aims to expand American territory.[24] Finally, the Jackson monument is directly adjacent to the White House, making a symbolic connection between the two. The connection is redemption. While the White House was burned by the British, General Jackson redeemed this embarrassment by soundly defeating the British at New Orleans. Nonetheless, these symbolic connections at Lafayette Park are not immediately obvious.

While the Chesapeake Bay and southwestern campaigns are commemorated with national symbolism in Washington, the Great Lakes battles have received national recognition at the U.S. Naval Academy in Annapolis, Maryland. Commodore Perry's Don't Give Up the Ship banner, which flew in the Battle of Lake Erie, is displayed in Bancroft Hall. Most of the War of 1812 was fought in the three landlocked campaigns, but fighting on the high seas has not been forgotten. At Annapolis one of the academy's first war memorials was the Macedonian Monument, which commemorates Captain Stephen Decatur, who commanded the USS *United States* in its victory over the British frigate, the *Macedonian*. The monument characterizes a victory trophy. The statue is a stone version of the *Macedonian's* masthead with captured cannons on all four corners of the monument's pedestal. While the War of 1812 is specifically remembered, the monument suggests a more poignant message of what the U.S. Navy can and will be expected to do in future encounters.

The most popular war memorial to the battles on the high seas, however, is not in Washington or Annapolis but in Boston harbor. The USS *Constitution*, anchored in the Charleston Navy Yard, is best remembered by its nickname, "Old Ironsides." Known as a fighting ship which could withstand physical punishment, the USS *Constitution* has become a national symbol of naval strength and preparedness. Like other historic ships that have been preserved, visitors can go aboard to learn about life at sea. Visting the USS *Constitution* is similar to visiting a historic fort.

4.4 General Andrew Jackson Monument at Lafayette Park, Washington, D.C. (Author's Collection)

While the ship is the historical artifact, the nearby USS *Constitution* Museum makes its history more explicit. Here the ship's role in the War of 1812 is presented in a slide show. There are also diverting displays of how the ship was built. Visual displays of artifacts then attempt to account for its naval action. More elegant ship artifacts and personal mementos of its famous commander, Isaac Hull, are displayed in a trophy room. As with "The Star-Spangled Banner," the War of 1812 made the USS *Constitution* a national symbol, "Old Ironsides," although Americans may remember little about the purpose of the war itself.

The War of 1812 is perhaps the most deceiving of America's wars of Manifest Destiny. Great Britain gave the United States a legitimate reason for declaring war, and the major war memorials which have been built emphasize this rationale. Defense against the British, victory over the British, and peace with the British echo the loudest. Some credence, although very little, is given to peace with Canada, but there is no portrayal of the United States as the aggressor. Finally, the territorial gains are barely remembered at all. Americans are distracted by national symbols to the War of 1812 without regard to its aims, whether legitimate or questionable. The United States needed patriotic symbols, and the War of 1812 provided the catalyst for their creation.

THE MEXICAN WARS

Western expansion inevitably produced conflict between the United States and Mexico. These were two young countries that had freed themselves from colonialism, the United States from Great Britain and Mexico from Spain. Both nations saw the need to settle their frontiers, and it was clear that Americans would move west for more land while Mexico needed to stabilize settlements in its territories, especially Texas and California. Both the Texas Revolution and the Mexican War of 1846 enabled the United States to expand its territory westward at the expense of Mexico.

The Texas Revolution has been well commemorated, but the Mexican War has been barely remembered. In 1836, Texans were fighting for independence as the state of Texas. In comparison, the Mexican War has been often thought of as little more than a U.S. police action against a weak and unprepared opponent. In terms of American identity, the War of 1846 was insignificant, but in concrete terms, the war reaped the greatest land harvest of America's expansionist period. For these two wars, honoring the past and acknowledging political results are inversely related to one another.

The different perceptions of these two wars are reflected in the war memorials built to remember them. The pattern of memory for the Texas Revolution has been to recognize independence, endurance, victory, and specific heroes, just as was done for the American Revolution. Memorials for the Mexican War of 1846 are best characterized by their rarity, although far more people died in it than in the Texas Revolution.

The Texas Revolution has been the traditional source of identity for Texans, but before the state's centennial in 1936, there were no major memorials to remember the fight for independence. Texas had few monuments for anything. Until the oil boom in the 1920s, Texas was economically poor. The state of Texas wasted no time once money was available, and state pride meant that something had to be done to celebrate 100 years of independence. Instead of taking a moderate pace, Texas organized a commission and built all of its major memorials for the 1936 centennial.[25] Texas completed in fewer than ten years what the New England states took decades to accomplish for the American Revolution.

Texas independence is memorialized at the sites where the fighting began and where its declaration was signed. Gonzales is to Texas what Lexington is to the entire United States. The First Shot of the Texas Revolution Monument is a simple design of two classical figures framing a bronze relief of the first battle. Common citizens are shown holding weapons in readiness for battle, standing by the cannon used to fire against the Mexican army. The first part of the inscription below the relief gives the historic facts and the famous citizen's defiant reply to the Mexicans who demanded the cannon's return: "COME AND TAKE IT." The second part of the inscription, however, reveals both Texas pride and the realities of Manifest Destiny: "THIS SHOT

STARTED THE REVOLUTION AND WAS DIRECTLY RESPONSIBLE FOR ADDING MORE TERRITORY TO THE UNITED STATES THAN WAS ACQUIRED BY THE FREEING OF THE ORIGINAL THIRTEEN COLONIES OF ENGLAND.'' The memorial relief visibly magnifies the importance of the Texas commoner while devoting just a small space for the inscription which describes the enormous land gains which resulted from the war.

Texas has preserved the original site of the writing and signing of its Declaration of Independence. Washington-on-the-Brazos is not Philadelphia, nor does it have a respectable Independence Hall to point to as a symbol of state pride. Instead, there is a simple duplicate of the building where the declaration was signed in 1836. The impression is that Washington-on-the-Brazos was never sophisticated, and that little occurred here except the making of the declaration. Nonetheless, there is a museum and a simple monument to remember those Texans who signed the declaration, but the document itself is in the state capitol in Austin. Washington-on-the-Brazos presents a subdued impression which is in contrast to the independent image that Texans have created for themselves.

If Texas has modest memorials to its independence, the opposite is true for its battles symbolizing endurance. The foremost image of Texas history is the Alamo. Located in downtown San Antonio, the old mission was refurbished in 1936, and a plaza was made to include a museum and a cenotaph.[26] For Texans, the Alamo is the state's most sacred space. In this more than in any other conflict, Texans were willing to follow commandant Colonel Travis's cry: "Victory or Death." It was the Battle of the Alamo that united settlers to see their conflict with Mexico as freedom through sacrifice. The Alamo was a church, but the battle transformed it into a different kind of holy place. The names of those who fought are engraved on brass plaques on the interior archways, and as a result, the Alamo's entire interior has become a hall of heroes. Immediately adjacent to the mission is the Alamo Museum, built for the Texas centennial. It contains some hero portraits and many artifacts from the past, such as the Bowie knife made famous by its designer. The artifacts in the Alamo and the museum capture some sense of the way it was in 1836, but the meaning behind them is not articulated in a symbolic sense. The Alamo has become more important as a symbol for the state than for the battle which was fought there. For Texans, it symbolizes self-reliance and sacrifice in the pursuit of greatness.

The mission's symbolism is captured by the Heroes of the Alamo Cenotaph, which sits at the edge of the plaza. On the east facade James Bowie and James Bonham are portrayed, while the west side glorifies David Crockett and William Travis. Behind these well-known men are other figures used to portray the lesser known men who also died. On each facade, the image is mainly one of preparedness and strength as if to imply that death was incidental to the purpose of their fight. On the main facade,

4.5 The Alamo Cenotaph, San Antonio, Texas (Author's Collection)

facing south toward Mexico, is a figure known as the Spirit of Sacrifice.[27] The figure stands on a funeral pyre which is symbolic of those Texans who died, and with arms stretched upward, the male figure conveys the message "We shall not forget." As the embodiment of Texas, facing toward the enemy, it may also be more stridently interpreted as the infamous cry, "Remember the Alamo." Such an interpretation can be criticized as conjecture, but two other symbolic elements support this view. On the north side is a peaceful, classical figure respectfully holding the shields of the United States and Texas as if to say: "We embrace the same principles." The inscription makes the point more directly:

ERECTED IN MEMORY TO
THE HEROES WHO SACRIFICED THEIR LIVES AT THE
ALAMO, MARCH 6, 1836
IN THE DEFENSE OF TEXAS
"THEY CHOSE NEVER TO SURRENDER NOR RETREAT, THESE BRAVE
HEARTS WITH FLAG STILL PROUDLY WAVING PERISHED
IN THE FLAMES OF IMMORTALITY THAT THEIR HIGH SACRIFICE
MIGHT LEAD TO THE FOUNDING OF TEXAS."

The Alamo Cenotaph indirectly portrays Manifest Destiny. The "founding" of Texas is meant to be on American terms as portrayed by the defiant Spirit of Sacrifice and the empathetic figure holding U.S. and Texas shields. The heroic figures on the east and west facades, famous and anonymous, are portrayed as being secondary to the main purpose, the independence and the "founding" of Texas as a step in American expansionism.

If the memorials for the Alamo glorify the Texas Revolution, the Goliad Memorial remembers sacrifice more somberly. Fannin and his men were executed in front of a firing squad, not slain in battle. Beneath the monument are the collective remains of those Texans who were executed, and the memorial is actually a collective tombstone to remember the massacre ordered by General Santa Anna. Along its horizontal wall are the names of the 340 men who were executed, and in the center is a vertical structure of two columns supporting a stone relief.[28] Between the two columns at the base is a carved wreath to represent remembrance. The stone relief atop the two columns attempts to symbolize that the Texans at Goliad did not die in vain. An angel holding a Texas star stands over a chained man. He is in pain, and the angel is attempting to remove his chains. The visitor can easily interpret the relief as if it could speak: "These men suffered and are now released from their fighting for Texas independence." More simply, the angel is Liberty, the chain is Mexico, and the man is a Texan. The Goliad Memorial portrays Texas's interpretation of Mexican injustice.

The Texas fight for independence can be understood in modern times as part of Manifest Destiny, but the Goliad Monument reaches emotions beyond unjust expansionism. Texans who know Goliad's history often do

4.6 Goliad Memorial to Massacred Texans, Goliad, Texas (Author's Collection)

not look fondly upon Santa Anna and Mexico, and they often say: "We wanted Texas for ourselves, but we damn sure didn't play dirty like Mexico." Yet most people, even Texans, pay less attention to Goliad than they do to the Alamo. Goliad had no glory, but the Goliad massacre and the resulting monument give a gloss of legitimacy to American expansionism by recalling Mexico's inhumane actions. Goliad enables Texans to think: "God was on our side, and that includes both Texas and the United States."

After numerous defeats, the Texans redeemed their losses with the 1836 victory over Santa Anna. The San Jacinto Victory Monument near Pasadena celebrates the winning of Texas independence, and it is one of the largest war memorials in the United States. The obelisk towers 570 feet above the battlefield.[29] With its reflecting pool, it is reminiscent of the Washington Monument in the nation's capital, but like many things in Texas about which its natives brag, the San Jacinto monument is bigger. Atop the obelisk is a three-dimensional five-pointed star, the symbol of the Lone Star State. The star and the monument boldly pronounce victory for Texas.

The monument is so large that its visible base is actually a museum building. Just above the museum and part of the shaft is a carved frieze depicting the Battle of San Jacinto. Within the museum a variety of items are displayed from the battle to honor those who fought. A bronze plaque

4.7 San Jacinto Victory Monument, near Pasadena, Texas (Author's Collection)

with all the names of those who fought at San Jacinto is mounted as a centerpiece in the display room as a means of combining individual as well as collective honor. The museum is a symbolic vault to remember explicitly Texas's final victory and the sacrifice of those who fought there.

The long-range meaning of San Jacinto and Texas independence to Manifest Destiny is clear to the visitor who looks for it. On the exterior walls of the monument the inscription ends:

> MEASURED BY ITS RESULTS, SAN JACINTO
> WAS ONE OF THE DECISIVE BATTLES OF
> THE WORLD. THE FREEDOM OF TEXAS FROM
> MEXICO WON HERE LED TO ANNEXATION
> AND TO THE MEXICAN WAR. . . . ALMOST ONE-THIRD
> OF THE PRESENT AREA OF THE AMERICAN
> NATION, NEARLY A MILLION SQUARE MILES
> OF TERRITORY, CHANGED SOVEREIGNTY.

While the inscription is emphatic, the glory of Texas is exalted through allegiance to the United States. Close by sits the USS *Texas*, used in World Wars I and II. The USS *Texas* and the San Jacinto Victory Monument are visibly connected by proximity as if to say: "What Texas fought for in 1836 is the same as in other wars—liberty and freedom." Texans did indeed fight for their freedom in 1836, but ultimately they also fought for more than this. Mexico was being pushed aside by Americans who felt that God had destined them to expand the nation's sovereignty. The USS *Texas* is a symbol for two of America's wars of justice. On the other hand, the San Jacinto monument partially commemorates Manifest Destiny, although this incongruity in symbolism between a just war and a questionable war is not apparent.

The Texas Revolution and its memory are finally embodied in the glorification of its heroes. The state of Texas decided to erect memorials for its founding heroes in east and central Texas. Some were located at appropriate historical sites while other hero monuments were dispersed into separate counties to distribute these remembrances. These memorials enabled Texans throughout the state to commemorate their heroes as part of the state centennial.

In addition to these dispersed memorials, the state of Texas also decided that a collective memorial to the most notable people in the fight for independence should be made at one place. In conjunction with the new state fairgrounds in Dallas, the state of Texas built the Hall of Texas Heroes. Inside the hall are statues of James Fannin, Mirabeau Lamar, Stephen F. Austin, Sam Houston, Tom Rusk, and William B. Travis standing in front of columns. On the cornice above and between the columns are the names of battle sites where Texans fought. With the Lone Star as a unifying symbol on the floor and other visible places, the hall has the character of the famous phrase: "All for one and one for all." Texans have the opportunity to capture a sense of who fought and died for their current freedom. While the hall was a well-intentioned project, it is mostly visited when events take place nearby, such as the state fair or the Cotton Bowl. The Texas Hall of Heroes, the architectural centerpiece of the fairgrounds, has a contradictory message since it is located in one of the most economically depressed areas of Dallas. Remembering Texas independence with its heroes at the state fairgrounds has a hollow ring since it is located in a public refuge from poverty.

For native Texans, identification with Texas independence is a matter of justifiable pride. The search for and molding of that identity had much to do with the state government's role in coordinating the design and construction of its war memorials. More than anything else, Texans derive their regional image from the state's fight for independence, and San Jacinto Day, April 21, is still celebrated as a state holiday. Overwhelmingly, Texans see this period of their state's history as being equivalent to the American Revolution. Yet, American expansionism was the political reality, and memorials such as the Alamo and San Jacinto cannot help but convey this message. In the end, however, Texans see their revolution as a war of justice, not one of Manifest Destiny.

If war memorials for the Texas Revolution are considered to be coordinated remembrance, the opposite is true for the Mexican War of 1846. Like some other American wars, it was a victim of timing as well as indifference. The United States had not devoted much attention to public monuments in the mid-nineteenth century.[30] Few monuments existed for the American Revolution and fewer still for the War of 1812. The building of war memorials was just beginning when the Civil War broke out. During the late nineteenth century, Americans finally began to build their war memorials, but few people were particularly concerned with the Mexican War. While the patterns for commemorating this war are quite weak, three forms of remembrance did emerge. First, there were local memorials for combatants, and second, battlefields were remembered. Finally, national recognition was made.

Individual states erected most of the combatant memorials, with some unusual results. South Carolina sent its Palmetto Regiment to fight in Mexico, and as a memorial an iron palmetto tree was placed on the state capitol grounds with a commemorative plaque at its base.[31] In Frankfort, Kentucky, in 1850, a marble shaft with a statue of Victory at the top was built at the state cemetery to remember all Kentuckians who had fought in the nation's wars. While it incorporated many wars, the victory monument was essentially associated with the Mexican War, because the memorial is surrounded by the graves of Kentuckians who fought and died in Mexico.[32] In some memorials the Mexican War was sandwiched between other wars of greater importance. For example, the Mexican War is commemorated with all American wars up to the Spanish-American War on the Indianapolis

Soldiers and Sailors Monument. In Salt Lake City, Utah, the Mormon Battalion Monument was dedicated in 1927 not only to remember soldiers from Utah who fought in the Mexican War of 1846 but also to demonstrate that Utah soldiers could be both Mormons and patriots.[33] Standing almost 30 feet in height, it is actually the largest memorial to the Mexican War. The front statue of the monument is a standing infantryman; behind and above him Columbia holds a Union shield symbolizing the United States. The monument remembers both Mormon men and women who were part of the regiment's long but rather uneventful campaign. The reliefs to the left and right of the infantryman are entitled "The Enlistment" and "The March" to depict the volunteerism and hardships of the battalion. In the end, the Battalion Monument is an affirmation of Mormon faith and its dedication to national endeavor. These examples of collective remembrance are among the very few that were built, but even rarer are monuments to local heroes, which are almost nonexistent.[34]

Most of the war was fought in Mexico, and while some battles occurred in the United States, commemoration for these battlefields has been slight. Most of the battles took place in California, and war memorials for these events are mainly state historical road markers. The Chino Battle Site, Rio San Gabriel Battlefield, and the Battle of Santa Clara are all marked in this manner. The San Pasqual Battlefield has fared better, because it is a California State Historic Park with a visitors' historic center still to be built.[35] Yet, even at this park, the battlefield is only commemorated with a simple obelisk and two historic markers made of stone. Most Americans are unaware of these battlefields, and they know even less about the few memorials that exist upon these grounds.

Although not known by most Americans, California was—for less than a month—an independent republic, and some Californians have commemorated that independence from Mexico. On the Plaza in Sonoma, California, the Bear Flag Monument shows a statue of a citizen–soldier in a pose of readiness, holding the California Bear Flag. It was at Sonoma that a band of citizens first rebelled on June 15, 1846, and began what is now known as the Bear Flag Revolt. The restored Sutter's Fort at Sacramento is remembered as the spot where the Bear Flaggers raised their flag of independence. In the Old Town Plaza at San Diego, a flagpole and an old cannon commemorate that city's independence. Finally, Monterey's Custom House is the site where an American flag was raised on July 7, 1846, to declare the city's independence, and local citizens have continued the tradition of the flag-raising since the 1880s. The most lasting war memorial in California is its state flag. The bear and red stripe on the original Bear Flag are still used today, and the banner historically symbolizes not just independence but triumph over Mexico. California's historical connections to the Mexican War ultimately share the symbolism expressed in the state flag. Californians thought that they had the right to rebel against Mexico and their state symbolism reflects that belief.

4.8 Mormon Battalion Monument, Salt Lake City, Utah (Courtesy of the Utah State Historical Society)

Two reasons for the paucity of memorials for the Mexican War in southern California are timing and urban growth. In the mid-nineteenth century the United States had not yet built many memorials, and cities such as Los Angeles were merely small towns. During the expansionism of the period, many battle sites succumbed to development. Only later did a public consensus for war memorials and historic preservation surface. In addition, the Californian's role in the Mexican War has never inspired the kind of state pride that Texans feel about their fight for independence.

In New Mexico and Texas, commemoration of this confrontation is equally rare. On the plaza in Santa Fe a simple marble marker marks the spot where General Kearny "annexed" New Mexico as an American territory during the war. The Palo Alto Battlefield near Brownsville, Texas, will become the most important battle site commemorating the Mexican War, because it has been designated as the site of the as yet uncompleted national monument to this war. The Mexican War of 1846 is the only war fought on American soil for which there does not currently exist a national battlefield site. While this project will ultimately be completed, there is little to see at the present site. In a small clearing, a vertical slab of weather-stained concrete is mounted with a small bronze plaque which proclaims that the Palo Alto Battlefield is registered as a national landmark. Nearby is a nicer stone monument provided by the state of Texas which declares what the place is and that the U.S. Army won the fight. The only recollection of Palo Alto as a battlefield is an old cannon on a concrete mounting. There is little to remember about the Mexican War in Texas and even less in New Mexico.

Commemoration of the actual events of the War of 1846 in the United States is minimal since most of the war was fought in what is now Mexican territory. These campaigns in Mexico could not be commemorated at the actual battlefields, so the embodiment of these campaigns took other forms. These commemorations have followed the pattern of honoring heroism and sacrifice.

In Washington, D.C., many military leaders from the American Revolution and the Civil War are celebrated with monuments, but Lieutenant General Winfield B. Scott was the only national hero to emerge from the War of 1846. An equestrian statue was erected on Scott Circle, and another on the grounds of the United States Soldiers' Home. Both memorials were made of bronze taken from captured cannons.[36] Other monuments in Washington honor military leaders who also fought in Mexico, such as Kearny and Hancock, but these leaders gained their fame in the Civil War. While Scott was a distinguished officer, most Americans who are unaware of his accomplishments can easily assume—mistakenly—that he was a Civil War general. The Mexican War's lack of identity has made Scott an anonymous figure to most Americans.

The Mexican War is more reverently commemorated at the service academies than in Washington. While there is no actual memorial for the war on campus, West Point's image as an excellent institution for military leaders was due to the performance of its graduates in Mexico.[37] While only an indirect memorial, West Point itself can be conceived as a memorial to the Mexican War in the metaphorical sense that the war gave birth to its distinguished reputation. General Winfield Scott, who was a strong supporter of the academy and was the war's hero, is buried in West Point's cemetery. To new cadets who must learn academy history and trivia, Scott's grave of honor is essentially the academy's Mexican War monument. At the U.S. Naval Academy in Annapolis, remembrance is more specific. The Mexican War Monument is at the center of the Ellipse, the traditional heart of the U.S. Naval Academy's campus. The monument is a small obelisk with four stone cannons used as a miniature colonnade about the pedestal base, and about two feet away from each corner of the pedestal, cannons are deployed defensively pointing away from the monument. The pattern of four is symbolic of the four graduates who died in the Mexican War. The Mexican War Monument appears to be one of the academy's most important monuments since it is located in the sacred center of its campus. The Mexican War Monument's existence and location are due to fortunate timing. The U.S. Naval Academy was moved to Annapolis in 1845. The monument was erected in 1848 and served conveniently as a means to establish both an esprit de corps and a tradition of honorable remembrance. For both academies the Mexican War provided the impetus to establish military traditions on their campuses.

The most enduring commemorations for this unevenly commemorated war are national cemeteries. Although no single memorial for the war exists in Arlington National Cemetery, some servicemen who fought were buried in Section One alongside men from every American war, from the American Revolution to Vietnam.[38] This old portion of Arlington is the symbolic method of treating all wars equally, and the Mexican War graves do not stand out but fade into the regimented rows of collective remembrance.

The Mexican War did include one inevitable innovation in American war memorials. In Mexico City, the first national cemetery was established in 1851 to bury the remains of 750 Americans who fought in the war with Mexico.[39] Only one acre in size, the cemetery has the unusual distinction of being the only American cemetery to be maintained on the enemy's soil.[40] In 1980, the Mexico City National Cemetery was reduced to its present size to make room for a city expressway. To do this, some remains had to be exhumed and placed in wall crypts. To safeguard the site, it was entirely surrounded by a wall. The existing grounds have the feeling more of an outdoor room or private garden than a cemetery. Yet, subdued commemoration does remain. American flags are flown, but their flagpoles are so short that the flags can only be seen by visitors within the walls. The single dedication to the Mexican War is a modest obelisk over the remaining collective grave of the dead. Its inscription on a marble plaque now says:

"TO THE HONORED MEMORY OF 750 AMERICANS, KNOWN BUT TO GOD, WHOSE BONES, COLLECTED BY THEIR COUNTRY'S ORDER, ARE BURIED HERE." But before the expressway project, the obelisk's old marble plaque said: "TO THE MEMORY OF THE AMERICAN SOLDIERS WHO PERISHED IN THIS VALLEY IN 1847 WHOSE BONES COLLECTED BY THIS COUNTRY'S ORDER ARE HERE BURIED."[41] While the Mexican government paid for changes to the cemetery, it rejected the old inscription, and the U.S. embassy had to negotiate a new one. The monument's modest size and new inscription are symbolic repetitions of the cemetery's reduced scale and walls of privacy. National glory can be proclaimed, but it must be done on the home turf, not in the opponent's backyard.

The Mexico City National Cemetery as a memory box typifies how the Mexican War has come to be remembered in the United States. Americans create a small black box in their minds that the Mexican War did occur and that somewhere and somehow those who died have been remembered honorably. Yet, many Americans are unaware that the United States ever fought Mexico after the Texas Revolution.

Both of the Mexican wars convinced Americans that Manifest Destiny was the nation's divine mission and not just a romantic idea. With the end of the War of 1846, the nation's geographical identity had been neatly framed. The Canadian border to the north had been finalized with the Buchanan-Pakenham Treaty of 1846. California formed the western boundary when it became a state in 1850, while the New Mexico territory and the state of Texas defined the southern border. All that remained for the United States was to mop up the American Indians to organize the remaining territories which eventually became states. The ultimate irony is that these wars did little to shape America's symbolic identity, but they significantly influenced the nation's geography. The Mexican wars resulted in more land for the United States, and this territory was the ultimate war memorial for Americans.

AMERICAN INDIAN WARS

Although the battles lasted over 100 years, the United States inevitably defeated and dominated the American Indian. Even before the American Revolution, the English, French, and Spanish tried and usually succeeded in making territorial gains in this New World. The problem of settler versus Indian did not seem great in the beginning, because America was seen to be a beautiful land with room for all. In time, however, the settler's new frontier was the Indian's traditional land, and conflicts occurred constantly. The American Indians were unable to stop the westward movement of settlers, and U.S. armed forces intervened to protect these settlers. As the nation's economic and military power grew, victory for the United States was inevitable.

The U.S. strategy toward Indian tribes was relatively simple and dishonest. Make a treaty for peace, allow settlers to expand where they wanted, get angry at Indians who retaliated against the broken treaty, have a war, and then make a revised treaty in which the Indians lose some or all of their former lands. In time, this strategy was legitimized under the rubic of Manifest Destiny, the right of American rule to determine the Indian's fate and property.[42] The pressure for property was great. General George Crook, an experienced Indian fighter, once said: "Greed and avarice on the part of the whites—in other words the almighty dollar, is at the bottom of nine-tenths of all Indian troubles."[43]

The United States was decidedly victorious in its wars with the American Indian, but today, there are divided feelings over the need for and justice of these past conflicts. Even if conflict was inevitable, the bad faith of Americans to begin, stop, and renew war for territorial gains can hardly be called victory with honor.

Commemoration of the American Indian wars is uneven in symbolism. The United States maintains historical markers, forts, and battle sites to remember these wars. In comparison, the American Indian has primarily used traditional rituals as war memorials. Mainstream America has a culture of maintaining and building war memorials while the Indian culture does not.

In a few places in the United States, there are historical markers that depict the forced movement of the American Indian. For example, near Lima, Ohio, a state marker announces: Shawnee Indian Reservation, 1817-1831, and the inscription describes the tribe's arrival and departure. The sign is a paradox. With a sturdy well-made appearance, the sign demonstrates local pride in Indian history. Yet this same design quality gives an air of legitimacy to the removal of the Indians, since the inscription does not explain motivations behind the illegitimate removal of the Shawnee. This contradictory pattern is also seen in the statue of Chief Menominee of the Pottawatomie tribe near Plymouth, Indiana. In tribal dress and a chieftain's bonnet, Menominee is portrayed as the great Indian whose memory is honored, but the inscription describes results more than honor.

IN MEMORY OF CHIEF MENOMINEE
AND HIS BAND OF 858 POTTAWATOMIE INDIANS
REMOVED FROM THIS RESERVATION
SEPT. 4, 1938 BY A COMPANY OF SOLDIERS
UNDER COMMAND OF GENERAL JOHN TIPTON
AUTHORIZED BY GOVERNOR DAVID WALLACE

The Menominee Monument is more elaborate than the historic road marker, but as political messages, they are both the same. These memorials to the Indian obscure the illegitimate actions of the government. There are no apologies in these official messages.

By the 1970s, over 100 fort and battlefield locations were either designated as national historic landmarks or considered historic sites of national significance.[44] The major artifacts are fort buildings and their remains.

Forts were orderly in design and purpose. Most of the military installations used during the Indian wars were west of the Mississippi, and their site designs resulted from two forces. First, U.S. military engineers borrowed the European tradition of a rectilinear parade field surrounded by army encampment buildings.[45] Second, the grid system of surveying townships and sections in the West often imposed itself on the orientation and layout of fort sites.[46] Eastern U.S. forts were surrounded by stone walls or wood stockades, but later western forts were usually without these protective barriers.[47] This openness was due not only to lack of materials but also to lack of need. The federal troops could do without them. More often than not, the weakening position of the Indians meant that battles were fought on their turf, not on the government's. Today, some of these forts have cannon displays, well-kept grounds, and nicely restored buildings. The restored appearance of these places depict their past. Forts were centers of power, and their orderly arrangements symbolized their enforcement of national authority.

At renovated fort sites, the central element is the American flag. It is as if one is seeing one verse of "The Star-Spangled Banner," " . . . that our flag was still there." It provides no history to the site, but as a symbol it functions as a form of national baptism, legitimation, to the events that took place.

A museum usually exists to present the fort's role in history. Topographical maps show historic trails to convey field operations of the period. Photographs depict the daily life of the fort and its occupants. Guns, uniforms, and other equipment are displayed to help capture the historic time. There have been recent efforts to include portrayals of the American Indian in these museums so that history may be seen from both sides, but the displays are usually dominated by fort artifacts. A diorama at Fort Davis, Texas, positions the visitors behind federal troops, symbolically protecting them. The diorama seems to say: "It is the United States versus them." This and other fort museum presentations subtly reinforce the legitimacy of the fort's mission, which often came at the expense of the Indians.

Fort life was not particularly glorious or exciting, and historic forts try to convey how soldiers actually lived. Uniforms, footlockers, bunks, horse stables, and cavalry gear portray the soldier's everyday life. From the barracks to the stables or mess hall a regimented architecture is always present. Some buildings may stand out as being aesthetically more pleasing, and they are typically officers' living quarters. Sometimes the remains of a chapel remind the visitor of the spiritual sustenance provided to soldiers to relieve the ever-present monotony of garrison routine.[48] In moral contrast is

4.9 Fort Davis National Historic Park, Fort Davis, Texas (Author's Collection)

the guardhouse where soldiers were punished. Remains of privies in a historical fort do not make one think of patriotism. To the modest, it may be embarrassing. Visitors do not see these presentations of fort life as visible symbols of war and defense. These places are only the backstage scenery of military life.

While restored forts from the American Indian wars are simple in design and have little aesthetic merit, they do convey the sense of visiting the locker room for the home team. Being on federal turf rather than Indian land, visitors are spatially conditioned to identify with the United States rather than the Indians. American Indians and people empathetic to them can consciously reject this conditioning, but others may find that the immediate experience awakens or reinforces their selective patriotism.

While forts under the management of the U.S. National Park Service are meticulously kept and articulate some history, many western forts are merely rubble. Flood control and irrigation have done the most damage to historic sites. Many forts were dismantled by settlers seeking building materials after the Army cavalry moved out. Cut stone and wood were especially sought after. Finally, time has taken its toll on buildings left unmaintained.[49] This neglect is due in part to a lack of concern with historic preservation which prevailed until the latter half of the twentieth century. Moreover, other wars, such as the Civil War and the world wars, were considered more important. The army trooper was forgotten along with his defeated foe, the American Indian.

Beyond the forts, these wars are marginally depicted at battlefields. Over 50 sites have been marked where engagements occurred.[50] Battlegrounds have experienced a fate similar to that of many fortifications, as farms and ranches have sprung up over some historic sites in the plains. Battlefields

4.10 Remains of Fort Union, New Mexico (Author's Collection)

have been identified with historic monuments, but these are usually little more than markers.

Most Indian battlefields are not conveniently located near a city or by an interstate highway. Tourists must go out of their way to visit these sites. After driving there, they find a historical marker, usually made of cast metal, and read about the events that took place. They look about, and after leaving, may come to Gertrude Stein's conclusion (about Oakland, California) that "There is no there, there." Unlike Civil War sites, there are no grand statues or rows of cannon. Visitors see farmland or, at best, an unchanged natural landscape which has no artifacts from the battle. They learn who fought, won, and lost without grasping a visual sense of what happened. Place and event have been tied, but little more.

The emptiness of landscape symbolism, however, is largely that of the non-Indian. Some Indians are able to give these places enhanced symbolism through oral histories. For example, some battlefields are on or near Indian reservations. Older tribal members often pass on stories telling what events happened as they walk to stones marking these sites or pointing to a given place on a battlefield.[51] Indian storytelling at the historic place becomes a temporary war memorial, a ritual to be passed on.

Indian battlefields are remembered either as a step in the westward movement or as a climactic ending to the Indian saga. The currently maintained battlegrounds are those that not only had national notoriety at the time but that also continue to be part of the national memory. More importantly, American recollection has shaped attitudes toward the American Indian and has often rationalized how the west was won. Two battles that most

Americans easily remember are Tippecanoe, which symbolizes the westward movement, and the Little Big Horn, which is seen as the Indian's last hurrah.

The Battle of Tippecanoe was the result of certain Indian tribes ceding land to the U.S. government without the approval of other tribes. The Shawnee chief, Tecumseh, and his brother, the Prophet, were particularly angry with federal tactics to expand U.S. territory. Tecumseh attempted to persuade Governor William H. Harrison of the Indiana territory that Indian lands ceded by the Treaty of Fort Wayne should be refused, but Harrison turned him away. Both whites and Indians then prepared for the unavoidable conflict. The Prophet was primarily a spiritual leader rather than an organizer, and Tecumseh warned the Prophet to wait until the various tribes could organize themselves to fight. But the Prophet did not wait, and on November 7, 1811, the gathered tribes attacked General Harrison's troops by Burnett's Creek. The U.S. troops won decisively, and the Indians were no longer a force to be reckoned with in Indiana.[52] Moreover, Tecumseh's dream of an Indian confederacy died at Tippecanoe.

The Battle of Tippecanoe was made famous by William H. Harrison in his successful presidential campaign in 1840. His campaign slogan was: "Tippecanoe and Tyler too," and he actually launched his political campaign on the battlefield itself.[53] Most Americans felt that Harrison had beaten a diabolical enemy, and this logic was extended to campaign fighting. Few people examined the Indians' motives in fighting to preserve their lands and their autonomy.

The Tippecanoe Battlefield Memorial park has the calm feeling of a typical county park. Well-landscaped and trimmed, the battlefield is bounded by a black wrought iron fence, and at its entrance is an arched gateway upon which is perched a spread-winged American eagle colorfully painted. On the arch a painted inscription in old styled letters says simply: Tippe Canoe Nov. 7, 1811. It is clear that the U.S. victory is what is being honored. Once inside the gate, people are immediately drawn to the Tippecanoe Monument. While all American soldiers who died are honored, General Harrison receives heroic treatment with a statue in front of the obelisk and upon a classical cornice. Yet, the inscription is not florid. Because it reports only the facts, one gets a sense of reading scores in a newspaper's sports page, although the inscription ends with an incomplete note:

LOSS: AMERICANS, KILLED   37
"   WOUNDED 151
INDIAN LOSS UNKNOWN

After leaving the monument, visitors can walk along a trail system and read markers identifying what took place in the battle at that particular point. Visitors constantly see a neatly aligned fence with well-mowed grass inside, and they walk on a well-defined, well-kept trail along the way. The whole scene, with its fences and large oak trees, is reminiscent of a late nineteenth-century park. It is difficult to grasp a sense of the horror of battle when visiting this well-manicured, tranquil park.

Near the battlefield entrance is a small museum which is run privately by a local association. The displays have a homemade look compared to those provided by the National Park Service. A slide show explains the problems leading up to the Battle of Tippecanoe, and the description of American expansion actually lends a pro-Indian bias to the presentation. A nearby diorama repeats this empathy for the Indian. It depicts the battle with Indians running toward the viewer with one warrior carrying another in his arms. Most dioramas have the reverse—American soldiers on the viewer's side. Although the diorama's construction is not sophisticated, the effect is that of a plea for help. These displays, along with other Indian artifacts, provide a subtle contradiction to the heroic character of the Tippecanoe Monument and the ornamental gate. The neutral ground in this dialectic is located outdoors between the gate and the museum. There is a nondescript boulder with a mounted plaque which simply describes Tippecanoe's historical events. The museum counterbalances the Tippecanoe Monument's pro-federal victory symbolism while the boulder is a simple scoreboard to tell who won the battle.

In the end Tippecanoe will be popularly remembered and associated with Harrison's famous campaign phrase. The battlefield is symbolically a political trail marker. For some it represents the inevitable march of progress, while others see it historically as a blazed path on the trail of Manifest Destiny.

The Custer Battlefield National Monument is the best-known memorial to the American Indian wars. After Colonel Custer's unsuccessful attack and defeat in 1876, most of the troopers' bodies were simply covered with earth by fellow soldiers of the Seventh Cavalry. In 1879, the U.S. secretary of war ordered the establishment of a national cemetery, and later in the same year, a simple wood pyramid was built as a temporary memorial at Little Big Horn. In 1881, a permanent memorial was dedicated, and the battleground became a national monument in 1946.[54]

The battle hill, the cemetery, and the museum building are all visible upon entering the grounds on Battlefield Road, but the hill is the primary attraction. It is the exact place which is popularly thought of as "Custer's Last Stand." Atop the hill is a stone monument inscribed with the names of cavalrymen who died at the battle. The monument is symbolically enhanced not only by its high elevation but also by the surrounding grave markers. Yet, these markers are not really gravestones. Instead, each marks the place where a given soldier was known to have died, and beneath each name, every marker says, Fell Here, June 25, 1876. The irregular placement of markers, which symbolizes the chaos of war, is counterbalanced by the dominating monument—order prevails over disorder. Intentional or not, this visual order is emblematic of what occurred after Little Big Horn. In spite of Custer's defeat, federal troops eventually imposed their order on the Indians.

In contrast to the battle hill, the cemetery portrays the orderly symmetry of all national cemeteries. The neatly aligned graves are punctuated by the inscription at one end:

> THE MUFFLED DRUM'S SAD ROLL HAS BEAT
> THE SOLDIER'S LAST TATTOO.
> NO MORE ON LIFE'S PARADE SHALL MEET
> THAT BRAVE AND FALLEN FEW.

Standing in the cemetery viewing the scattered markers on the hill below the monument gives the immediate sense of standing amidst order against a scene of disorder. That a certain soldier's hill marker cannot be visually matched to his gravestone in the cemetery is not important. Collectively, the disorderly past has been redeemed through the symmetry of grave rows, even though many of these graves are for people who died in other wars. The poem for the soldier's last tattoo is an embellishment to reinforce the cemetery's symbolic order.

The simple small museum is geared to the 300,000 visitors who come to Custer National Monument each year. Exhibits of cavalry and Indian artifacts provide glimpses of events leading to Little Big Horn. The messages portrayed are in the neutral national style that tourists have come to expect from the exhibits presented by the National Park Service. Books and art prints devoted to the cavalry and the American Indian are available for purchase.

Except for trees planted near the cemetery, the battle site is much as it was a century ago, but some citizens are concerned about retaining its undisturbed character. The Custer Battlefield Preservation Committee, Inc., is attempting to buy surrounding property and scenic easements to ensure the historic and natural character of the area. Much of this land is owned by people of Indian ancestry. Landowners' names such as High Kicker, Medicine Trail, and Spotted Buffalo make it clear that this historic area could easily—and perhaps should—have been called Crazy Horse or Sitting Bull Battlefield. Most interestingly, the committee has primarily sought to purchase the land which includes Custer's route to the Little Big Horn battleground. Little of this land included the original grounds of the Sioux and Cheyenne encampment, although it is part of the proposed scenic easement. Symbolically, Custer and his Seventh Cavalry regiment are still surrounded by the Indians. The historic site of the battlefield is located in a Crow reservation and not a Sioux or Cheyenne reservation. Nonetheless, it is ironic that present-day Indian landowners have symbolically kept sacred the battle refuge and graves of their ancestors' conquerers by not despoiling the surrounding land. If promotional tourism occurs in the area, the Custer

4.11 Custer Battlefield National Monument near Crow Agency, Montana (Author's Collection)

Battlefield will be profaned by the hamburgers and kitsch of the white man, not by the traditional American Indian way of life.

While forts and battlefields have been preserved largely through government efforts, American Indians have mainly chosen to remember their wars through ritual. As mentioned before, battle sites are remembered by storytelling. Victory dances were done to remember battles and to honor fellow tribesmen, and warriors told their tales by counting coup feathers or scalps. In time, the Indians who fought these wars died, and veteran dances at powwows now honor those who have fought for the U.S. armed services. Indian rituals symbolically honor individuals rather than any particular war.

The most lasting war memorials that American Indians have are their reservations. These lands have become a refuge for many sacred sites and for Indian culture itself. Many contain the centuries-old tribal grounds while others are sites of forced relocation. In the past, these areas have been depicted as places of despair, but in recent times, some Indian lands have proven to be rich in minerals. As before, many non-Indians would like to gain access to these lands, but American Indians are protected by law more diligently now than in the nineteenth century. Some critics argue that Indian reservations are the leftover crumbs of America's Manifest Destiny. Metaphorically, the reservation is the land of the losers.

The American Indians historically have not built permanent war memorials, but there is one notable exception, the Crazy Horse Memorial near Custer, South Dakota. Of all American Indians, Crazy Horse is perhaps held in the highest esteem by his fellow people. As DeWall has said: "In essence Crazy Horse was an Indian's Indian. . . . He never surrendered, never signed a treaty and never went on a reservation. Also, he never allowed his picture to be taken."[55] The Sioux Indians were aware of the mountain carvings at Mt. Rushmore and decided that the American Indian deserved a memorial as well. Chief Henry Standing Bear of the Pine Ridge Reservation in South Dakota asked Korczak Ziolkowski to carve a memorial for all American Indians. The memorial is intended to be the image of Crazy Horse as he was remembered by tribesmen. Work began in 1947, and Ziolkowski worked on the monument until he died in 1982. His family is now continuing the project with no fixed timetable for its completion.

While Indians have not traditionally adopted war memorials or been able to afford them, the Crazy Horse Memorial appears to be a singular exception. The monument is quite literally being carved from a mountain, and when completed, it will easily be the largest sculpture in the world. For the Indians, it makes no difference if the monument is critically acclaimed. What is important to them is that its conception and execution have been totally independent of federal aid or intervention. The monument may be seen not only as a tribute to the American Indian but also as a symbol of spite against the federal government's bureaucratic treatment of Indians.

4.12 Crazy Horse Memorial Model and Mountain, near Custer, South Dakota (Author's Collection)

The monument's proposed symbolism is meant to reflect the pride of the American Indian. Crazy Horse is shown proudly pointing over his horse's head to sacred Indian lands. The theme comes from the story of a white trader who mocked Crazy Horse for not going on the reservation after the Battle of Little Big Horn. The trader taunted Crazy Horse by asking him: "Where are your lands now?" Crazy Horse replied: "My lands are where my dead lie buried."[56] The Crazy Horse Memorial ultimately symbolizes more than pride. The monument is an act of defiance. American Indians are having an approved image created for themselves, in defiance of the U.S. government. Crazy Horse's finger pointing east might just as easily be construed cynically as accusing the source of guilt, the belief and practice of Manifest Destiny as it came from the east, particularly Washington, D.C. To the American Indian, however, the monument wil serve a simpler purpose. It will portray them as they wish to be seen, a proud and peaceful people.

The American Indians and their wars have been primarily portrayed to the American public through a distorted fantasy. Hollywood movies have so fictionalized places and events that people take for granted the common day occurrence of children playing cowboys and Indians. Much of the place symbolism of the American Indian wars has been lost or forgotten. While the American Indian's way of marking battle events with stones is very personal, oral histories are not always passed down, and the stories become distorted. The true meaning of the stories is often lost. Some sites were never marked. Few people outside the Indian culture are aware of the ritual folk practices of remembrance. As a result, American Indians are unable to counter the stereotypical images of their past which are created by the mass media.

For many Americans, the Indian wars are viewed romantically as the rugged growth of a country in its halcyon days. Historic sites bring dignity to the past, and rituals such as the anniversary ceremonies at Little Big Horn attempt to bring dignity to all who were involved.[57] Yet, there is a lingering of hate. When driving in the western United States, a person may see a bumper sticker on a car or truck saying Custer Got Siouxed or Broken Treaty Score, Red Man O, White Man 391. These accusations are the war memorials of the modern Indian, memorials that will question the government's victory for as long as American Indians feel they are oppressed.

THE SPANISH-AMERICAN WAR

Before the war with Spain, American Manifest Destiny was geographically limited to the North American continent. Wars with Great Britain, Mexico, and the Indians were part of western expansion. American politics became isolated from international events, especially after the War of 1812. The establishment of new states and territories and the Civil War fully occupied the American political conscience for most of the nineteenth century.

When western settlement finally conquered the great frontier, the American desire for expansionism was still alive. To be a world power in the nineteenth century meant that a country had to be a naval power, but America's navy was weak. After 1890, however, the United States began to build warships which "could meet a potential enemy anywhere on the high seas."[58] Americans became more confident of their nation's worth as the country increased both its industrial and its military strength. Americans were aching for a fight, as E. L. Godkin, the anti-imperialist editor for the *Nation* magazine, said: "The number of men and officials in this country who are now mad to fight somebody is appalling."[59] The sinking of the USS *Maine* in Havana Harbor gave the United States the excuse it needed to go to war. When Spain was defeated, John Hay, an American ambassador in London, said: "It has been a splendid little war."[60] The United States was aching for a chance to show its strength, and Spanish problems in Cuba gave American expansionists and imperialists a chance to exploit their ambitions.[61] The Spanish-American War was the result of a renewed interest in Manifest Destiny, which was redefined beyond the American frontier.[62]

In retrospect, the Spanish-American War was the United States' first effort to be a world power. Its previous wars of Manifest Destiny were conflicts over frontier. Much of the North American continent had been unsettled, and while political boundaries existed, they were not steadfast. Justly or unjustly, American expansion allowed for the United States to define its continental limits. The war with Spain, however, meant that the United States was practicing what the American revolutionaries fought against—intervention and control by a world power.[63]

Americans did not feel that their fighting endeavors were "interfering," and after the war they built memorials which reflected their ambitions. The memorial parade which followed had three basic patterns. First, the United States wanted to glorify its heroes. Second, revenge was portrayed through memorials to the sunken USS *Maine*. Finally, the common means to win the war, men and weapons, were commemorated.

In all wars, certain individuals and military units tend to gain notoriety over others. People want heroes. Almost as quickly as the Spanish-American War was declared, the first hero emerged. Commodore George Dewey and his U.S. Pacific Fleet attacked the Spanish Fleet in Manila Bay and totally destroyed the enemy without any casualties. After leaving the Philippines, Dewey came home as an admiral to a gala celebration in New York City. To honor Dewey, the city of New York provided the largest and most ornate memorial for the entire Spanish-American War. A temporary memorial arch and a plaza colonnade made of plaster were constructed at Fifth Avenue and Twenty-third Street for Admiral Dewey's triumphant hero's parade on September 30, 1899.[64]

Although similar to the Civil War Soldiers and Sailors Arch in Brooklyn,

4.13 The Dewey Victory Arch, New York City (Courtesy of the New York Historical Society, New York City)

the Dewey Victory Arch had primarily a naval theme befitting the admiral hero. Atop the arch, the quadriga had four horses leading an angel of victory riding on a giant seashell. Statues along the cornice displayed sailors and officers. On the arch's piers, two sculpture groups located on the colonnade side depicted "Triumphant Return" and "Combat," and on the reverse, paraders faced "Departure for War" and "Peace" as they marched through the arch. The plaza colonnade of Corinthian columns continued the arch's victory themes with sculpture groups for the U.S. Army and the U.S. Navy. Like the Roman Caesars, Admiral Dewey paraded through the arch and colonnade, with 25,000 officers and men behind him.[65] The flowery inscription on the arch captures the essence of the memorial's symbolism and the public feeling at the time:

> TO THE GLORY OF THE AMERICAN NAVY
> AND IN GREETING TO OUR ADMIRAL
> A GRATEFUL CITY RELYING ON THEIR VALOR
> HAS BUILT THIS ARCH MDCCCXCIX

Despite all the victory hoopla in New York City, Dewey's arch was torn down within a year. The admiral's victory at Manila Bay was important, but not important enough in a city where celebration is embraced like fashion, which lasts only a season. The grandest memorial to the Spanish-American War, and one of America's largest, was gone.

Dewey's victory has been remembered unevenly ever since. In Dewey's hometown of Montpelier, Vermont, a statue of him was to be built at the State House, but was never erected. For years, his boyhood home was preserved. Pressures for public building in Montpelier caused the house first to be moved to make room for a new state office building, and finally to be destroyed n 1969. Nonetheless, Montpelier has not totally forgotten its heroic son. Two cannons which were captured at Manila Bay sit on the State House lawn to commemorate Dewey's victory.[66] The most enduring memorial to Dewey is seldom recognized for what it is. In the frequently visited Union Square in San Francisco, the Victory Monument commemorates Dewey's triumph at Manila Bay. It is a tall Corinthian column topped with an angel standing on a globe, holding a mariner's trident in one hand and a victory wreath in the other. At the base, the long inscription is a chronicle of Dewey's endeavors. The Victory Monument is a simple trophy which has become valued more as a design centerpiece for an urban plaza than as a monument to Dewey. With the coming of the world wars, Admiral Dewey was quickly forgotten.

While most of the naval acclaim was given to Dewey, others were also remembered, although to a lesser degree. In Erie, Pennsylvania, townspeople dedicated a park and monument to their own Captain Charles Vernon Gridley who commanded the USS *Olympia* in the Battle of Manila Bay.[67] Gridley was best known through Dewey's then well-known battle command, "You may fire when ready, Gridley." The Gridley Park and Monument embellished the town's local naval history, which included the Commodore Perry Memorial and the War of 1812 ship, *Niagara*. Besides Gridley, others were honored. In Greensboro, Alabama, the home of Rear Admiral Richard Pearson Hobson—known as Magnolia Grove—was preserved as a museum to recount his naval career and his efforts to blockade the harbor at Santiago, Cuba.[68] Both of these "favorite son" memorials enhance the patriotic feelings and civic pride of the local community.

While the Navy played a crucial role in the Spanish-American War, the heroes of the U.S. Army are better remembered. Colonel Theodore D. Roosevelt and his Rough Riders were the Army's glory boys. Made famous by their successful capture of Kettle Hill, wrongly popularized as the charge on San Juan Hill, Roosevelt and his Rough Riders were remembered for their zeal and heroism. The Rough Riders continued to be remembered and glorified when Roosevelt became president of the United States.

In contrast to memorials for Dewey, those for Roosevelt and the Rough Riders have endured. Roosevelt is best remembered through the equestrian statue in Portland, Oregon, entitled "The Rough Rider." A duplicate stands in Roosevelt Park at Minot, North Dakota.[69] Displayed in his actual battle dress, Roosevelt's symbolic image is not appreciably different from other equestrian memorials for military leaders in earlier wars. With the horse standing alertly, Roosevelt's pose formally proclaims: "I am prepared." The Arizona Rough Riders Monument in Prescott, Arizona, however, is more emphatic. Popularly known as the Buckey O'Neill Statue, this memorial conveys preparedness amidst danger. The soldier is wearing wrinkled field dress and looks ready to fight; his horse appears startled. More simply, the message is one of earthy courage, as if the soldier is saying: "Let's get them damn sonsabitches!"[70] More solemnly, a simple stone monolith with a bronze plaque stands in Arlington National Cemetery to honor those Rough Riders who gave their lives in Cuba in 1898.[71] As a tribute to the United States and the Rough Riders, Cuba made the top of San Juan Hill into a memorial battlefield park with an observation tower, with cannon raised in symbolic salute. Roosevelt and the Rough Riders were popular heroes, as these memorials attest. In comparison, Dewey was made a hero temporarily, but his naval fleet did not capture American imaginations as the Rough Riders did.

Many heroes of the Spanish-American War are honored by having streets in Arlington National Cemetery named for them. Dewey, Hobson, and Sigsbee drives honor the U.S. Navy's heroes, while Roosevelt, Lawton, and Miles commemorate the U.S. Army. Even McKinley Drive refers indirectly to the war, since William McKinley was president at the time. Although this symbolism is subliminal, knowing that it exists makes it apparent that the heroes of this rather small war have been honored extensively in Arlington National Cemetery. This connection is strengthened by the grave markers

4.14 Rough Riders Monument, Prescott, Arizona (Author's Collection)

for Spanish War dead along some of these streets, especially Lawton Drive. The streets for heroes symbolize unified direction while their soldiers' and sailors' markers lend real support to the claim.

While the United States wanted to glorify its heroes, they also felt the need to remember why they went to war in the first place. With flagrant press coverage, the American cry "Remember the *Maine*" was not only patriotic but also full of the desire for revenge. Not until Pearl Harbor did Americans so fervently associate revenge with a physical symbol.

The USS *Maine* provided one of the most unique forms of commemoration of any American war; parts of the ship's remains have been incorporated in the design of war memorials. When the USS *Maine* was raised from the bottom of Havana Harbor, its cannons and other parts were salvaged and dispersed. In Arlington National Cemetery, the mainmast to the *Maine* was used atop a mausoleum, and more than 200 of the ship's crew are buried nearby.[72] Behind the memorial a decorative ship anchor appears to come from the *Maine* although it did not. At Annapolis the *Maine*'s foremast stands at one corner of Farragut Field on the naval academy's campus. The United Spanish War Veterans got one of the ship's anchors and made lapel pins from it for its membership.[73] A variety of other ship parts were dispersed among numerous cities. For example, on the state capitol grounds in Columbia, South Carolina, a small bore cannon was mounted.[74] As part of its Spanish-American War memorial, Woburn, Massachusetts, has a ventilator cowl.[75] Canton, Ohio, was the boyhood home of William McKinley, U.S. president during the war. To honor their favorite son, Canton's *Maine* memorial was made from the base of the battleship's conning tower.[76] In Pittsburgh, one of the *Maine*'s torpedo tubes protruding from its armored porthole was used as a centerpiece for a memorial wall with inscriptions carved in decorative tablets.[77] All these separate memorials have the common symbolism of sacrifice for the nation.

While the *Maine*'s artifacts were scattered about the United States for use in various memorials, the ship's major armament was saved for the Plaza del Maine memorial in Havana, Cuba. To express its gratitude, Cuba built the Plaza del Maine memorial and dedicated it to the United States in 1928. The ship's cannons and broken chains were laid at the memorial's base. On the north side of the pedestal base a ship's bow was placed to symbolize aid from the United States, and directly above was mounted a memorial plaque with the names of those who died on the *Maine*. Above the plaque is a statue of a mourning woman holding two bodies, symbolizing those who died on the *Maine*, and on the south side two figures, representing the United States and Cuba, symbolize their joint mission and joint victory. On the east and west sides of the base are bronze reliefs showing first the *Maine* coming into Havana Harbor and then its remains after being sunk. Above the base are two Corinthian columns supporting a spread-winged American eagle which, until Castro's takeover, faced Havana Harbor. The eagle's posture symbolizes the beginning of its flight back to its nest, the United States.[78] To the east and west of the *Maine* monument are semicircular courtyards. A bust and pedestal of President William McKinley stands in one, while a bust of President Theodore Roosevelt was placed in the other. Both face the *Maine* monument, as if to say: "The *Maine* has been redeemed." As a whole, the Plaza del Maine symbolically legitimizes the United States' war with Spain.

With the Communist revolution in the early 1960s, the Plaza del Maine was seen by Cubans as a symbol of American imperialism. Soon after Castro took power, the American eagle atop the memorial was removed. Its pose was interpreted as symbolically maintaining a perch of U.S. power instead of flying back north to its American nest. Yet, the Plaza del Maine is still properly maintained in remembrance of those who died.[79]

The physical scattering of the USS *Maine*'s parts to make war memorials

4.15 Plaza del Maine, Havana, Cuba (Author's Collection)

has a religious equivalent. Some Catholic churches in Europe have a sacred place, known as a reliquary, to display a supposed splinter from the cross on which Christ was crucified. The USS *Maine* was a symbolic cross upon which the sons of America were sacrificed for their country. While comparison can only go so far, the *Maine*'s fragments were not valuable as aesthetic elements. Instead, the fragments themselves symbolize a sacrifice which had to be redeemed.

Not all *Maine* memorials included the ship's artifacts. In the southwest corner of Central Park in New York City, the *Maine* memorial portrays sacrifice quite gloriously. The sculpture group atop the fountain is a triumphant Columbia in a shell-shaped chariot led by sea horses. On the fountain's north side is another sculpture in which figures symbolize Peace, Fortitude, Justice, and History; a weeping boy in the arms of Fortitude symbolizes the loss of the *Maine* in a classical manner.[80] But like many memorials with classical symbolism, the meaning is easily missed. While New York's memorial fountain is quite large, not all *Maine* memorials were grandiose. Along the Mississippi River, a park in LaCrosse, Wisconsin, contains a stone mounted with a small plaque. Decorated with a bowed figure of Liberty holding a shield, it says simply: "MEMORIAM USS MAINE." Communities wanted to remember the sacrifice of the *Maine* even if they did not have parts from the ship.

The final tribute for the USS *Maine* took place in 1912, but the final event in the *Maine*'s history did not occur until 1976. The U.S. Congress appropriated funds in 1911 to recover the remains of the U.S. sailors and to dispose of the battleship hull properly. After raising the hull of the ship, the USS *Maine* was towed out to sea four miles from Havana Harbor with an escort fleet. On that afternoon of March 26, the *Maine* was sunk with an American flag draped over its masthead.[81] Yet, what is cruelly ironic about the *Maine* and its resulting memorials is contained in a research report published in 1976 by Rear Admiral Hyman G. Rickover. The report concluded that the *Maine*'s sinking was due to an internal explosion and not a Spanish mine.[82] The reason for starting the Spanish-American War was proven to be false.

Memorials to "Remember the *Maine*" no longer have authentic symbolism. The *Maine* memorials were as much emblems of revenge as they were tributes to the men who were killed on the ship. While Americans dedicated these memorials in the sincere belief that Spain was the guilty party, these monuments are now contradictory. Remembering those who died is legitimate, but treating the *Maine* as a sacrificial cross is not. History has invalidated the symbolism.

While memorials to the USS *Maine* and honors for particular heroes give a unique quality to the Spanish-American War commemorations, the most enduring memorial is the anonymous soldier portrayed in the Hiker monument. These statues were erected in many local communities, and were even available through foundry catalogues. Designed to portray what the common soldier wore and did, the Hiker was to its war what the Doughboy monument was to World War I. In 1965, after construction of these monuments in many other communities, a Hiker statue was finally dedicated in Arlington National Cemetery.[83] The Hiker is typically a soldier standing relaxed in field dress with an open collar. He looks prepared for battle instead of a military parade. Often a bronze Spanish War veterans' cross and seal is mounted on the pedestal base. The Hiker's lasting popularity among veterans and other Americans is most likely due to its clarity in intent, a collective symbol of the common soldier as he was in the war.

To a lesser extent, monuments with the angel of Victory were dedicated as collective memorials, such as the Spanish War monuments in San Francisco and Newport, Rhode Island. Moreover, Victory appeared in New York's Dewey arch and *Maine* memorial. Even more subtly, Victory appears in a bank sign in Ybor City, Florida, which is near the site where U.S. troops embarked for Cuba. The most flagrant expression of Victory, however, was the monument for California volunteers in San Francisco. The proud inscription boasts, "FIRST TO THE FRONT," and the memorial expresses a fervent nationalism. The angel of Victory is thrusting a sword straight forward in her right hand, and she holds an expressively furling flag in her left hand. If this was not enough, she is precariously positioned atop a winged horse whose reared front legs give the impression that it is about to gallop forward. Beneath the horse is a dying soldier who is defiantly holding his rifle in the air. Alongside the horse is a soldier with a pistol and sword, and he seems to express a stern willingness to fight. The entire expression of the sculpture is valor for a noble cause. In retrospect, the Spanish-American War occurred during the period of classical revivalism inspired by the Columbian Exposition of 1893. Critics have argued that the American use of classicism in architecture and its symbolism expressed the American imperialism of the time. The angel of Victory not only symbolizes victory in the war but also glorifies the doctrine of Manifest Destiny.

Weapons were used as collective memory memorials, but few Americans are now aware of these commemorations. A captured cannon from Santiago, Cuba, stands nearly forgotten in Hanscom Park in Omaha, Nebraska.[84] At the other extreme, the USS *Olympia* is docked at Penn's Landing in Philadelphia, near Independence National Historic Park. The park symbolizes liberty and freedom while the *Olympia* supposedly portrays the purpose of preserving these values in war, albeit a war that embodied American Manifest Destiny. While no intentional connection is made between the two Philadelphia sites, tourists who visit one place and then the other psychologically join together these places as symbols of nationalism. The connection is quite easy to make since many tourists leave their cars directly by the *Olympia* in the Penn Landing parking lot to visit Independence National Historic Park. Onboard the *Olympia* a plaque is inscribed with Admiral

4.17 Victory Monument for the Spanish-American War, San Francisco, California (Photograph by Jim Rowings)

4.16 Hiker Monument in Arlington National Cemetery, Virginia (Author's Collection)

Dewey's famous command: "You may fire when ready, Gridley." The *Olympia* was not the only battleship saved as a memorial from the Spanish-American War. The USS *Oregon* gained notoriety for its 15,000-mile run from the state of Washington, through the Straits of Magellan, to Key West, Florida, in 47 days. Soon afterwards, it sank Spain's flagship. In 1925 the battleship was given to the state of Oregon, which maintained the ship as a memorial.[85] The USS *Oregon*, however, "was stripped during an over-zealous World War II scrap drive," and the ship then became a barge and was finally dismantled in 1956.[86] The stripping of the USS *Oregon* was emblematic of public opinion at the time. The Spanish-American War was important, but it paled in comparison to the cause and stakes in World War II. The weapons from the Spanish-American War were also dwarfed by those that were developed for the world wars. At the turn of the century, Americans saw their battleships as grand symbols of American power. They were powerful, but bigger weapons from later wars have replaced Spanish-American War battleships and cannons as symbols of U.S. world power and bigger wars have displaced the Spanish-American War in our memory.

Collective memorials to those who fought in the war took many forms throughout the United States, but a national memorial could only be in one place, Arlington National Cemetery. The Soldiers and Sailors Monument at Arlington is neither large nor exceptional in design. It is a Corinthian column upon which an American eagle sits perched atop a globe of the world, and on the pedestal base is a bronze plaque which has an accurate but uninspiring inscription for those who fought and died. While the dead are remembered, the memorial is essentially a victory column in the Roman style. The eagle upon the globe can easily be seen to mean contradictory things. A patriotic American might interpret it to be the United States protecting democracy in the world, but a critic can just as easily conclude that it symbolizes the arrogance of American imperialism at the turn of the century. Most people, however, probably consider the eagle and globe to be just a nice American decoration and nothing more; meaning in the Soldiers and Sailors Monument is multiple and unclear.

Another collective memorial in Arlington is dramatic but easier to interpret. American nurses wanted to remember those of their profession who died in the war. The rough stone Nurses Monument makes a simple statement. Its Maltese cross contains the words, "USA SPANISH AMERICAN WAR NURSES," and the inscription reads: "TO OUR COMRADES." Above the inscription, a victory wreath is laid upon a palm leaf, symbolizing peace, in modest remembrance of the war. About five feet in height, the Nurses Monument has the feeling of a large grave marker as if to say: "Thanks for your sacrifice in this war to achieve peace."

Neither the Soldiers and Sailors Monument nor the Nurses Monument are as well remembered as the memorials built in local parks. The Hiker monument at Arlington was built and dedicated over 60 years too late for people to know of its existence. Too many other wars have occurred since the war with Spain. Still, the national collective memory is perhaps best embraced at Arlington National Cemetery. All Americans assume some soldiers and sailors from this war—as from all wars—are buried there, even though they probably do not personally know of anyone whose remains are in the cemetery. In this sense, collective memory for the Spanish-American War is expected just as it is for other wars, even though it may not be explicitly recognized.

The idea of expectation of memory helps explain how Americans perceive commemorations for the Spanish-American War. Most people assume that memorials for this war exist, but they are often hard-pressed to recall having seen a monument for the war with Spain. Compared to other American conflicts, the Spanish-American War is minuscule in importance. Yet, at the turn of the century the United States was experiencing prosperity and expansion in industry and even agriculture. Moreover, the nation was ready to spend money to upgrade the unsophisticated image of American cities by building monuments and civic improvements. War memorials were being built everywhere, but they were for the American Revolution and the Civil War. America was catching up with its history. The country's prosperity finally allowed cities and states to build the memorials that people had been wanting to commemorate America's great wars of the past. More memorials for the Spanish-American War might have been built during this period, but World War I began. Considering the options, most communities decided that a Doughboy monument made a more important statement than a Hiker memorial to a splendid little war. World War II followed quickly, and America's memory for the Spanish War faded fast, as seen by the scrapping of the USS *Oregon* for war material in the 1940s. Today, this war is somewhat of a Victorian curiosity to Americans. Why was it fought and where? Why all the pomp and circumstance at the time? Yet, the Spanish-American War is important to remember because it was America's first war as a world power, a new form of Manifest Destiny. Memorials to this war do share many qualities with monuments for all wars, but its unique memorials, such as those for the USS *Maine* and the Dewey arch, reflect a desire for revenge, glory and power.

SYMBOLS OF MANIFEST DESTINY

Memorials for wars of Manifest Destiny often reflected political changes in America. The United States was experiencing national growing pains. It was politically unstable, although the country's political principles were basically formed in the American Revolution. Some national symbols emerged from the War of 1812, but this symbolism basically fulfilled the unfinished business of national identity which had begun in the American

Revolution. Americans were attempting to consolidate the nation's historical image with war memorials at the very moment that the image was being changed by territorial expansion.

War memorials in the United States evolved as the nineteenth century passed, and classicism was the style. While American memorials have their own style, classicism was an international phenomenon and not just an American one. Yet, the style fitted comparatively well with the United States, a Western Roman Empire with its own style of democracy. Classical symbolism was used to portray the nation's values, but this visual language is no longer understood by most Americans.

Memorials to these wars are few when compared to the enormity of political changes they brought about. Fewer Americans fought and died in the wars of Manifest Destiny than in the great wars, such as the world wars. Historically, Americans have built more and larger memorials when more people were involved in the conflict. The wars of Manifest Destiny usually resulted in huge territorial gains rather than long lists of war dead, and it was the latter purpose for which most memorials were built.

While these wars each have particular patterns of commemoration, mixed political meanings surrounding these wars prevent clarity in meaning and common understanding. American aims in these wars were neither totally unjust or just. For example, the memorials for the USS *Maine* were dedicated in the false belief that the ship had been sunk by the Spanish. On the other hand, Texans have a just cause to commemorate the Goliad massacre. In the American-Indian wars, both sides had reasonable claims of justice and injustice to defend their aims and actions, although the Indians suffered the most indignities. Political meaning behind these wars was mixed, while memorials for these wars were used to legitimize American actions. Yet, underlying contradictions often emerge in spite of coordinated images. When the real facts of history become known, people view memorials to the wars of Manifest Destiny with some skepticism. Remembering those who died is valid, but the justness of the particular war must be valid as well. In the end, American expansionism and greed taints the symbolism in memorials for these wars.

CHAPTER FIVE

MONUMENTS TO DEFEAT

W̶HEN A COUNTRY IS DEFEATED IN WAR, its people experience not only disgrace, but other, more divided feelings as well. They examine the justness or unjustness of the cause. They question the inevitability of the defeat. A defeated people do not simply reduce a war's outcome to winners and losers; they are compelled to find a way to redeem themselves.

A nation can believe that defeat was justified, especially when the country's people decide that the cause for war was immoral. The best American example is the Civil War. The Union was split, and after the war there were bitter feelings both in the North and South. After many years of division, northerners and southerners have eventually decided that the Confederacy's aim, the preservation of slavery, was unjust. On the other hand, a nation may decide overwhelmingly that its defeat was justified and quickly divorce itself from its lost cause as soon as the war is over. While Americans have not experienced this dilemma, other nations have. Few Germans now feel that their country should have won World War II under the tyranny of nazism. A nation's people may continue to argue or they may decide quickly whether a defeat was just or unjust. In either case, they will question the moral reasons for allowing such a war to occur.

People have differing opinions over the inevitability of their nation's defeat. Some citizens believe that their country could have defeated the enemy but chose to settle for a compromise or a withdrawal. Others will say the war was a lost cause from the beginning. Americans have demonstrated this dilemma in their divided views of the U.S. involvement in the Korean War and the Vietnam War. These were wars of restraint. While political rationalization was used to justify restraint in military force, many Americans still asked: "Why did so many die without victory?" Americans have been embittered toward their government and each other over the outcomes of these wars. Proponents of these wars felt that American honor was preserved, while opponents said that the United States should not have become involved in such obviously hopeless causes. Under these circumstances remembering victory and defeat for particular battles is redundant; what is at issue is the legitimacy of the war itself.

Defeat in war cannot be forgotten, and a nation's people must find ways to redeem those who died for their country, to make defeat honorable. This can be done by honoring the individuals who fought rather than the country's lost cause. The many Confederate memorials on county courthouse lawns are tributes to the fighting man regardless of his cause. Servicemen from the wars in Korea and Vietnam have been vocal in wanting their wars to be remembered with memorials of the same quality as those for previous American wars. Soldiers who fought and were defeated are not concerned with redeeming a lost cause. Instead, they want citizens to acknowledge the willingness the soldiers showed in fighting for their country.

Memories of defeat produce mixed feelings; thus, memorials for these wars pose critical questions. What was remembered, and what was forgotten? How was honor portrayed and then embraced in a context of defeat? The Civil War, Korean War, and Vietnam War are each remembered differently in light of the historical circumstances which caused them. As a result, memorials for these wars often reflect the problems which caused these conflicts.

THE CIVIL WAR

The Civil War was the most devastating conflict in American history. Approximately 1.5 million northerners and 1 million southerners fought from 1861 to 1865; of these, 359,000 Union enlisted personnel and 259,000 Confederate enlisted personnel died.[1] It was a bitter war. Two economies, the industrializing North versus the agrarian South, were pitted against one another. The southern economy depended upon slavery, and it was this issue that ultimately began the war even though many northerners did not oppose slavery. Due to its industrial superiority the North eventually won, and the Union was again united and slavery abolished. The cost in U.S. lives to achieve these ends was greater than in any other American war.

Southerners are today more willing to believe that the South should have lost the Civil War, since a victory would have perpetuated the inhumane institution of slavery. While Confederate rituals linger, such as singing "Dixie," they are increasingly considered to be in bad taste.

The American poet laureate, Robert Penn Warren, argues that the South's defeat was also a loss for the North, producing communal guilt as a nation. Warren says,

the Civil War is . . . the story of a crime of monstrous inhumanity, into which almost innocently men stumbled; of consequences which could not be trammeled up, and of men who entangled themselves more and more vindictively and desperately until the powers of reason were twisted and their very virtues perverted . . . there is a reconciliation by human recognition.[2]

The Civil War is an example of the defeat of humane reasoning to achieve humane results, "an image of the powerful, painful, grinding process by which an ideal emerges out of history."[3] The realized ideal is a free society without slavery, and both the North and South have come to embrace it.

Memorials to the Civil War evolved differently in the North and in the South. Today, we can see in a town square the typical soldier on a pedestal in both the North and South, but historically their placement was unevenly timed. After the war, the North was in a better financial position to build memorials than the South. The construction of Confederate memorials did not fully begin until the 1900s.[4] The lack of Confederate memorials immediately after the Civil War might have given the impression that southerners did not care. Nonetheless, southern communities did memorialize their townscape when it was possible, and they were willing to pay a high price to do so.[5] Economic recovery from the war significantly influenced when memorials were built.

Town memorials in both the North and the South did not directly proclaim victory or defeat. Their purpose was to bestow dignity on the war dead. Regional animosities did exist, but for today's visitor, Civil War memorials tend to hold one united meaning, the remembrance of the loss of life. These monuments represent the lost attempt to resolve the political conflicts which caused the war itself. This interpretation becomes more accepted as regional animosities pass, and Warren's notion of communal guilt gains credence. American communities ultimately felt it was more important to recognize who died than who won.

Beyond the typical town memorial, other major patterns of providing memorials to the Civil War emerged. These commemorations were national military parks, grand city memorials, and the formation of Arlington National Cemetery. While these patterns provided the foundation for future war memorials, the unique historical circumstances of the Civil War led to war memorials that often reflected the division between the two halves of the nation, one the victor and the other the loser.

National military parks which were set aside to remember battles from the Civil War have many similarities in their design and commemoration. The battlefields of Gettysburg, Pennsylvania, and Vicksburg, Mississippi, allow interesting comparisons. Both battles were won by the North and provide northern and southern parallels and contrasts for war memorials and landscape design. The Gettysburg and Vicksburg battlefields contain many patterns for commemoration which are also found at many less well-known battle sites.

The landscapes at Gettysburg and Vicksburg reflect the landscape of battle itself. Visitors to these parks see statues and artillery pieces that face the battle zone. On the battle line there are memorials to the common soldier and regimental monuments that collectively remember military units. In a zone behind this line are monuments to commanders. Beyond this are monuments to the campaign generals. The monuments, except for state memorials, are often less grand the closer they are to the battle line. Equestrian statues for generals are located behind the lines while regimental monuments are smaller in scale and closer to the battle line. The battle zone, no man's land, is largely empty except for small markers where specific skirmishes took place. War memorials oriented to the battlefield reflect the place history of the battle itself.

Some memorials express a variety of individual roles and group allegiances. Infantrymen, artillerymen, cavalrymen, buglers, and even civilians are commemorated as part of the scene in monuments. Cannons, cannonball stacks, and rifle stacks are used in memorials to remember companies and regiments. Ethnic groups are remembered in such monuments as the Gaelic cross at Gettysburg which commemorates a military unit with a large number of Irish soldiers. Unit symbols were sculpted. The Forty-Second New York Infantry Regiment, recruited by the Tammany Society, was symbolized by Tammany, a Delaware chief of great bravery. After the monument's unveiling at Gettysburg, all regimental veterans were referred to as braves to symbolize their proven nobility.[6] These memorials reflect social allegiances that existed before and during the war. Veterans were often proud of their ethnic backgrounds and their particular contribution to a battle. Beyond which side won or lost, they wanted their battle efforts to be commemorated.

Visitors to these parks are constantly reminded of which military front they are on. Directional signs and historical markers are color-coded to identify each army. In Vicksburg, Union signs are blue, while those for the Confederacy are red. They are constant reminders that the battle turf has been stratified without trying to imply friend or foe. At both Gettysburg and Vicksburg, Confederate Avenue marks the South's line of defense. Union Avenue at Vicksburg identifies the North's line of defense. The names of Union generals are used to delineate Union territory at Gettysburg. Partisans of one side or the other may view only one side, while visitors who are more indifferent or ambivalent about state or regional alliances may regard the whole battleground as a monument to the Americans who died there. Thus visitors may have multiple interpretations of the memorials' meaning.

The natural landscape itself has been reconstituted. Park administrators have made efforts to restore battle sites authentically. Trostle's Woods and Ziegler's Grove at Gettysburg have been reforested to replace farm lands plowed after the war.[7] The visitor gains a sense of the landscape that soldiers actually occupied during battle. One battlefield other than Gettysburg and Vicksburg deserves special mention in this regard. The Battle of Antietam by Sharpsburg, Maryland, was one of the most vicious battles in the Civil War. The Miller cornfield where the line of battle swept back and forth 15 times is still maintained. Less than a mile away is Bloody Lane where 4,000 Confederate and Union soldiers were killed in battle within four hours. These two famous killing grounds are so physically distinct and famous that visitors can easily ignore nearby monuments. The landscape itself is the memorial.

The states who sent soldiers to these battles have commemorated state involvement by erecting memorials; the number, size, age, and style of these monuments reflects the extent of each state's participation, particularly the extent of its loss.

At Gettysburg, there are many Pennsylvania monuments, and at Vicksburg, many from Mississippi. Both states fought valiantly on their home turf, and their numerous monuments reflect this effort. Other states who sent large numbers of troops have proportionately more or larger memorials than less involved states. New York and Virginia have larger monuments at Gettysburg; Louisiana and Pennsylvania are strongly represented at

5.1 Bloody Lane at Antietam Battlefield, Maryland (Author's Collection)

Vicksburg. The scale of these memorials reflects not only the scale of each state's involvement, but also—and more importantly—the scale of its loss.

The age of these memorials goes hand in hand with state commitment. Those states most heavily involved in the battle tended to build their memorials sooner than other states. While the North could afford and did build memorials more quickly than a reluctant and poorer South, the pattern of commemoration for each side tends to follow the pattern of the state's involvement.[8] For example, New York and Pennsylvania built their memorials at Gettysburg before other, less involved Union states. Virginia built its state memorial in 1917 while Texas added a memorial as late as 1964.[9] The same pattern tends to be true at Vicksburg for both the Union and the Confederacy. Not unexpectedly, Mississippi built its memorial in Vicksburg before many other southern states even though it could not easily afford a major monument.[10] Eventually all states involved at Gettysburg and Vicksburg built memorials.

The age of a battlefield memorial usually dictates its style. The earliest memorials were classical in style; later memorials, usually those erected by the less involved states, reflected the shift from classicism to modernism.

In the late nineteenth and early twentieth century, memorials paralleled classical design in architecture and other sculpture. Early memorials demonstrated the European training of the sculptors who executed these

5.2 Pennsylvania Memorial at Gettysburg National Military Park, Pennsylvania (Author's Collection)

works. All the major memorials were done by sculptors who were educated or who later studied in Vienna, Rome, or (especially) Paris.[11] Their works combined both idealism and realism. Many monuments contain angels of liberty and peace. Known figures, such as Grant or Lee, are grandly posed, but the reality of war was symbolized through the common soldier. Early classical sculpture work portrayed soldiers in the circumstances they experienced; hats are bent, arms are in slings, clothes are tattered, and bodies are often slouched. Even in these informal poses, soldier figures tend to reflect a stern determination to endure. They symbolize the dignity of the common man upon whom falls the brunt of battle. Classicism provided a realism that many states wanted in their monuments, because these sculpted figures in poses of fighting or dying clearly represented the symbolic meaning, sacrifice. The common soldier's experience of war was captured but not overglorified. Sculptors of these early memorials also had the benefit of observing actual veterans of the war, many of whom were scarred or were missing limbs. Keenly aware of these painful realities, these sculptors used classical realism in their monuments to reflect the harshness of the Civil War.

Later memorials tended to be built in a modern style. This was especially true for Confederate memorials which were often built later than Union monuments. The Arkansas and Georgia monuments in Gettysburg and Vicksburg have an overtone of art deco, while the Florida monument has nondescript markers in a modern vein. As has been mentioned, these states took longer to erect monuments because their involvement in the battle was not as great as other states. A notable example is Texas, which has usually used the same monument, changing only the inscription, in its commemoration of these far-off battles. These more modern and less decorative memorials are less articulate in their symbolism, often leaving the impression of a state name and an inscription and little more. The stylized modern monuments, such as those from Texas, reflect not only a changing fancy—modernism—but also the perceptions of people. The war became more distant in people's memory, and as a result the commemorations of it became less vivid. The feelings of division and defeat were no longer foremost in people's minds. These battlefield monuments often appear to be signposts of participation more than sincere expressions of honoring the dead.

Some exceptions to latter-day styles do exist. The Alabama monument at Vicksburg and the Louisiana and Mississippi monuments at Gettysburg have all been completed since 1950. These memorials are in a classical style. The Mississippi monument at Gettysburg, completed in 1973, is especially striking. One soldier lies dead while another stands fiercely ready to use his rifle as a club, representing both the sacrifice and proud gallantry of Mississippians.[12] With no inscription to verify its meaning, the heroic sculpture appears to say "never surrender." Unlike earlier Civil War sculptures, the standing soldier is extremely athletic. To some the Mississippi monument expresses defiance as much as bravery. The sculptor, De Lue, was heavily influenced by Bourdelle, a romanticist sculptor, during his studies in Paris.[13] The Mississippi monument is characteristic of the work of some sculptors who designed memorials in the classical style during the time of modernism and who sometimes romanticized heroism and death in the Civil War. War scenes were not expressed as directly as in earlier classical monuments. Bent figures covered with the dirt and grime of war gave way to athletic figures in the Greek style. These romanticized sculptures confuse the purpose of honoring the dead with classical themes and poses that suggest a just political cause.

Some memorials, both classical and modern, attempt to depict reconciliation. At Vicksburg, the Missouri memorial remembers both Union and Confederate soldiers from the state. Victor Holm, the sculptor, was willing to depict both sides fighting one another, but he was unwilling to support the state's original recommendation of two separate memorials. Instead, he emphasized brotherhood between the North and South in his single memorial by depicting an angel of peace between the memorial's bronze reliefs symbolic of North and South.[14] The Wisconsin memorial at Vicksburg has a bronze relief depicting ". . . a Union and Confederate soldier with hands clasped in friendship to symbolize the peace which exists now between North and South."[15] Finally, the Kansas memorial at Vicksburg is a modern sculpture with two whole rings joined by a broken ring to symbolize union, war, and union once again.[16] In these memorials, communal peace is an integral part of commemorating the dead. These monuments attempt to go beyond honoring those who fought, but visitors to Vicksburg and Gettysburg are largely unaware of these expressions of peace and conciliation. There are too many monuments around them which honor who fought but little else.

While some differences between northern and southern monuments do exist, memorials for both sides generally tend to emphasize dignity and gallantry in their designs. This theme is especially apparent in the earlier classical monuments, although modern southern memorials tend to be less graphic. This is primarily the result of monument committees on both sides attempting to be evenhanded. The visitor unaware of history could just as easily perceive that the South had won these major battles. If defeat is meant to be seen here, it is the defeat represented by communal loss rather than the defeat of a humiliated Confederacy by a righteous Union.

The symbolic proclamation of Confederate guilt is not at the physical core of Civil War battlefields but is more often at their periphery. This is best seen with cemeteries, commercial development, and holidays.

Most battlefields which have become national military parks have cemeteries at their edge which tend to include only Union soldiers. The Confederate dead are buried elsewhere, or their bodies remain unidentified

5.3 Mississippi Memorial at Gettysburg National Military Park,
Pennsylvania (Author's Collection)

in makeshift graves in the battlefield itself. For example, there is no explicit graveyard for Confederates at Gettysburg, and at Vicksburg the Confederate cemetery is totally separated from the military park. Union soldiers are conspicuously associated with the nearby field of honor while the Confederates are not. Immediately after the battle, Union troops made graveyards by the battlefields, and after the war Union soldiers were recognized first when these graveyards were made national cemeteries. In time, both northern and southern soldiers from other wars, such as World War I, were allowed to be buried in these national cemeteries. Yet, most of these later burials were for southerners, since national cemeteries exist all over the United States to serve local needs. In the southern national cemeteries, such as Vicksburg, southerners from later wars are buried and honored as Americans without legitimizing past Civil War deeds. National military parks are symbolic landscapes that honor the Union but declare the Confederacy to be guilty of fighting for an unjust cause.

Confederate graveyards typically exist in southern towns and contain those who died in battle and veterans who died afterwards. The Vicksburg Confederate Cemetery deserves special mention. Graves are arranged by state, and grave markers of high ranking officers are conspicuously displayed along the pedestrian pathway. Certain devices make it clear that these Confederate dead are being honored. The area which contains the Confederate graves is set apart from nearby civilian graves and is surrounded by heavy black chains. More importantly, the United Daughters of the Confederacy have attached their Cross of Honor at numerous places on the chains. While each soldier received this medal, the crosses on the chain convey a sense of collective, rather than individual, honor. These defeated soldiers were dignified through this symbolism, and the soil has been made sacred so that these Confederate soldiers may be protected from the profane. Small Confederate flags are placed at the grave site each Fourth of July in memory of Vicksburg's fall on that day in 1863. Confederate cemeteries such as this are counterclaims to national military parks which refuse to honor Confederate dead. These cemeteries proclaim that southern soldiers deserve to be recognized for their efforts regardless of northern opinion.

In the past, the communities surrounding Civil War battlefields were as tranquil as the battlefield itself. Recently, however, battlefields in the South have been used to encourage tourism, particularly those near large cities; Stone Mountain, near Atlanta, and Lookout Mountain, near Chattanooga, are two examples. At other sites nearby tourist attractions have made such developments unnecessary to attract business. More isolated places, such as Gettysburg and Vicksburg, offer a stark contrast. Tourism in these communities has developed quite differently, and history offers some reasons.

Gettysburg has become highly commercialized given the community's small size. In spite of strong objections by the National Park Service and legal action by the Commonwealth of Pennsylvania, private developers built a 300-foot observation tower overlooking the battlefield in 1974. Despite opinions that the tower destroyed the area's scenic beauty, there is no question that it sparked commercial development of business geared to tourism which was previously nonexistent.[17] Visitors to Gettysburg can now visit the Soldiers National Museum and National Civil War Wax Museum. There are bus tours, displays, souvenir shops, and other such ventures. The city of Gettysburg has taken advantage of its history as the site of an important Union victory to promote tourism.

Vicksburg offers a contrast. While it is a much larger town than Gettysburg, there is no commercialism that promotes the nearby battle. In time, such enterprise might develop, but Vicksburg's history tends to suggest otherwise. The Confederate surrender at Vicksburg on July 4, 1863, has never been forgotten, but neither is it celebrated. The military park has been preserved primarily through federal efforts. Before the surrender, Vicksburgers celebrated Independence Day enthusiastically; after 1863, it became little more than a day off. Since World War II, Independence Day has regained some of its old flavor, but remembrance is still subdued.[18] In Vicksburg, the Fourth of July still symbolizes the defeat of the Confederacy more than victory in the American Revolution. This persistent attitude suggests that local businesspeople will not exploit this defeat, because they do not want to discredit their southern forefathers.

All Civil War battlefields tend to convey communal guilt, the inability of reason to win over aggression. Southern defeat is given dignity by portraying the Confederate soldier as a brave and heroic figure. Yet, the exclusion of Confederate soldiers from national military cemeteries near Civil War battlefields makes this communal guilt explicit. In some cases, the presence or absence of commercialism surrounding these battlefields reflects a desire to remember victory in the North and to subdue the memory of defeat in the South. Yet, even if these situations represent the last remnants of regional views, these animosities are outweighed by the triumph of freedom over slavery. Perhaps the lasting impression that visitors have of Civil War battlefields is the loss of human life. Today, visitors see all those who died more as Americans than as northerners or southerners. Civil War battlefields reflect Warren's concept of communal guilt as people increasingly ignore regional allegiances.

The Confederacy's surrender at Appomattox on April 9, 1865, ended the Civil War, and the town has been preserved to remember this event. After a number of disjointed attempts to make Appomattox a memorial, it finally became a national Historic Park in 1954. After the war, Appomattox deteriorated; it is now more a replication of the past than a restoration of it. Still, old messages are conveyed. In the reconstructed County Courthouse, museum displays present the history of Appomattox. The actual signing of the instrument of peace took place in the McLean House, which has been rebuilt as it was in 1865; but visitors only walk by the house and must conclude for themselves that this is where General Robert E. Lee signed the surrender. Appomattox is the nation's symbolic landscape which proclaims a merciful end to this difficult period of our history.

On the opposite side of the courthouse is Surrender Triangle, where over 28,000 Confederates laid down their weapons and ceremoniously furled their battle flags on Old Richmond Road. At the triangle, a marker provides an etched illustration while a prerecorded tape relives the event. The visitor can try to imagine how Confederate soldiers went through the sorrowful ritual of surrendering arms and flags. The triangle was the ritual space to bury the Civil War. While the McLean house made the Confederacy's surrender official, the triangle was the place of its requiem mass. Oddly, there is no monument to remember this significant place and event. The absence of a monument leads the visitor to conclude that southerners were not particularly eager to memorialize their surrender while northerners were not willing to embarrass the South by building a monument which would ultimately say: "This is where the Confederacy decided to quit."

Beyond the reconstructed village and small courthouse museum, visitors are primarily attracted by live entertainment. Employees of the National Park Service perform a living history program to enable people to recapture what it was like in the summer of 1865. A Union soldier, a Confederate soldier, and a village resident take turns speaking in native dialect about life in those times. For a moment, Appomattox becomes a stage, a very real one, in which people can temporarily feel that they are time travelers.

The Appomattox National Historic Park is a reconstruction of the end of the Civil War and the beginning of the new Union. This radical change of history is experienced at Appomattox as frozen time in space. There are no nearby towns to disturb the mood. No elaborate stone memorials exist in Appomattox, because the place itself is the memorial to the Civil War's end.

Beyond the typical town memorials, battlefields, and Appomattox, the Civil War spurred American cities to begin the first attempts in the nation's history to build major war memorials. Two main patterns emerged. Large cities commemorated the war, and Washington, D.C., began to become the center for national memory.

Some large American cities built war memorials to the Civil War not only as a matter of civic pride but also as a way to improve the physical image of their cities. While the City Beautiful movement did not gain strength until the early part of the twentieth century, even in the late 1800s city leaders were beginning to consider the need for urban design in their communities. They saw war memorials as a means to remember the Civil War and simultaneously beautify their cities.

The grand city war memorials were known as soldier and sailor monuments, and not surprisingly, these monuments were built in northern cities.

New York City's Soldiers and Sailors Monument, located in Central Park, is modeled after the Monument of Lysicrates in Athens, which was actually a monument used to honor winners in athletic and music competitions rather than soldiers.[19] Across the East River in Brooklyn, the Soldiers and Sailors Memorial Arch was built in the Grand Army Plaza. Its design is a combination of Roman victory arches and the Arch de Triomphe in Paris. The plaza and the arch use traditional symbolism to celebrate victory, with equestrian figures of the great heroes, Lincoln and Grant, recessed within the inner walls of the arch.[20] On the south side of the arch atop pedestal columns are sculpture groups. On the right is the Navy group which portrays a variety of sailors, including a black man, all posed as if to say: "We are ready to fight." Behind them is a sea goddess who poses as a protector for their purpose. On the left is the Army group which portrays a similar set of soldiers set for battle with a protective angel behind them. Atop the arch is a sculpture group known as a quadriga. A triumphal angel, flag in one hand and sword in the other, stands in a chariot led by horses. Beside her are two trumpeting angels with winged horses at their side.[21] This grouping, with its recollection of a Roman triumphal arch and its bold sculptures, conveys a feeling of strength and conquest. The inclusion of President Lincoln in the motif gives the further impression that this was a just and moral victory as well. These memorials had a deeper meaning than the celebration of victory. Like the triumphant victory arches and columns in Rome, northern soldiers and sailors monuments recollect northern sentiment that they had defeated an immoral enemy and saved the Union. The large monuments in northern cities enabled their citizens to capture in a symbolic capsule the huge costs in human life which had been exacted to eliminate injustice.

Some of the largest memorials for the Civil War were erected in two midwestern cities, Cleveland and Indianapolis. The states of Ohio and Indiana sent many soldiers to fight in the Civil War. With so many deaths, the citizens of Cleveland and Indianapolis naturally wanted to commemorate the sacrifice. However, these cities probably had motives beyond remembrance; they were young cities and had no public structures that they could point to with great pride. Civil War memorials provided these two cities with a modest way to express civic improvement.

In Cleveland, the Cuyahoga County Soldiers and Sailors Monument is a memorial relic room topped with a victory column. At the base are two sculpture groups depicting soldiers and sailors in battle. On the column are the names of major Civil War battles and on top is an angel named Liberty holding a shield. In the relic room, there is a roll of honor on each of the four walls identifying those who died.[22] Throughout the memorial, military paraphernalia is incorporated into pseudoclassical motifs. Military service insignia are even part of the heating grates.[23] When the memorial was dedicated in 1894, it dominated its site in Cleveland's downtown rather than

5.4 Soldiers and Sailors Arch, Brooklyn, New York (Author's Collection)

integrating with surroundings.[24] High-rise buildings eventually made the memorial small in comparison, but in its time the Cuyahoga County Soldiers and Sailors Monument documented ". . . the showy materialism of the epoch—the taste for display and literalism. It is the product of a society that fervently believed in the values it glorified."[25]

The grandest city memorial built to commemorate the Civil War was the Indian Soldiers and Sailors Monument in Indianapolis. While it was initially conceived to remember the Civil War, veterans' organizations ultimately recommended all of America's previous wars be remembered in this monument. The final design included commemorations to the American Revolution, the War of 1812, the Mexican War, and the Civil War.[26] It was this country's first major combined memorial, grouping many wars together. One tablet at the base was solely inscribed for the Civil War while the other tablet combines inscriptions for the other three wars. The Civil War commemoration ultimately dominates this monument, with the years of that conflict—1861 and 1865—being the only dates on the shaft.

The symbolism of this Indiana monument is intense and complex.[27] The memorial is composed of three major parts which are the upper shaft, the pedestal, and supportive sculpture and inscriptions. These elements are integrated to tell the story of the Civil War.

The shaft is a symbolic representation of who fought and won the Civil War. At the top, standing on a globe, is the statue of Victory. It is also known as Miss Indiana. While some conflict occurred over the statue's orientation, the ultimate decision was to face it south.[28] The cynic might say that Victory—sword in one hand and raised torch in the other—is gloating over the defeated enemy. The shaft is ringed by three ornamental bands known as astragals. The top astragal is just below the monument's capital and displays the war's dates with 1861 on the north and south sides and 1865 on the east and west. The middle astragal represents the U.S. Navy in the Civil War. Sailors, weapons, and boats are displayed between ship bows which are at each corner of the shaft. The bottom astragal is a memorial to the Army, and it is the largest and most ornate. Cannons, rifles, and banners are arranged to give a feeling of battle on all four sides of the shaft. On the north and south facades, a huge eagle with outstretched wings atop a shield symbolizes the United States. Miss Indiana and the eagle on the upper shaft announce the Union victory, the army and navy scenes display who fought, and the dates say when. More simply, the shaft is an elegant scoreboard.

Below the three astragals is the monument's pedestal, and its message is more political than the shaft. On the east side is a huge sculpture ensemble called the war group. Various types of soldiers are being led by a war goddess with a raised torch, and behind and above all of them is an angel of war clutching arrows and the American flag.[29] The ensemble seems to shout: "God is for the Union," and since the memorial primarily commemorates the Civil War, it further implies: "but not for the Confederacy." Below the war ensemble is another statue group known as "The Dying Soldier."[30] Soldiers are bent over to care for a dying comrade; the message is that war has a price. When both sculpture groups are seen together, the impression is not limited to the cost of war. The composite symbolizes sacrifice for a righteous cause. On the west face of the pedestal is the peace group sculpture. In the center a goddess of peace holds a flag wrapped by an olive branch in one hand and the U.S. Union shield in the other. The surrounding figures portray many images of war's end, such as soldiers with no headgear, but one image is clearly a political comment on the Civil War. A slave sitting below the goddess lifts his unlocked chains in gratitude to her.[31] Below the peace group is a sculpture ensemble known as "The Return Home." It is a simple scene depicting a young soldier being greeted by what is obviously understood to be his parents on the family farm. It symbolizes relief, but when seen with the more dramatic peace group, the message is: "relief from war with righteousness fully served." The upper shaft announces victory, but the pedestal tells the visitor that a

5.5 Indiana Soldiers and Sailors Monument, Indianapolis, Indiana (Author's Collection)

just cause was won at a great cost in human life. More importantly, the pedestal's dramatic character leaves the visitor with the impression that the war was worth the price to achieve the political end, abolition of slavery.

The remaining elements of the monument consist mainly of sculpture and inscriptions which embellish past American victories. These parts enhance the symbolism presented on the upper shaft and pedestal. On the pedestal's south side there is a memorial tablet for the Civil War, which was later updated with an inscription for the Spanish-American War, and two sculpture pieces, the cavalryman and infantryman, stand by an entranceway to the downstairs museum. On the other side, a tablet memorializes the American Revolution, the War of 1812, and the Mexican War with two sculptures, the artilleryman and the sailor, at an entrance. Surrounding the monument are four sculptures to commemorate distinguished Indianans who fought in or lived during the country's first four wars. These remaining elements on the monument symbolically but falsely connect the American Revolution, wars of Manifest Destiny, and Indiana politicians with the Civil War. The principles fought for in the American Revolution did not lead inevitably to the Civil War, although both wars were based upon defending moral principles. Neither of these wars justify why wars of Manifest Destiny were fought. By grouping these wars together, the overall message is: "Americans for the Union have always won, because their wars were always just." The Indiana monument symbolically unifies facets of American war history that ultimately contradict one another.

Most visitors do not recognize all the intricacies of the monument's symbolism, but what they do experience is its complexity and the beauty of its fountains. For most people, it is an enjoyable urban plaza rather than a place to contemplate in silent remembrance. In some respects, the monument has become utilitarian, because it's viewed as a part of downtown beautification; some of the city's most expensive commercial properties surround it.

The Indiana Soldiers and Sailors Monument achieves what similar monuments in New York, Brooklyn, and Cleveland attempted to convey. They were symbols of the prosperous North and demonstrations of public concern with improved city design prior to the City Beautiful movement. There were no huge memorials in southern cities, because the South was still trying to regain its economic strength. These grand memorials of the North were promoted and often financially supported by the Grand Army of the Republic, an organization of Union veterans which had as one of its many aims the remembrance of fellow soldiers through war memorials.[32] While remembering Union soldiers was important, the dramatic style of these memorials said something more basic to their builders: "We won and they lost."

Some cities built memorials to remember heroic figures. New York City has its statue of General Phillip H. Sheridan on Grand Army Plaza at Fifth Avenue, and a few other cities have similar sculptures of military figures. The most important cities to erect this type of memorial, however, were the two capitals, Richmond, Virginia, and Washington, D.C.

Richmond was the capital of the Confederacy, and has more monuments to the Confederacy than any other city.[33] While the city's Soldiers and Sailors Monument is the South's only counterclaim to similar memorials in the North, Monument Avenue is the most elaborate urban design project built in memory of the Confederacy. Beyond being a tree-lined boulevard,

Monument Avenue is a tribute to Confederate leaders. Even visitors who know little of the Civil War unavoidably realize the war's importance to Richmond as they drive by equestrian statues dedicated to well-known confederate heroes such as generals J. E. B. Stuart, Stonewall Jackson, and Robert E. Lee, and a large memorial to President Jefferson Davis. These memorials evoke feelings of valor, and for southerners, these monuments are sources of pride, carrying the message that these were brave people who fought with honor. Yet, to outsiders such monuments memorialize Confederate patriots at best and fighters for an unworthy cause at worst. In the end, the collection of Richmond monuments reflects an attempt to redeem honor amidst the reality of defeat for those who wish to empathize with the South's dilemma of remembrance.

Although only completed in 1979, Stone Mountain Park outside of Atlanta, Georgia, demonstrates an even larger scale of Confederate grandeur than Richmond. The park's main attraction is the colossal relief carved from Stone Mountain itself. Confederate President Jefferson Davis and generals Robert E. Lee and Thomas "Stonewall" Jackson are gallantly portrayed on horseback. Their hats are held over their hearts in a gesture of remembrance for the dead. Without a doubt Stone Mountain is currently the largest war memorial in the United States. If the South was unable to afford large monuments like northern cities at the turn of the century, Georgians have attempted to redeem the past by honoring the Confederacy with Stone Mountain.

At the mountain's base, the Memorial Plaza and its trails articulate more clearly what is remembered. State memorials for the Confederacy are stone monoliths lain in paved trials which lead to the plaza. On one side of the plaza, a statue of a woman holding her child is inscribed on its base: "THE COUNTRY COMES BEFORE ME." On the other side, a young man holds a raised broken sword with the inscription below him: "MEN WHO SAW NIGHT COMING DOWN ABOUT THEM COULD SOMEHOW ACT AS IF THEY STOOD AT THE EDGE OF DAWN." The man, woman, and child symbolize the tragic reality of the Civil War coupled with the hope of a better life. The huge relief honors the past while the Memorial Plaza articulates the future. Nonetheless, most visitors are overwhelmed by the mountain, and the nearby War of Georgia Museum repeats the message of the past. In the end, Stone Mountain Park is a recreation center for boating, swimming, and relaxation. Its war memorials are important, but many people see them as scenic stage sets for a tourist center rather than shrines.

While Washington, D.C., is also the nation's capital, it was clearly the capital of the North in the Civil War. That allegiance was not forgotten. The capital contains 25 statues of Union officers while only two commemorate Confederates.[34] Compared to Richmond's three equestrian statues to commemorate Confederate generals, Washington has eight equestrian memorials. McClellan, Kearny, Thomas, McPherson, Logan,

5.6 Confederate Memorial on Stone Mountain, Georgia (Author's Collection)

Sheridan, and Sherman were Union generals who could not be forgotten, but the most lavish memorial was made for the Union's best remembered military leader, Ulysses S. Grant.[35]

Located at the east end of the Mall at Union Square, the General Ulysses S. Grant Memorial stands before the U.S. Capitol. At the Mall's west end is the Lincoln Memorial. If Lincoln was the symbol of the Union during the Civil War, then Grant was its military defender. The Grant Memorial is a complex of sculptures depicting a forward charge. To Grant's left is the cavalry group and to the right is the artillery group.[36] The equestrian statue of Grant is surrounded by four lions, classical symbols of honor. On each side of the pedestal are bronze relief panels known as "Infantry" which commemorate the average soldier. The sculptor, Henry Shrady, portrayed General Grant as former soldiers remembered him, "sitting calmly with slouched shoulders and with an old battered hat observing a battle in the distance."[37] The Grant statue is placed strategically between the artillery and cavalry groups to further evoke the feeling of a general watching a battle. The understated inscription at the base of the pedestal is a testimony to the importance of its subject. It says only "GRANT," and to students of the Civil War that is enough. The distant view of the Grant Memorial portrays a scene of victory, but the details—the expressions of the soldiers,

5.7 General Ulysses S. Grant Memorial, Washington, D.C. (Author's Collection)

the tired-looking horses, the well-worn equipment—convey a more profound message: Even victory exacts a high price in human suffering.

Two memorials in Washington commemorate the political ideals of the North. The Emancipation Monument in Lincoln Park symbolizes the cause of the war. Abraham Lincoln is shown standing over a kneeling slave who is beside a whipping post, chains, fetters, and a frayed whip—the symbols of slavery. In contrast, the Arlington Memorial Bridge symbolically reunites the North and South. At one end of the bridge is the Lincoln Memorial and beyond the other end is the Custis-Lee house.[38] Yet the bridge decorations of eagles, axes bundled with rods, and bison keystones do not convey this message clearly, and few people ever note the bridge's symbolic intent. One message is quite clear. The bridge leads directly into Arlington National Cemetery.

Arlington National Cemetery was first established as a burial place for Union and Confederate soldiers. Two major memorials were built, one commemorating each side. The Confederate Memorial and the Union's Tomb of the Unknown Dead of the War Between the States both symbolize the loss in lives. The South's memorial proclaims an end to the Confederacy while the Union tomb established a future model of remembrance.

The Confederate Memorial was built by the United Daughters of the Confederacy and dedicated in 1914. It stands in Andrew Jackson Circle where the Confederate dead are buried. Of all the memorials built to remember the Civil War, this memorial best symbolizes not only what they had to resolve in their lives but also what they respectfully wanted to honor. At the top, a female figure holding a plow faces south, symbolizing peace.[39] Beneath her is the biblical inscription: "THEY SHALL BEAT THEIR SWORDS INTO PLOWSHARES, AND THEIR SPEARS INTO PRUNING HOOKS." Below these words is a circular frieze in relief that illustrates the inscriptions, with soldiers leaving for war, returning from it, and resuming a peaceful life. On one side of the monument's base, there is an inscription that says: "TO OUR DEAD HEROES BY THE UNITED DAUGHTERS OF THE CONFEDERACY." Beneath it, there is a Latin phrase that most visitors cannot translate. The inscription says: "THE VICTORIOUS PLEASED THE GODS BUT THE DEFEATED PLEASED CATO." As a Roman general, Cato was highly respected for his moral righteousness. Defending what he thought was right, Cato led an army against Caesar in the Roman Civil War, but he was on the losing side. The use of this classical phrase is a subtle symbol that praises the moral worth of southerners who fought in the Civil War. As a whole, the memorial is solemn rather than heroic. The inscriptions honoring the dead remember the past, and the biblical passage is a message of peace for the future. The sculpture and inscriptions are a combined message that acknowledges the Confederacy as political history rather than future reality.

The North's main memorial in Arlington is the Tomb of the Unknown Dead of the War Between the States. It contains the remains of 2,111 Union soldiers who died at Bull Run and along the route to the Rappahannock River. As a form of national spite, General Montgomery Miegs placed the memorial so near to the Custis-Lee Mansion in order to discourage the Lees, a southern family, from returning home. Another memorial, the Temple of Fame, honors the first Union officer buried in Arlington, and it was located in the Rose Garden for the same purpose.[40] The Union Tomb is most important as a forerunner of The Tomb of the Unknown Soldier to remember World War I.

Arlington National Cemetery is ultimately dominated by the North. More Union soldiers and former slaves are buried here than Confederates, and the streets are named after Union generals; no Confederate generals are commemorated in this manner. The Arlington Memorial Bridge may symbolize rejoining the North and the South, but Arlington National Cemetery's symbolism specifies that the North dictated the terms. Still, this memorial to the Civil War provided the spark of an idea: one main national cemetery near Washington.

Civil War memorials have served a multitude of symbolic purposes. Local monuments remembered friends directly but simply with allegiance depending upon the home region. National military parks have attempted to recapture the past as it was, but in some cases, glorification has been a barrier to remembering sacrifice. Soldiers and sailors monuments were city

5.8 Confederate Memorial, Arlington National Cemetery, Virginia (Author's Collection)

expressions of civic improvement in the North with clear overtones of remembering victory more than peace. Washington, D.C., used sculptures to remember the Union's military leaders as the nation's heroes while monuments in Richmond, Virginia, honor Confederate heroes. Finally, Arlington National Cemetery was a foundation for remembering all American soldiers, although a weak one. These various symbolic uses of Civil War memorials demonstrated that most Americans wanted war memorials to fit their own needs without a common purpose.

Civil War memorials generally have not reflected Warren's proposition of communal guilt, but people are beginning to have this unified perspective. Most of these memorials were built and dedicated when Civil War wounds were not entirely healed, although veterans from both sides commonly participated in dedication ceremonies. Memorials for both the North and the South put each side in a good light while rarely acknowledging the nation's common failure. The memorials have not changed, but American society has evolved beyond most of the old hatreds. Today, people are more distant from the past, and they are psychologically more able to accept the Civil War as history rather than a reason to bear animosities, although some prejudices still exist. In reflection, remembering the Civil War enables Americans to understand that the nation was rethinking its identity from an ideology of states' rights to a belief in the United States with equality for all. Nonetheless, the Civil War was a heavy price to pay for change. Americans are gradually beginning to interpret Civil War memorials as commemorations for the great loss in American lives, not just for those of North or the South.

THE KOREAN WAR

There is a Korean folk saying which says: "A shrimp is crushed in the battle of the whales."[41] The Korean War was such a battle, with North and South Korea caught between two major powers, the United States and the Soviet Union, and threatened by another, lesser power, China. But this was not a full-scale war, for neither the United States nor the Soviet Union wanted another major war. For this reason American troops never stepped on Chinese soil; the major powers would tolerate a little war but not a big one. In the end, the United States decided that the Korean War was a no-win situation. As General Omar Bradley said: "[It was] the wrong war, in the wrong place, at the wrong time, with the wrong enemy."[42]

It was not a war that Americans wanted or were quickly willing to volunteer to fight. Many reservists in the armed forces who fought in World War II resented having to fight another war, because they thought one was enough. It was someone else's turn, but the younger generation was not eager. As one young man told his fellow high school classmates: "Boys, there's two things we gotta avoid: Korea and gonorrhea."[43]

Americans not only physically avoided the war, afterwards they avoided it mentally as well. There were no grand parades to greet returning soldiers. Yet, they were not treated badly. The 1950s were good times in America, and people wanted to pay more attention to how they could better their lives than to think about a war that nobody cared about.

Some memories would not fade away. There were names such as Heartbreak Ridge, Fox Hill, No-Name Ridge, and Pork Chop Hill that people knew were fought over with bravery and at great costs in American lives. People saw on newsreels and television the devastating cold under which soldiers had to survive and fight. Yet, the hard-earned memories were figuratively shoved aside by President Truman's firing of Douglas MacArthur as commanding general of the U.N. forces. When MacArthur came home, he got a ticker-tape parade in New York City, but the common GI did not.

In the end, Americans were left with the satisfaction that they had not allowed communism to expand. At the same time, the United States had not defeated the North Koreans, the Chinese Communists, or ultimately the Soviets. The war can be seen as a tie. For Americans, however, a tie is often seen as a loss, especially after the winning streak of wars in the nation's brief history.

The Korean War has mainly been a forgotten war, and there are significantly fewer memorials for it than for any American war in the twentieth century. It was the smallest war, since more Americans were killed in the world wars and Vietnam. Nonetheless, patterns for commemorating the Korean War have emerged which are mainly reifications of past traditions.

One pattern of remembering Korea has been for military units to embellish their memorials from previous wars in the District of Columbia and Arlington National Cemetery. The First Division Memorial in the Ellipse along Constitution Avenue in Washington was originally dedicated for World War I. After the Korean War, two wings were added to the original memorial. The west wing commemorates World War II while the east wing memorializes the Korean conflict.[44] When the Marine Corps War Memorial was dedicated in 1954, the Korean War was inscribed on its base along with the other wars in which Marines have participated. The 101 Airborne Division Memorial in Arlington National Cemetery is an eagle-topped monument, and behind it, a wall lists the wars in which the division has been engaged. The wall is divided into equal sections, and on one of them is an inscription for the Korean War. Each war in which the division has participated is treated the same, conveying the message that combat is hell in all wars. Embellishment of war memories after the Korean War was an expression of this brotherhood among the military.

The main memorial to the Korean War is the Tomb of the Unknown Soldier in Arlington National Cemetery. Unknown soldiers for both World

War II and the Korean War were entombed there. The dedication took place on Memorial Day 1958 when, as with the Unknown Soldier for the First World War, both unknowns were awarded the Congressional Medal of Honor.[45] Within the Memorial Amphitheater Hall a separate section was set aside to display all the medals dedicated by other countries to the Korean War Unknown Soldier. While the dedication ceremonies gave equal weight to both conflicts, remembering World War II easily outweighed memories for Korea. The Second World War was the big war, and far more Americans were killed in it than in Korea. Korean veterans had their day of honor, but it was not the same as having a separate ritual. Yet, this symbolically connected the two wars, and the Korean War was publicly made more legitimate by having a joint ceremony with "the Good War."

The remainder of Arlington National Cemetery was used for remembrance as in past wars. The Argonne Cross, first dedicated in the first World War, has been continuously updated, but unlike other memorials, the cross is inscribed with "Korean *Campaign.*" It was important to remember, but not large enough to give it equivalent status as the Great *War* and World *War* II which appear on the Cross base. While previous wars were remembered by street names in Arlington National Cemetery, the Korean War indirectly received the same honor. There are Eisenhower Drive, MacArthur Drive, and Marshall Drive. All of these men were involved with the Korean War, but their fame is more with World War II than the Korean War. This is made more apparent when the visitor notices nearby streets—Patton, Halsey, and Nimitz—which are strictly associated with the Second World War. Among all this indirect commemoration, the actual graves of Korean dead in Arlington put memory in perspective. A cross for a Korean veteran is the same as for a veteran of any other war. Many died in battle regardless of the war's size or popularity. The Korean War has been respectfully remembered in Arlington National Cemetery. Nonetheless, this remembrance symbolically parallels the size of the Korean War. Other than the Tomb of the Unknown Soldier, small commemorations have been provided for a small war.

The commemorative patterns used in American foreign cemeteries was also continued. Most Americans who fought and died in Korea were returned to the United States, but some were not. The unidentified remains of 800 service people and those whose kin requested overseas internment were buried at Honolulu Memorial National Cemetery of the Pacific. While known mainly by the public as a cemetery for World War II, over 8,000 names are inscribed on the walls of Courts of the Missing for the Korean War.[46] Up the steps from the Courts of the Missing is the chapel which is flanked by map galleries enclosed by roofed colonnades. Above the colonnades are the names of significant places of battle. While the names predominantly ring out memories of the Second World War, at the north end visitors see "KOREA." In the North Map Gallery are two maps with straightforward descriptions of military events in the Korean War.[47] Collectively, Korean War dead have been given an equal place of honor at the Honolulu cemetery. The tradition of symbolizing God with the chapel and country with the map galleries enables Korean veterans to be seen as the same as veterans from the Second World War. Nonetheless, visitors are overwhelmed by the number of graves for the Second World War and with the simple fact that not so far away is the place that Roosevelt said would live in infamy, Pearl Harbor. While the Korean War is remembered honorably, most visitors link Hawaii's history more strongly with the Second World War. The Korean War dead are symbolically treated the same as all war dead within the cemetery, but the American people do not perceive this war to be equal to World War II in importance.

The Korean War was largely forgotten in the 1960s and 1970s in the United States, but American servicemen began to be recognized in Korea. Two main memorial sites were developed.[48] First, the Republic of Korea specifically dedicated a memorial in 1975 to American armed forces in front of the Ministry of National Defense at Paju. In 1978, the United Nations Forces Memorial at Pusan was dedicated. Both memorials symbolically thank the United States for preserving the Republic of Korea.

The symbolism of the American memorial at Paju recognizes all states within the United States and all the nation's armed forces. The memorial plaza is laid out in a circle. A perimeter wall is created with 50 flagpoles, and at the base of each flagpole is a state seal for each of the 50 U.S. states. Radial lines in the plaza floor symbolically connect each state to a central circular paving area where the main monument sits. In a simple way, the memorial demonstrates that America is a body of states united in purpose. The monument itself is comprised of four black marble triangles standing on their tips which support a square plate which has a circular opening. Triangular bronze reliefs for each of the armed services—Army, Navy, Air Force, and Marine Corps—are placed upon the monument's standing triangles. The reliefs depict battle scenes.

Inside and underneath the monument's structure is a flat circular stone made of white marble. Upon the stone is an inscription dedicating the memorial to the U.S. troops who lost their lives in the defense of the Republic of Korea. The American memorial at Paju is in keeping with Asian customs of gift giving. Each state and each armed service branch is separately thanked by its representation in the memorial, and by coordinating these symbols, the United States is commemorated for its sacrifice.

The United Nations Forces Memorial at the United Nations Memorial Cemetery at Pusan honors those nations that helped the Republic of Korea. The memorial is made of three concave walls which form a triangle. At each of the three corners is a repeated sculpture of two figures which sit and hold one another with one figure holding up a hand. These figures may be seen as nations united in upholding the principle of freedom. Upon the two back facades are 22 bronze plaques which present a brief history of the allied nations' role in the war. On the memorial's front facade are two doves in bas-relief holding branches symbolic of peace, and between them is an inscription in Korean and English saying:

IN MEMORY
OF THOSE MEMBERS OF
THE UNITED NATIONS FORCES
WHO GAVE THEIR LIVES
IN THE KOREAN WAR
1950-1953

While some Korean War dead are buried at Pusan, no American soldiers are buried there; nonetheless, the memorial commemorates all who died. On the dedication day, the allied countries provided bound volumes which contained the names of their countrymen who were killed in Korea, and in a solemn ceremony, the memorial volumes were placed within the monument. The symbolism of the monument is consistent with itself. It tells visitors to remember and to honor those who died. In the end, it is primarily a memorial for the Republic of Korea, because 237,686 names are from South Korea while the other 37,936 are from allied countries. American servicemen represent 33,629 of the allied dead.

While the Korean War was commemorated nationally in Washington, D.C., and in Korea, American communities did little to memorialize it. There were no Doughboy statues erected to remember servicemen as there had been after World War I. Some cities have statues to honor General Douglas MacArthur, but he is remembered more for his successful efforts in World War II than for his criticized leadership during the Korean War. A few armed forces reserve centers were dedicated to Americans who fought heroically in Korea, and in the past, passersby might see an F86 Sabre jet in front of a U.S. Air Force reserve center. The most common jet fighter used in Korea, these jets could be seen as subliminal reminders of the war in Korea. All of these remembrances of the Korean War were essentially secondary or hidden.

Formal commemorations to the Korean War have largely been combined memorials, those where two or more wars are grouped together. When the Vietnam War was over, some communities became sensitive to the fact that Vietnam veterans received no traditional welcome home. The decision to remember Vietnam led to the realization that earlier wars had to be remembered as well. Two extreme examples of this are Unionville, Connecticut, and Van Buren, Arkansas. Both communities had Civil War statues but had no other memorials. To catch up, each town dedicated one monument to remember simultaneously World War I, World War II, the Korean War, and the Vietnam War. The Korean War is remembered in

5.9 Combined War Memorial, Unionville, Connecticut (Author's Collection)

these monuments, but it seems more like a historical footnote. Memory for the Korean War is sandwiched between the Second World War and the Vietnam War, conflicts which have received significantly more attention.

The most prominent city commemoration to the Korean War is the Milwaukee County War Memorial. This combined memorial was built and then dedicated in 1969 to honor the war dead of World War II and the Korean War. This is most noticeable on the front facade where a spectacular mosaic mural incorporates large Roman numerals which record the dates of World War II and the Korean War. The memorial building is essentially a square doughnut on stilts, and within its exposed center is a memorial fountain. The fountain's edge is trimmed in black marble, and the names of those from the county who died in World War I, World War II, Korea, and Vietnam are inscribed. Within the pool a constantly lit lantern symbolizes continued remembrance. The Milwaukee County War Memorial building commemorative motto is: "HONOR THE DEAD. SERVE THE LIVING." While some may come to see the memorials, its primary function is utilitarian.[49] It houses an art museum, the Rotary Club headquarters, the local opera company offices, Veterans' Military Order of the Purple Heart, and numerous other organizations. Although the Korean War is remembered in the war memorial building, its memory is amidst

5.10 Milwaukee County War Memorial with Years of the Korean War, Milwaukee, Wisconsin (Author's Collection)

those of other wars and the civic organizations which have their own symbolism. The building's mosaic facade showing the war's dates makes it one of the largest memorials, if not the largest, to the Korean War in the United States. Yet, this utilitarian memorial's functions are so many that it is easy to forget that part of its Roman numeral facade commemorates Korea: "MCML—MCMLIII." The numeral's purpose is further obscured by the abstract design arrangement, which makes the numeric message hard to decipher. The symbolism in this monument is abstract and minimal. Most Milwaukee residents know its meaning, but outsiders can have difficulty identifying the building as a memorial which commemorates the Korean War.

Memorials to the Korean War are typically collective commemorations rather than separate ones. Quite often, the Korean War is remembered jointly with World War II, from the combined burial of Second World War and Korean Unknown soldiers in Arlington National Cemetery to the combined memorials in local communities. Memorials for the Korean War are victims of timing. This war began so shortly after World War II that it never had an identity which sufficiently separated it from other wars. It was more convenient and efficient to include the Korean War in memorials to other, larger conflicts.

Attempts to commemorate the Korean War were even overshadowed by the Vietnam War. Some Korean veterans and interested citizens tried to obtain support for a Korean War memorial in Washington, D.C., in the

1960s, but politicians and public officials were not eager to support it. The political upheavals and war protests against U.S. involvement in Vietnam made that war a much more pressing concern. After the Vietnam War, veterans and the public wanted a memorial for the forgotten servicemen of that conflict. Their requests were answered with a memorial in 1982 and a commemorative statue in 1984, but there was still no Korean War memorial in Washington, D.C. The American Battle Monuments Commission and a private committee have separately pursued funding for such a memorial. The funding process has been beset with problems similar to those experiences in funding a memorial for the USS *Arizona* at Pearl Harbor. These problems were eventually resolved in 1986 when the U.S. Congress authorized the American Battle Monuments Commission to administer private fund-raising and public funds to build the memorial. Government officials expect the monument to be completed and dedicated in 1992. Even though a national Korean War memorial is to be built, the Korean War will continue to be overshadowed by other wars in recent American history.

THE VIETNAM WAR

Vietnam was an unpopular war. Thousands of young Americans demonstrated to pressure the United States to withdraw from a war that they they thought to be immoral and without relevance to their lives. The burning of draft cards and protests against military ROTC programs on college campuses were common sights in the late sixties and early seventies. Some soldiers, especially black Americans, opposed this war in which they claimed that they were not respected and that their fellow GI's deaths were seen as meaningless.[50] After coming home, many Vietnam veterans felt that they were treated as outcasts. They thought that they had fought for nothing and had been forgotten, but they themselves could not forget.

Support for remembering and then commemorating the Vietnam War was fragmented. Highly patriotic groups, such as the American Legion and the Veterans of Foreign Wars, embraced Vietnam veterans, but such symbolic gestures were often seen as a typical right-wing response rather than as the sentiment of the average American. In spite of the many memorials in Washington, D.C., to more popular wars (such as World War II), there was little initial effort to commemorate the veterans of this unpopular conflict. In other communities people were beginning to recognize the human costs of Vietnam, but they were divided among themselves as to the best way to remember the war.

Commemoration of the Vietnam War began to follow three successive patterns: the search for meaning, official national remembrance, and finally civic articulation in the form of memorials. These transitions represented the stages of trying to understand what the Vietnam War meant and how it needed to be remembered.

Finally, memorials for the Vietnam War began to be developed. Local communities made the first modest gestures, mounting simple plaques in county courthouses naming those who had died, just as they had done for earlier wars. The eternal flame at President Kennedy's grave in Arlington National Cemetery had popularized that device, and a few communities chose to use memorial flames. In other cities, the desire to commemorate Vietnam led to the erection of combined memorials for that and other wars.

But in fact, most often communities did nothing to remember Vietnam; Americans preferred to forget this episode in their history. Remembrance for the Vietnam War at the national level began quite early, not with the federal government, but rather with the armed forces and veterans' organizations.

If there was any armed service group uniquely associated with Vietnam, it was the U.S. Army's Special Forces, more popularly known as the Green Berets. In 1969, while the war was still being fought, the Special Forces commemorated themselves by dedicating the Green Beret Monument at Fort Bragg, North Carolina. Although it had no direct reference to Vietnam, the memorial's style and its proximity to a monument inscribed with the names of Special Forces personnel killed in action, most of them in Vietnam, leave little doubt which war was being remembered. The statue portrays an athletic-looking sergeant in combat fatigues, resting an M-16 automatic on his hip. The soldier is looking over his shoulder and his resolute expression seems to say: "Let's move on." The latent symbolism is unflinching preparedness, regardless of the obstacle. It is clear that this monument is intended to honor the Vietnam War dead; the soldier's combat fatigues are the style worn in Vietnam, and the inscribed names of those who died in action are overwhelmingly from that war. The implicit message of the Green Beret memorial is that if the American people are unwilling to honor the Vietnam dead, then their comrades-in-arms will take up the cause. Until and unless another war adds the names of many other fallen Green Berets, this monument will be mainly regarded as a Vietnam War memorial.

While honor is an important function of memorials, another of their purposes—humanitarianism—was being addressed at this time in a peace memorial for those who were dying in Vietnam. Dr. Victor Westphall lost his son, David, in Vietnam. He saw the need to remember not only his son but also others who had died and were still dying. Dr. Westphall began in 1968 to build a chapel in Eagle Nest, New Mexico. Others donated funds; a few, using a design provided by architect Ted Loma, actually worked beside Dr. Westphall. In 1971 the project was completed and on May 21, 1972, it was dedicated as the Vietnam Veterans Peace and Brotherhood Chapel.[51] Vietnam veterans were drawn to Westphall's efforts, and the memorial's operation and upkeep are now guaranteed by the Disabled American Veterans organization. On Memorial Day in 1983, it was rededicated as the D.A.V. Vietnam Veterans National Memorial.[52]

5.11 D.A.V. Vietnam National Memorial, Eagle Nest, New Mexico (Photograph by Ralph Clement)

The chapel sits in New Mexico's Sangre de Cristo Mountains, and it is a symbolic sanctuary from war. Alone on a hillside, its restful curved lines may be seen as a peaceful statement.[53] On each step up the hill to the chapel there is a small sign; each sign has the name of a veteran whose picture has appeared in the chapel. Inside the chapel this individual remembrance is continued. An interior wall contains pictures provided by families in memory of their dead sons. At one end of the chapel is a cross; its top is an eternal flame. The symbolism of heroism is absent; instead, remembrance is joined with the symbolism of peace. Dr. Westphall has said: "If those who died can, in any measure, become a symbol that will arouse all mankind and bring a rejection of the principles which defile, debase, and destroy the youth of the world, perhaps they will not have died in vain."[54]

The memorial uses remembrance of a war—the Vietnam War—to make a symbolic statement against all war. As an artifact, the chapel and its surroundings do not fully convey the message, but a poem written by David Westphall and displayed at the chapel's entrance speaks to the cost of war regardless of who is involved:

> Greed-plowed cities desolate.
> Lusts ran snorting through the streets.
> Pride reared up to desecrate
> Shrines, and there were no retreats.

So man learned to shed the tears
With which he measures out his years.

The visitor leaves with a feeling that more was lost in Vietnam than battles; a great wealth of human potential was lost, along with a sense of purpose. This memorial was an important event, but recognition in Washington, D.C., had yet to occur. Vietnam veterans did not forget, and change was on the horizon.

War veterans took into their own hands the issue of official recognition and remembrance of those who died.[55] The Vietnam Veterans Memorial Fund was formed, and in 1980 it gained an endorsement from the U.S. Congress to build a memorial on two acres in the Washington Mall.[56] Roughly $7 million were privately raised to finance the project. The veterans decided to open a competition for the monument's design.

First, the Vietnam Veterans Memorial Fund established the memorial's purpose and the procedures for its selection. The design jury was composed of distinguished architects, landscape architects, sculptors, and a critic. The absence of any Vietnam veterans on this jury was a circumstance which later haunted the final selection. The people selected for the panel were mainly from the design world, and their design critique was independent of the opinions or desires of those who fought the war. If this division were not enough, the purpose and philosophy of the memorial's design was to stem the controversy caused by the war. In the competition rules, potential designers were told: "The memorial will make no political statement regarding the war or its conduct. It will transcend those issues. The hope is that the creation of the memorial will begin a healing process, a reconciliation of the grievous divisions wrought by the war."[57]

While the philosophy of unity without political overtones was honorable and the jury selection procedures appeared to be sound, they did not reflect the spirit of the times. For the country, the Vietnam War was over, but for many veterans it was still a painful part of their lives. These veterans were still angry and felt that those who had not shared their experience of war were unable to understand it. They anticipated a memorial whose symbolism expressed the real experiences of those who had fought and those who had died. How could those who had not experienced Vietnam design and then judge how veterans should be remembered?

Maya Ying Lin, a Yale architecture student of Chinese-American descent, submitted the winning design. The design was simple and direct. It is shaped as a descending V which is ten feet deep into the ground at its vertex. One wall points to the Washington Monument, a symbol of independence, while the other points to the nearby Lincoln Memorial, a symbol of a reunited Union. The names of the 57,939 dead or missing servicemen were to be carved into the granite walls in the order in which they were declared dead. The first casuality's name is at the apex, with the names of his comrades following until the wall is filled to its tip. The names then continue on the other wall's tip and end at the apex. The first casualty name from the first wall and the last name from the second wall are side by side. The V is united by a symbolic chain of names. While these visual orientations were included, Lin's main purpose was still quite simple. She wanted the names on the wall to be the memorial without other competing symbols.

The winning entry generated a great controversy among veterans and other citizens. The proposed monument was perceived as being in a ditch. From ground level, people would look "down" on the names of those remembered. This was perceived as a negative metaphor since visitors were unable to look "up," respect, these soldiers. The walls were to be black. The white in the American flag symbolizes purity while black often represents evil. Most war memorials are made of white marble or granite. The Marine Corps War Memorial has a black base, but its negative connotation is neutralized by the heroic bronze figures raising the American flag at Iwo Jima. The V shape was criticized by some as being a peace sign or as representing enemy Vietcong, especially since there was no American flag nearby.[58] A vociferous veteran who opposed the memorial called it "a black gash of shame."[59] Many veterans simply could not understand the memorial's intended symbolism.

Many Vietnam veterans and citizens could not accept Ms. Lin's design, which met the selection committee's criterion of being politically neutral. Although Ms. Lin was American by birth, some veterans cited her Oriental heritage and accused her of designing an anti-American memorial. The real problem was that the monument's contributors felt betrayed since they had not been able to choose the design and were unhappy with the solution. It was as if history was repeating itself. The American public had held a negative image of soldiers who fought in the Vietnam War. Once again, many veterans felt that the winning design further perpetuated negative images of them. This time, however, they resisted. Concerned veterans began to fight back.

The veterans wanted their own brand of dignity for their memorial. It was to be theirs, and they felt that it should symbolize what they wanted to express. The organizational battles began. The jury and the American Institute of Architects insisted on designer autonomy. In the meantime, the veterans were gathering popular support for their proposal, a memorial sculpture depicting soldiers in the Vietnam War. The original design by Lin gained approval from the Fine Arts Commission and the National Capital Planning Commission, but it needed approval from the National Park Service since the memorial would be on federal land. Secretary of the Interior James Watt had to approve it, and he sided with the veterans. Foes of the proposed wall memorial countered by adding to the memorial rather than changing it. Their first proposal was to have an American flag cast into the memorial's vertex with a sculpture placed on the ground below and near the vertex. While they accepted the concept of a flag and a sculpture, the U.S. Commission on Fine Arts rejected a number of specific plans.[60] Finally, the commission accepted a Vietnam Memorial Board compromise solution by placing a flagpole above and behind the monument's apex and siting the sculpture 120 feet away and uphill near the memorial's entrance.[61] All these design changes were symbolic battles. Vietnam veterans had been stigmatized by a lost war, but the war for the Vietnam Memorial was one that they fully intended to win. The veterans did not win every concession they sought, but the compromise solution recognized that the veterans would not back down. Many people felt that the final result was the best compromise that could be achieved and were relieved when the controversy was over.

While this controversy was being resolved, the Vietnam Veterans Memorial Fund appointed a panel to select an artist for the memorial sculpture. The committee was comprised of Vietnam veterans who were for and against the wall memorial, but the group was formed without the knowledge of Maya Lin, the original competition winner. The committee selected Frederick Hart for his sculpture of three GI's in a steadfast but casual pose.[62]

The wall memorial was completed and dedicated on November 13, 1982. Vietnam veterans were finally recognized in America's hallowed ground, Washington, D.C., although it had taken over seven years to accomplish. Determining the design for the entire Vietnam War Memorial had been problematic, but controversies made symbolic by the memorial emerged again before dedication ceremonies.

The Vietnam Memorial and its dedication day provided a political scene which leant itself to the purposes of veterans who wanted government action in Washington. Vietnam veterans gave public testimony about the physical effects of Agent Orange, a chemical defoliant used in the war. They wanted health benefits and used the dedication trip to make their views known. As some of them said to Veteran Administration officials:

Many of my brothers have died while you sat up there and played political bullshit . . . you will wait 'till most of us are dead . . . put the money where your mouth is.

The things that are happening to me and every other Agent Orange man didn't happen to him before he went to Vietnam. What are you gonna do?[63]

The formal dedication and informal happenings between Vietnam veterans were heart-rending and filled with conflict. At the National Cathedral, volunteers held a candlelight vigil while reciting each and every name of the dead and the missing in action.[64] Views from veterans about the wall memorial ranged from anger to respect and, finally, to release.

This country sucks as far as the Vietnam Memorial helping out. We're how many years into this before we even get recognized.

Came here to honor those guys living *and* dead. That's what I came here for.

I got mixed emotions. The monument. The only reason I'm here is that there're three names on it. I was to see if they're on there, that's all.[65]

These views of the wall memorial emanate from conflicts that the veterans held within themselves about the war itself. Veterans were heard to say "we won the war," "we lost the war," and "Washington lost the war. They turned their backs on us."[66] The emotional strain of protest, seeing old buddies, and participating in ceremonies created waves of both happiness and despondence. They wanted honor and respect. Some found it; others did not. The memorial dedication provided the day of remembrance that many veterans had wanted, but its events only revealed once again the conflicts and agony of the Vietnam experience, although in a general atmosphere of dignity which was absent before.

The wall memorial itself has become a peaceful experience. People feel the walls looking for the name of a lost friend or loved one. Some make rubbings of names to take home while others lay wreaths, or place a rose in a seam between the walls' panels. In the 1980s it has become one of the most frequently visited sites in Washington. Amidst the many visitors, there is a solemn quietness, and parents forewarn their children to behave during

5.12 Vietnam Veterans Memorial, Washington, D.C. (Author's Collection)

their visit. At one entrance veterans have displayed their own temporary memorial to those missing-in-action, MIAs, as a plea to have them returned from Vietnam. Under the ritual quietness, visitors can be seen crying or visibly shaken by the experience of seeing the memorial.

The Vietnam Memorial symbolizes social contradiction. The mixed feelings about the war eventually provided the groundwork for the conflict over the memorial's design. Its dedication and even visits to this day have proved to be unsettling. The Vietnam Memorial wall has been in place since 1982, and the statue was dedicated on Veterans Day, November 11, 1984. Although the wall memorial is unified in design, its symbolism can easily be seen to be in conflict with the memorial statue of three figures. The statue conveys a message of honor for those who served our country, but the wall makes people question the value of serving for such a questionable cause. The statue's critics had the opportunity to counter those who had argued that the wall's design was elite modernism. Frederick Hart's sculpture of three young soldiers, two white and one black, does not portray realism to critics. Instead, they see it as a "John Wayne" image of self-deception for those who wish to glorify and to justify the past.[67] These contradictions in meaning ultimately will or will not be resolved within the individuals affected by Vietnam, and the Vietnam Memorial can be seen as a symbol of personal resolve to live with a lost war. As Maya Lin wrote about the decision to build both the wall and statue: "In a funny sense the compromise brings the memorial closer to the truth. What is also memorialized is that people still cannot resolve that war, nor can they separate the issues, the politics, from it."[68]

One memorial to the Vietnam War may have put the American conscience at rest more than any other. On Memorial Day in 1984, an unidentified serviceman was buried in the Tomb of the Unknown Soldier in Arlington National Cemetery. During the ceremonies, the president of the United States awarded the Congressional Medal of Honor to the unknown American. No memorial wall or statue was able to accomplish what the Tomb of the Unknown Soldier dedication was able to do. For the first time, Vietnam veterans psychologically identified themselves as the equals of those who died in the world wars and Korea. The negative overtones of participating in a lost war were now symbolically gone. Vietnam veterans could feel that they were in the nation's hall of honor instead of waiting unnoticed outside, but their pain from the Vietnam War was not totally eliminated.

American communities had been groping for some way to commemorate the Vietnam War, and after the memorial controversies in Washington, some cities used that experience as a lesson. Rather than trying to resolve contradictory feelings about the war, memorials in Kansas City and New York City have attempted to articulate the conflicts. Remembering the experience of Vietnam was as essential as commemorating those who died.

The Vietnam Veterans' Memorial Fountain in Kansas City, Missouri, was designed to be a symbolic history of the war. The memorial begins with a path leading up to an American flag which symbolizes strength and dignity. From there, the visitor threads back and forth on a path between connecting pools each of which progressively symbolizes a period in the war. The first pool is small, representing the United States' initial involvement, and the middle and largest pools symbolize the height of the war. On one side of the biggest pools, visitors can pass by the wall memorial which lists the names of the 450 Kansas City soldiers killed and missing. Carved reliefs of the Vietnam Service Medal and the Purple Heart Medal frame the names on each side to convey the message of where they fought and at what price. Five evergreen trees separate the pools from the wall and symbolize the five armed services. After leaving the wall, visitors walk to the final pool which splits into two distinct pools to symbolize the divided opinions about the Vietnam War. Beyond these pools, a single pathway which can symbolize future unity leads the way out of the memorial.[69] All these sequenced messages are organized as a walk through the history of the Vietnam War.

5.13 New York Vietnam Veterans Memorial, New York (Author's Collection)

Critics can argue about how well the story has been told in the Kansas City Vietnam Memorial. Those who were against the war can argue that the split pool symbolism should be shown throughout the memorial rather than at the end. On the other hand, veterans were cognizant of the split feelings during the war, but they felt more pain and division after the war when Americans criticized their willingness to fight in Vietnam. The memorial does symbolize one version of the war, but it is a tale which cannot please everyone. Perhaps the biggest problem with the Kansas City Memorial is understanding that a story of any kind is being portrayed. Like the wall memorial in Washington, D.C., the fountain memorial is appealing for its visual simplicity, but its abstract symbolism lacks clarity.

While the Kansas City memorial tries to portray the war as a story, the New York Vietnam Veterans Memorial at 55 Water Street in New York City lets the veterans tell the story. The memorial is a symbolic window built with glass blocks. Across the blocks are inscribed the words of Vietnam veterans as expressed in letters to home. Since the glass blocks are somewhat opaque, each side of the structure could be inscribed. The multitude of experiences and feeling of Vietnam veterans are expressed; their comments convey support, criticism, and even apathy toward the war. More importantly, the veteran inscriptions describe immediate experiences of the war. The messages tell of a commitment to help their buddies and of losing friends in a war that they could not win. Whereas the Vietnam Memorial in Washington, D.C., was plagued with controversy because it attempted to portray a unified message, the New York wall memorial thrives on pluralism. The main inscriptions on each side of the wall, however, take a critical view of the war:

Take one moment to embrace those
Gentle heroes you left behind
And in that time when men decide and
Feel safe to call the war insane****

One thing worries me—will people believe
me? Will they want to hear about it,
or will they want to forget
the whole thing ever happened?***

The physical design of the monument enables visitors to come in close contact with the window memorial in order to read it and leave mementos. Two openings in the window wall enable visitors to see inscriptions on both sides easily without having to walk in a complete circle. Collective memory is encouraged not only by the arrangement of blocks but also by the provision of a place for visitors to pay their respects. Ledges on both sides of the structure enable people to leave flowers and mementos, and nearby there is a guard who makes sure that these items are not vandalized. The memorial is designed so that people will come close to it rather than distancing themselves from the messages that the monument attempts to convey.

The New York window memorial has a larger symbolic meaning evoked by the surrounding landscape. If the memorial symbolizes a window, what can be seen on the other side? The memorial is set in a plaza, and from one entrance point a fountain is located on one side of the window memorial. The white noise from the fountain adds a peacefulness, and visitors may patriotically conclude that the windowpanes of pain have ultimately returned this nation to a state of peace. Seeing the busy activity on the nearby street, visitors realize that they can stop to remember, but life must go on. Beyond the immediate landscape of the memorial is New York City with its skyline of high-rise buildings. New York City is the epitome of American capitalism. For critics, the window memorial is but a reminder that Vietnam was capitalist adventurism fighting against communism. For patriots, the memorial's larger meaning can be the continuation of American freedom as expressed in New York City's successes and opportunities. The New York Vietnam Veterans Memorial was purposely designed to allow plurality of meaning, but the context of its site introduces yet another pluralism. The window memorial has multiple and even conflicting messages and expresses reality as well as idealism.

Memorials to the Vietnam War are designed to remember the war itself rather than any one battle. Most of the fighting was guerrilla warfare, and all of Vietnam was the battleground. A few specific battles are remembered, but in the end, the real feelings are that people do not care to remember the battles won in this war. It is difficult enough to remember a lost war and then construct symbols to it. An honest effort and personal bravery are all that can be redeemed. Americans had divided feelings at the beginning of the Vietnam War, and these feelings still persist. Ultimately, the symbolism used in memorials for the Vietnam War reflects how Americans have politically judged this war.

SYMBOLS OF DEFEAT

Two kinds of defeat have been part of the American experience. Over time, the Civil War has become a war in which people have decided that the Confederacy needed to lose. Eliminating slavery was emancipation for all Americans in the spirit in which the country was founded. The communal guilt, however, is that emancipation was not accomplished politically under peaceful conditions. The Civil War brought a reformation of national identity, forging a collection of sovereign states into a united federation of states. A new patriotism emerged. The second kind of defeat has divided and fragmented meanings. The Korean and Vietnam wars were limited wars in which defeat was politically prescribed, as opposed to the forced defeat experienced by the Confederacy. To Americans, these wars lacked focus or purpose. War was not total, and the moral reasons for these wars were not clear. They could not be won. In all these wars, Americans have found some need to reassess American political aims.

Perceptions of the historical and political nature of these wars have determined how people have come to commemorate them. For the Civil War, a tremendous number of memorials were built. Many were opulent and designed to be civic improvements in a time when American cities were attempting to cast off their unsophisticated frontier images. Memorials were both general and specific. Town memorials and national memorials remembered everyone, but memorials to war heroes, battlefields, and military regiments further articulated the act of remembrance. In comparison, there are fewer memorials to commemorate the Korean and Vietnam wars. The aim of remembrance is more general than specific, although there is quite often a conscious attempt to list those who died. Yet, these wars do not have heroic figures such as Grant or Lee, and Americans more easily imagine the Battle of Gettysburg rather than the Battle of Inchon or the Tet Offensive. Moreover, many large American cities are already developed, and war memorials as civic improvements are now seen as marginal instead of central to urban development.

While these differences exist, common bonds between these wars are present. Americans who fought and died are commemorated regardless of the war's political results, and these soldiers are portrayed as being just as honorable as those who fought in wars of victory. A more subtle purpose is accomplished by building memorials to these wars. War is treated as past history, and political events since that time can be separated from the past. While these memorials mark defeat, it is impossible for them to convey the critical message that the political values which led to war may not be deterred or eliminated. On the other hand, memorials to these wars may remind some people that the United States should not find itself in a position where so many lives can be lost for so little reason. Death in victory provides moral purpose at best, and at the least, concrete accomplishments of peace or territorial gains. In comparison, people remember defeat with divided feelings, and their doubts are often reflected in what is commemorated in memorials for wars of defeat.

CHAPTER SIX
MEMORIES OF HORROR

WAR ITSELF IS HORRIBLE, but when defenseless people suffer imprisonment, humiliation, and worse, it becomes even more so. Civilians may be imprisoned for the duration of war, or imprisoned only to be executed later. Whole cities or towns may be massacred. Remembering these events is painful, and the places where they occurred become places of shame.

A country loses face after a war when it is forced to acknowledge that its soldiers and its government unjustly imprisoned or eliminated civilians. It is not easy for a country to recognize these victims or to construct memorials that unveil its sordid past. There is neither glory to exalt nor is there pride.

The greater the atrocities, the greater the need for a country to express humanitarianism in these memorials. Poor treatment in prisons is shameful, but the execution of defenseless people and community massacres are even worse. The following memorials are discussed to illustrate the escalation of horror and the mixed and multiple meanings of the tributes which have been made. Unlike the previous chapters, the memorials discussed here are not limited to the American experience. While prison camps have existed in the United States, it has never run execution factories in war as Nazi Germany did in World War II. The United States apparently has no war memorials within its boundaries dedicated to victim massacres under declared war, but U.S. armed forces have been involved in this type of war incident on foreign soil. It is true that the American Indians have been massacre victims of federal troops under cease-fires where the circumstances of war are unclear. The memorials chosen here exemplify social circumstances and memorial solutions which American society needs to understand. It is hoped that this country will never require such memorials.

PRISON CAMPS

Prison camps are used for the detainment of people who are considered to be the enemy. During war, they are designed to neutralize the enemy as captured men in a chess game. Perceptions of who is the enemy may be accurate, but at other times people may be incorrectly designated as foes. Being within a prison camp symbolically denotes guilt and shame even though these labels may not be deserved.

The preservation of these camps over time depends ultimately upon the wrongs which were done and upon who won the war. Losers often preserve their prison camps as a way to redeem their dignity by taking responsibility for their past war crimes. On the other hand, victors may not save their prison camps, especially when they imprisoned people who were wrongly thought to be the enemy. To preserve these prisons is to preserve a nation's mistakes. Guilt and shame are eventually put in their proper place through factual accounts of history, but the camps which held innocent victims are barely noticed or cared for by the victors. Defeated nations must confess their crimes to the victors and perhaps to themselves, but victors often forget their prison camp crimes.

World War II Japanese-American Camps

After the Japanese bombed Pearl Harbor on December 7, 1941, most Americans reacted with hate toward Japanese-Americans. In early 1942, the United States began the unconstitutional internment of Japanese and Japanese-American people in ten prison camps that were located mostly in the western United States; 110,000 Japanese-Americans were eventually imprisoned.[1] Among them, 73 percent were American citizens, while many others had been long-time residents. Their property was confiscated, and they had great difficulty in retrieving it or receiving compensation after the war. The U.S. government has made some reparation payments to those imprisoned, but most people have never been fully compensated. The irrational hatred many Americans felt against Japanese-Americans was converted into institutional prejudices which lasted many years through governmental neglect.

Japanese-American camps did not become "hell holes of starvation and death" as some have called them,[2] but to the Japanese spirit they surely were a form of hell. Saving face is an integral part of the Japanese culture. As prisoners, they were unable to preserve their self-esteem to the rest of America. Many Japanese-American men volunteered for military service and fought bravely in the European campaigns, but they were not trusted to fight against the Japanese in the Pacific. Within the camps, traditional Japanese life did exist, but only within limits set by prison project directors. The camps typically had a board of directors and other minor civil servant positions held by Japanese-Americans. In many ways, the camps operated much like any other community. They had schools, scouts, and organized sports. Even though they exercised a good deal of control "within" the rules of prison life, they were desperately lacking in human pride. In *The Minidoka Interlude* published in 1943 Tom Takeuchi wrote:

More than a year of racial segregation and living in camps—crowded, without privacy or conveniences, with inferior food and little income and with liberties curtailed—has held its effect on our morale. We have lost the pride that kept us away from charity. We have lost our initiative and self-confidence due to lack of meaningful work. We have developed an inferiority complex.[3]

Some Japanese-Americans reacted against their imprisonment. There were peaceful demonstrations at some camps to protest unsatisfactory living conditions.[4] Even hunger strikes occurred. At Tule Lake, incoming military units created stockades to control outbursts, and some prisoners did forced labor at the point of a gun.[5] While they protested the violations of their rights as citizens, Japanese-American internees were unjustly imprisoned until the war was over.

When the war ended, the prisoners were released, and the camps were closed. Lingering prejudices made it difficult for Japanese and Japanese-Americans to reenter the mainstream of American life. Many former prisoners fought back legally to be compensated for their unjust imprisonment and the unlawful confiscation of their property. Their cries were largely ignored after the war, because most Americans wanted to forget that the United States had participated in this injustice. Japanese-American prisoners saw the need to remember their people's suffering in the camps, but most Americans equally wanted to forget that these camps had existed.

The existing camp sites are now desolate landscapes. Most of the camps were located in remote places in order to isolate the prisoners and to prevent hostilities from the outside. In the west, the camps were mainly in desert country, while in Arkansas swamps were chosen.[6] There are few extant remains of the old camps. Most of the buildings were temporary structures, and those are now gone. On the old grounds, there are remains of fences, concrete footings to now absent watchtowers, and concrete slabs which are, in their way, gravestones for buildings which once stood on them. On the cemetery grounds grave markers are typically simple and most are in disrepair. The neglected camp grounds are now only a fading reminder of the past.

Some prison camp memorials were built by prisoners or with private

6.1 Desecration of the Gila River Relocation Center Memorial, Arizona (Author's Collection)

donations after the war, but vandals have marred these commemorations. In Arizona, Japanese-Americans have objected to memorials being erected, because there is no provision for their maintenance. The justification for their position is their memorial to Japanese-American soldiers at the site of the former Gila River Relocation Center. It is abandoned and scarred with graffiti. The federal government's failure to mark these places is worthy of note. At the entrance to the Rohwer camp cemetery in Arkansas, an old sign defaced with bullet shots identified the grounds in the past. A newer, unmarred sign was erected while the old sign was left standing. These two contradictory signs make it clear that while there was enough care to erect a presentable introduction for visitors, no one bothered to repair the vandalism. Neglect of these former camp grounds is more than the failure to police vandals. The lack of government care for these former prison grounds is a political commentary that citizens need not be reminded where American injustice occurred. What is publicly left unsaid is quietly forgotten.

Some memorials have been maintained, and these monuments often not only mark this episode in U.S. history but also enable the viewer to question the meaning of the camps. At Manzanar is a memorial marker, known as the Soul Consoling Tower, which was built by the Japanese internees in 1943. The California Department of Parks and Recreation has attached to a sentry house a bronze plaque briefly describing the camps and wrongs done to the internees.[7] Since its dedication in 1973, the plaque has caused some

6.2 Rohwer Relocation Center Cemetery, Arkansas (Author's Collection)

controversy, because it refers to Manzanar as a concentration camp.[8] The term is associated with the Holocaust camps, and it carries an obvious stigma that Americans do not want to claim. At the former Rohwer Relocation Center, prisoners hand-built concrete memorials for those who died in camps and for Japanese-American soldiers. The soldier memorial, which resembles an armored tank, is distinctly Japanese, with wheel cogs in the shape of chrysanthemums. After the war, a granite memorial was erected to commemorate soldiers who were initially interned at Rohwer. Its inscription describes not only the bravery of the fighting men but also the bitterness of suffering in the camps.

THIS MEMORIAL IS ALSO DEDICATED TO THE MEMORY
OF THE MANY JAPANESE-AMERICANS FROM ROHWER
THAT GAVE THEIR LIVES THAT OTHERS
MIGHT ENJOY THE FREEDOMS WHICH THEY
AND THEIR FAMILIES WERE DENIED.

We are unlikely to visit these war memorials of national shame. There are no major cities nearby from which to make such an excursion, and once at a former camp, there is little to see. The camps are out of sight and thus out of mind. For most Americans, the tragedies did not exist. In Washington,

D.C., there are many monuments to glorify our righteous acts, but none to declare our injustices. The symbolic meaning of this Japanese-American legacy must be provided through the media. These camps still permeate the lives of former prisoners. Some refuse to visit the sites, while others make an occasional visit. Perhaps the greatest shame is the federal government's absence of recognition for these places. The nation's misdeeds are not matched with dignified national memorials which properly remember these camps.

As war memorials, the camps have become increasingly invisible. The lack of attention to these sites has become a way to cover shame just as the dust or overgrown vegetation has covered the reality of the camps. Letting nature take its course is an appalling substitute for symbolizing past injustices during war.

Andersonville Prison Camp Memorial

Andersonville is the best-known camp for prisoners of war in the United States. Located in southwestern Georgia, it is remembered for its many casualties during the Civil War. During its 13-month existence from February 1864 to April 1865, more than 45,000 Union enlisted men were confined, and over 12,000 prisoners perished from disease, malnutrition, overcrowding, and exposure. On a single day in August 1864, 97 men died.[9] Andersonville was a disposal dump for people as much as it was a prison.

Andersonville is commonly seen outside of the South as a deliberate act of inhumanity by the Confederacy. The reason that Andersonville is most vividly remembered is that no other Civil War prison produced as many deaths. Over 40 percent of Union prisoner deaths occurred at Andersonville. They were the result of improper facilities, untrained personnel, and lack of medical supplies and medicine.[10] The reality of life at Andersonville was filth and human poverty. Prisoners made crude shelters and lived in mud. The stream flowing through the stockade was polluted by Confederate soldiers at its upper level and by Union soldiers at its lower reaches. Eventually, prisoners dug wells and sold the brackish water to other inmates. At its maximum capacity, the stockade was so crowded that only 30 square feet were available to each prisoner. While food was provided, the diet was so limited and repetitive that malnutrition developed. Prisoners were poorly fed, clothed, and sheltered. They inevitably became sick, and the lack of medical facilities and supplies resulted in their miserable deaths. One Union soldier wrote:

One man, who lies near our tent, . . . debilitated with swelled feet from exposure to the sun or dropsy, chronic diarrhea, and neglect of cleanliness was found to have the lower part of the body near the rectum eaten into holes by maggots, which literally swarmed on him.[11]

Economic conditions in the Confederacy offer important reasons for the inhumanity at Andersonville. The prison was established during the latter part of the war, when the Confederacy was in short supply of all forms of resources. It has been argued that Andersonville's horror resulted principally from the breakdown of the Southern economy.[12] On the other hand, the counterargument has been that when a nation is incapable of waging war, it should cease to do so.[13] Ultimately, the inhumanity at Andersonville was the result of the South's persistence in fighting a hopeless war for an inhumane principle, slavery.

In 1865, after the war, the burial ground for deceased prisoners was appropriated by the federal government. The prison, however, fell into disrepair and was purchased in 1890 by the Grand Army of the Republic, a veteran's organization. The prison site was donated to the United States in 1910 and was administered by the Department of the Army until 1970. At that time, the prison was placed under the jurisdiction of the National Park Service which has restored the site.[14]

The present stockade grounds present a tidy, organized facade which belies the historical reality of inefficiency and human filth. Earthworks are sodded and a meticulously neat arrangement of Confederate sentry tents are offered as a stage set. The infamous timber stockade and crudely built dead line (the boundary that prisoners could not cross) no longer exist. In their place, marked posts are symbolically placed to demarcate the stockade and dead line boundaries. At each of the stockade's four corners, simple but stout stone markers are used to delineate the limits of the prison grounds. A visitor can comfortably walk the 19 feet from a stockade marker to the dead line marker and then enter the prison grounds. For the visitor unaware of the prison's history, there is no visual sense of imprisonment or imagined danger of traversing the no man's land between the markers. Even knowing the life and death regulations which were enforced in this space, the absence of the actual barriers makes it difficult to imagine the crude shelters, mud, and even human excrement which were common sights within the prison grounds during the worst days of Andersonville. The prison grounds today are as carefully mowed and kept as the surrounding area. Nonetheless, the grounds are more realistically portrayed now than in the past. Until recently, a memorial grove of trees stood near the stream located within the prison. These have been cut down, and the visitor can now grasp the size of the stockade and its barren appearance even though the grounds are well kept. Visitors must imagine what Andersonville's horrors were like. They must mentally erase the green landscape and imagine the foul stench and filth of so many soldiers in a large stockade with a floor of mud. The well-kept landscape commemorates those who died, but it does little to enhance our understanding of their misery.

Within the stockade grounds there are numerous memorials erected by various Union States to commemorate former prisoners. The monuments here and in the cemetery were mostly erected during the early part of this century. The memorials on prison grounds were done in the classical style, and the angel of mercy was often used as a symbol of remembrance. While mainly identified with the states' names, these monuments typically do include inscriptions which use words such as honor, heroism, patriotism, and sacrifice. States felt the need to remember all of their native sons who suffered.

The most prominent structure in the stockade grounds is the Providence Spring Memorial. It commemorates the spot where lightning struck and a spring came forth when the water shortage was at its peak. The prisoners considered the event to be an act of Providence, which is the source of the memorial's name. The structure, its nearby fountain, pond, and trees are a symbolic ensemble of religious faith—God as provider amidst man's inhumanity to man. To a nonbeliever, the memorial simply represents past religious fervor, but to believers, the monument signifies an actual event that justifies their religious faith.

While the cemetery grounds contain some state memorials, the dominant image is the mass of symmetrically aligned tombstones. The grave markers are so closely placed to one another that each row visually appears to be a unified mass. It is false to interpret this design as symbolic of unity among soldiers. In reality, huge trenches were dug from 1864 to 1865 with the dead placed side by side without coffins.[15] The correct marking of graves is only known because a Union soldier secretly kept systematic records. Some soldiers, however, were not recorded and their graves are marked as "UNKNOWN SOLDIER." Ultimately, the historical events at Andersonville give a sadistic symbolism to this burial plot. The dead are honored by the careful maintenance of the grounds and by the quality of their markers, but their graves contradict this humane and honorable treatment. The cemetery commemorates defenseless victims, not honorable warriors.

One burial area is set aside symbolically to dishonor a group of prisoners who were called the Raiders. These traitors to their fellow Union soldiers stole personal possessions and even killed inmates to further their black market trade. The ring leaders of the Raiders were eventually caught and hanged. Near the center of the cemetery, the Raider gravestones are clearly set apart from other graves. The area is a symbolic prison. While the grounds are maintained in the same manner as the remaining cemetery, an annual ritual keeps the Raider graves in disgrace. On Memorial Day American flags are placed before each Union soldier's grave except for the Raiders. By placing these graves in a separate burial plot and denying them the honor of Memorial Day flags, the nation's sentiment is made clear: "We have the duty to bury and preserve the grave of any soldier, but we are not obliged to honor the disgraced."

On the roadway between the cemetery and the prison grounds, the state of Georgia has recently erected a prominent sculpture in remembrance of

6.3 Georgia Andersonville Prison Memorial (Author's Collection)

Andersonville. The sculpture is comprised of three gaunt figures who appear to be struggling in extreme pain. Their clothing and posture are not those we associate with good health or even human choice. The sculptor, William Thompson, expressed his design intent when he wrote: "This sculpture is dedicated to all American prisoners involved in all American wars from our country's birth up to the present. The sculpture is designed to have a universal quality, and no reference to any particular uniform or specific details have been made. The accent has been placed on the inner struggle and strength of the prisoners."[16] Design intent and perceived reality are not always the same. The visitor unaware of its purpose immediately associates the design with the horror of Andersonville although there is a religious scripture on the sculpture's base intended to convey the universal symbolism. The sculpture's location at Andersonville, rather than at a neutral site, weds the prison's historical horror to the sculpture's explicit expression of human suffering.

The town of Andersonville has expressed its own interpretation of the prison's history by remembering Captain Henry Wirz, the prison commandant at the end of the war. Wirz commanded the stockade from March 1864 to April 1865. Tried and found guilty of war crimes, Wirz was hanged in Washington, D.C., in 1865.[17] Ovid Futch, a Civil War historian, argues that the guilty parties were the previous commandant and the general for all Confederate prisons, and that Wirz was falsely accused of all the

atrocities at Andersonville.[18] Rightly or wrongly, Wirz had been thought of
by northerners as a villain. The United Daughters of the Confederacy led a
campaign to build a monument in memory of Wirz which was criticized by
northerners and southerners alike. Although various sites were considered,
Andersonville was finally chosen as the proper place to commemorate Wirz.
By allowing the memorial to be built, the town of Andersonville legitimized
Wirz as a victim of circumstances and ultimately reinstated him as an
honorable soldier. In the town center, a simple obelisk with his name was
dedicated in 1909.[19]

The Wirz monument is a symbolic protest in defense of Captain Wirz.
From a distance, the obelisk has no meaning and presents no contradictions
to visitors unaware of Wirz's history. Upon closer inspection, they see that
the inscriptions challenge Wirz's conviction for war crimes. Some passages
say: "TO RESCUE HIS NAME FROM THE STIGMA ATTACHED TO IT BY BITTER
PREJUDICE" and "CAPTAIN WIRZ BECAME AT LAST THE VICTIM OF A
MISDIRECTED POPULAR CLAMOR." Other passages speak of Wirz doing his
duty, and suggest that his unjust trial will be overthrown one day when time
softens prejudice. While visitors may agree with these sentiments, as they
stand nearly in the shadow of Andersonville Prison they may cynically ask:
"If Wirz was not responsible, who was?" There is no monument in the
town of Andersonville to proclaim who was guilty, only the one arguing for
Wirz's innocence. Guilt is subtly glossed over in a passage from the
monument's inscriptions which describe Wirz working under "THE HARSH
CIRCUMSTANCES OF THE TIMES." History has proven that Wirz was not
totally responsible for the crimes at Andersonville, but the monument's
inscriptions still fail to address responsibility for 12,000 Union dead in
Andersonville Prison. The Wirz monument announces the innocence of one
man, but in so doing it convicts the many by ignoring criminal responsibility.

The Andersonville Prison is now a memorial ensemble to past history. All
of the victims and the guilty parties are dead, and the passing of time has
healed many wounds of hatred both in the North and South. Joining the
National Park Service system in 1970, Andersonville Prison has become a
legitimate element of our national heritage. Audio and visual presentations
at the historic site enable visitors to think about what happened here so that
history does not repeat itself. Andersonville as a historical lesson, however,
is effective only if people are willing to put aside regional allegiances, both
North and South. The dedicated monuments teach little to the visitor, but
the prison grounds and the collective mass of gravestones offer substantial
evidence of how humankind can be cruel to itself.

The atrocities of Andersonville should not be forgotten, but the
victorious North is not without blame. Some historians have argued that the
Union's Elmira Prison in New York had a higher death rate than
Andersonville.[20] At Elmira, New York, a national cemetery contains the

remains of those Confederate soldiers who died from prison mistreatment, and the United Daughters of the Confederacy have provided a memorial to remember them. The actual prison, however, no longer exists. On the lawns of two residential homes, one-foot cube blocks are symbolic surveyor markers to identify where the prison once existed. There is nothing else. The town necessarily expanded physically over time, but northern neglect is hardly justified, especially when southerners are honor-bound to remember Andersonville. Both the North and South were criminal in their treatment of prisoners. In modern times, the North is guilty of not applying the same principles of judgment for Elmira which were demanded for Andersonville. All nations whether they win or lose or, whether their cause was just or not, are capable of inhumanity to victims.

EXECUTION FACTORIES

Memorials for execution factories portray brutality and terror. The preservation of these places represents a country's willingness, and even the pressure from others, to take responsibility for war crimes. By admitting guilt, a country can restore some human dignity to the victims of its crimes and to the nation itself. Younger people who did not live during the atrocities, however, often resent their social heritage since they were not responsible for the war crimes. Nonetheless, they carry their country's social burden, and memorials to war crimes are physical reminders that they cannot easily avoid.

Plotzensee Prison Memorial

The Plotzensee Prison in Berlin stands as a memorial to executed Germans and other Europeans who fought to resist nazism in Germany. The memorial was dedicated in 1968. Some 2,500 men, women, and adolescents were guillotined or hanged within the prison confines from 1933 to 1945. On one day in 1943, 186 condemned prisoners were executed.[21] Plotzensee was an example of the final solution for Germans who resisted nazism.

A cycle of prisoners were executed at Plotzensee. In the early years, Communists, the Nazis' traditional arch rival, were killed. Social Democrats, union leaders, bureaucrats, Christians, military officers, students, professors, and others were eventually executed for their involvement in the various resistance groups that emerged. The most famous group executed here was the Stauffenberg circle which attempted to assassinate Hitler on July 20, 1944. Plotzensee Prison was a processing plant that the Nazis used to confront protest and resistance by eliminating their political enemies.

The resistance circles often had their minor victories, but they all suffered the consequences of being captured and executed. Their efforts present a contradiction to the stereotypical image of the blindly obedient German. Hans Rothfels, a Jewish historian who wrote a seminal book on the German opposition, estimates that between 750,000 and 1.2 million Germans were imprisoned for anti-Nazi activities.[22] The late Federal President Theodor Heuss stressed the importance of executed members of the resistance at Plotzensee when he said: "The shame into which we Germans were forced by Hitler was washed from the sullied name of Germany by their blood. . . . The legacy remains a living force; our obligations have not yet been fulfilled."[23]

The Plotzensee Memorial is a symbolic composition incorporating German guilt, resistance, and horror. Visitors to the memorial must know of Plotzensee in advance. To reach the memorial, the visitor walks along a narrow side street which is framed on one side by a high red brick fence. In time, the visitor reaches the memorial's stone entrance which simply says "PLOTZENSEE MEMORIAL GROUNDS." Past the gate is a simple garden, and just beyond are the memorial grounds. On the grounds is a stone plaza and a stone wall which bears the inscription: "TO THOSE SACRIFICED UNDER HITLER'S DICTATORSHIP, 1933-1945." The message is intended to include Germans and Jews, because to the right of the wall stands an urn containing earth from National Socialist concentration camps. The implied message is that no one should have been allowed to die for the sake of such an inhumane cause.

The wall memorial is more than a built wall. It is a proclamation of guilt that is physically and symbolically part of the building behind it. The building is the place of horror. The first entrance is nondescript, but once through the entrance the visitor is suddenly in the execution chamber. It cannot be compared to those that still exist in state prisons. An iron beam with hanging hooks makes it immediately apparent that the room was a small death factory. The hooks are the production line. Death was treated systematically as in a slaughterhouse, and the chamber "has become the principal memorial to German resistance against Hitler."[24] The execution chamber has changed over time. Originally, it was divided into two areas, one for the gallows and the other for the guillotine, which is no longer there. The chamber's starkness has been softened with commemorative wreaths, ribbons, and flowers from various German institutions. The floral compositions form a symbolic altar of remembrance enhanced by chapel-like windows which give light from behind. The execution chamber provides remembrance but not an account of historical events.

By walking outside and then entering the adjoining room, visitors can see what was once the waiting chamber to the execution room. It is starkly simple with no furniture. There is a wall exhibit which explains the history of Plotzensee, and free pamphlets are available in a variety of languages so that visitors can interpret the exhibit. In viewing the room and its exhibit,

6.4 Execution Chamber at Plotzensee Prison, West Berlin, West Germany (Author's Collection)

one has a morbid sense of anticipation, since the adjoining room's contents and history are known. It is easy to imagine that you are the next victim.

Any visit to Plotzensee memorial is punctuated by the discomforting reality that the Plotzensee Prison still exists, although as a modern-day prison. Nearby watchtowers, incinerator stacks, and barbed wire fences provide a physical presence which evokes the prison's terrible past even though the memorial's grounds are physically set apart from the remaining prison. Beyond the practical need to separate and protect visitors from a prison, the wall can be interpreted as a visual statement about the memorial grounds: "What has happened on this side of the wall is history which should not be forgotten. The prison on the other side is testimony that it has not."

Beyond the memorial's tribute to guilt, resistance, and horror, its continued preservation symbolizes German society's need to regain its honor and to exemplify the values of those who fought but failed. For many young Germans, Plotzensee signifies that their fellow Germans were capable of worthy deeds under tyranny. But it is also an ever-present reminder of a younger generation which must bear a nation's guilt, even though they were not responsible.

Dachau Concentration Camp Memorial

The Dachau camp is West Germany's best preserved prison in remembrance of the Holocaust. Located only 15 kilometers from Munich, it is the most visited prison in the Western world and has been called the show camp of Europe.[25]

While the number of deaths in Dachau seems minuscule to camps in Poland, it is a complete statement of the Nazis' final solution. From 1933 to 1945, 225,000 prisoners passed through its gates; 50,000 victims died during their internment, a low figure in comparison to major death camps.[26] Dachau was Heinrich Himmler's model camp where the SS experimented with the science of death; it was the beginning. Because many commandants of more infamous prisons received their training here, Dachau became known as the staff college for administering concentration camps.

Even though established primarily for political prisoners rather than extermination, Dachau's functional elements were used extensively in other prisons. The SS camp, prison barracks, barricade systems, disinfection buildings, and the crematorium were first developed here. Also, doing medical experiments and using prisoners for small industries were perverted innovations at Dachau. Most importantly, its camp regulations were the model for all subsequent prisons. Dachau was the rational prototype for implementing Nazi Germany's final solution for the Jews.

Most camps are remembered for their gas chambers, but not Dachau. The SS began construction of a gas chamber in 1942, but due to sabotage, it was not completed until 1945. It never functioned properly and was never used for killing. As a result, prisoners were sent to Austria to be gassed.[27]

Dachau is best known for its inhumane medical experiments. Prisoners were exposed to high altitude atmospheres, and experiments were done to find a human being's ability to withstand freezing temperatures. Twelve hundred subjects died or suffered permanent disabilities after being inoculated with malaria and then being treated with experimental drugs. Some prisoners were used in tests to produce drinkable sea water and suffered great pain and injury.

Our graven image of Dachau comes from its last six months of existence. Masses of Jews and other condemned people came to Dachau from the Balkans and from evacuated camps in the immediate path of Allied forces. In a short time, starving people jammed the prison barracks. The death rate rose quickly, with the SS using crematorium ovens night and day to burn human bodies as quickly as possible. Those who broke regulations, were sick, or were exhausted were thrown directly into the ovens. In the last six weeks, prisoners at Dachau were burned like rotting garbage.

When Dachau was liberated, American troops found 30,000 prisoners, mostly starved, and 8,000 corpses. Many present-day photographs and films of Holocaust victims are from Dachau, even though greater travesties took place in other camps.[28]

From 1945 to 1965, the grounds at Dachau were unimproved. Except for a Catholic memorial and a visitors' center, barracks were left in disrepair. Roads were muddy from rainfall. In the mid 1960s, the grounds were rehabilitated as a national historic site. During this entire time, however, the former SS camp was converted and maintained as a training center for Bavarian police. The oldest crematorium is now preserved in its crumbling state. For 20 years Dachau was remembered for the Nazi crimes which were committed there, but the prison itself was largely forgotten.

Dachau is now a symbolic assemblage of preserved buildings, landscaped grounds, and memorial chapels and monuments. Their messages reflect the camp's past horror, but the symbolic expressions convey multiple messages.

The preserved buildings are immaculate. An old administration building has been converted into a museum with artifacts and photographs. These neatly ordered displays are in sharp contrast to the filth and misery they depict. Old barracks, watchtowers, and the newer crematorium with the unused gas chamber are tidy and clean. It is difficult for visitors to Dachau to imagine that people were despicably mistreated in this place, because present-day officials have taken great care to make tourists feel comfortable during their visit.

The museum is the first stop at Dachau. After pausing to get a pamphlet guide, the visitor begins a tour through a designed maze that tells the history of the Holocaust. Most of the panel displays are photographic reproductions, but the first artifacts are in a simple display case. The case contains two books: Arthur Gobineau's *The Inequality of the Races* and H. S. Chamberlain's *Foundations of the Nineteenth Century*. Both books highly influenced German thought in the nineteenth century and early twentieth century, when one form of Social Darwinism, the superiority of the Aryan race, was in vogue. The books symbolize the seeds of destruction. Metaphorically, they are the rational DNA which structured the replication of hate against the Jews. These important documents go unrecognized by many visitors, because they have never heard of Social Darwinism or do not know the history of how this social theory was transformed into the practice of genocide. Beyond this case, other displays recount the repression of the Jews. After passing a number of large photographs, visitors see hard evidence. A whipping table and cane are displayed as weapons of terror. The visitor's realization that he or she could be the one on that table makes the horror of Dachau palpable. It is no longer merely a historical fact. Further into the exhibit, there is a display of drawings by a former prisoner that depicts the fear and helplessness of prison life. In contrast to the table and cane, visitors can rationally attempt to interpret the artist's message. They try to understand Dachau's inhumanity rather than feeling actual suffering. Nearby is a memorial room. Behind a glass wall are

6.5 Watchtower and Prison Barriers at Dachau, West Germany (Author's Collection)

commemorative ribbons on the upper wall, with plaques, pictures, and flowers on and along the table below. It is an international collection of mementos with separate but similar recognition from a variety of institutional sources, mainly European. It is not immediately apparent what is being commemorated in this display, but one surmises that the purpose is the same as the purpose for preserving Dachau—to assure that the horror will not be forgotten. At the tour's completion there is a movie presentation which brings to life much of what has already been presented in photographs and text. While the educational aspects of these presentations are important, many visitors to the museum are already familiar with some of Dachau's history. Such visitors are more affected by how the museum is designed to make you react rationally, physically, and emotionally, than by the presentation of the historical facts themselves.

From the museum visitors can inspect the grounds, and they first see where prisoners once lived. The barrack grounds have been starkly simplified from the camp's original paths and buildings. The camp road is now paved with gravel, while former barracks are simply identified with white concrete curbs, and the grounds are covered entirely with white gravel. The graveled barrack sites suggest collective burial plots, even though no one is buried there. Each barrack's area has a stone marker with a number that resembles a generic grave marker, such as number 13. Two actual barracks have been restored, and their interiors recapture a distant glimpse of prison life. One room contains a rigid display of wall lockers, tables, and stools where work and eating probably occurred. In another area, there are neatly arranged stacked bunks made of wood. The rigid arrangement portrays modular efficiency, and visitors learn that prisoners were brutally forced to conform to the immaculate cleaning of these barracks, at the same time that their own bodies were subjected to starvation and filthiness. The Dachau barrack grounds were not the site of the slaughterhouse, but rather stockyards where victims were systematically deprived as they awaited slaughter. The nondescript buildings and grounds appear to be nothing more than simple warehouses and a big parking lot. The deceptive normalcy of the surroundings makes it difficult for the visitor to imagine the hunger and pain which occurred in the actual places where they are standing.

While the barrack displays and curb boundaries demarcate where prisoners lived, it is the outer wall that physically defines the denial of human freedom. From the inside, the barrack grounds are surrounded first by a concrete lined trench, then by barbed wire fences, and finally by a concrete fence that is periodically interrupted with watchtowers. This fence now imprisons the visitor in the historical experience, just as it once emprisoned the victims of Dachau. Originally the only passage was through the gatehouse arch, and historically it was an entrance but seldom an exit. Worked into the grill gate entrance at the camp's guardhouse is the infamous phrase, "ARBEIT MACHT FREI," work makes one free. Yet the visitor knows that the only real freedom here was death.

From the vantage of the guardhouse gate, the narrow prison building behind the old administration building is visible. Inside its door is a long corridor lined with cell doors which have guard peep slots. Visitors can enter one cell which is blocked off by a grate. The display is both congruent and contradictory to the preservation of Dachau. The cell's existence conveys what it was like to be put behind bars. On the other hand, the cell's walls are marked with graffiti. Comments like "Down with tyranny," "Freedom," and "Liberation," are visitor commemorations which denounce the crimes of Dachau. Unlike the other well-kept grounds and buildings in the camp, it is obvious that the cell's graffiti is allowed by officials as a form of legitimate rebellion, the need for spontaneity in a memorial which preserves the image of repression.

Just beyond the barbed wire fences of Dachau is the nearby crematorium. The building at first appears innocent enough, but in front is a square marked off by curbs, shrubs, and grass. In its center are the remains of a simple vertical structure now laced with vines. A plaque announces that this is where prisoners were hung. The first impression of innocence quickly disappears. Once inside the building the visitor can see the never-used gas chamber. It is surprisingly small given our impressions that millions were killed in these killing rooms. The spartan design screams its potent reality as experienced in other camps. Concrete surfaces and shower spouts evoke the cold and single-minded aim of the SS executioners. Upon leaving this death chamber, there is still no relief. After walking out, visitors come to the ovens. The ovens are more frightening than the gas chamber, because visitors can see explicit tools of inhumanity. Pullies, oven doors, and handled pallets speak to human work, but against humanity. The work space appears efficient, like a factory producing a product. It is easy to imagine people doing the work of stoking the fire, putting in bodies, and removing ashes, while getting an A-1 rating from an efficiency expert. Visitors are relieved to leave the crematorium, but once again they face the hanging post.

Behind the crematorium, a garden offers momentary relief from the death factory, but even here there is no escape. Two memorials, one Jewish and one Christian, commemorate the collective remains of those who were executed. Farther down the path is what appears to be a nicely landscaped memorial. There is a concrete wall softened by a hedge. In front of this backdrop is a well-kept row of greenery in a low area. Sloping up and parallel to the path, there is a well-trimmed row of red flowers growing low to the ground. In the middle of the flower row, there is a simple stone marker which says: "EXECUTION RANGE WITH BLOOD DITCH." It is here that thousands were shot and then sent to the ovens. The religious memorials and blood ditch are visually respectful commemorations of the horrors which occurred. Unlike the regimented barrack grounds and crematorium, these victim memorials beautify the actual places where mass executions took place. There is beauty as well as order here, and this can have a disturbing effect. People can want a beautiful place to remember victims, but it is difficult to resolve how this commemoration can express beauty while simultaneously demonstrating anger at the ugliness of inhumanity. Pretty, aromatic red flowers to symbolize the blood ditch conflict with the attempt to imagine the sight of blood and the harsh smell of gunpowder after an execution. The visual order imposed to create a place of respect is paradoxically paralleled by a historical order of place to implement inhumane ends.

After completing the garden walk, visitors again pass by the crematorium, and then face a memorial statue of a withered prisoner. Inscribed in German on the statue's base, is this simple statement: "TO HONOR THE DEAD, TO WARN THE LIVING." Visitors see this statue before they leave the crematorium and the garden, and it reminds them that this was the last stop in the implementation of nazism's final solution. It was here, as in other concentration camps, that the Holocaust was successfully practiced on a day-by-day basis. The perverted idealism of Social Darwinism was made real in the daily horror of Dachau. Social Darwinism was reduced to a concentration camp, and the prisoner statue is symbolic of the ideology's explicit results. The inscription induces visitors not only to recognize history but also to challenge the worth of ideologies.

6.6 Crematorium Ovens at Dachau, West Germany (Author's Collection)

Dachau has been criticized for being too hygienic in its restoration. White buildings with black roofs and white gravel convey a sterile, neutral image. Feig notes that it is hard for the visitor to imagine how people were brutally treated when the camp's environmental messages are antiseptic.[29]

Yet this hygienic image in no way contradicts Dachau's despicable history. This is the prison where human death was made a science and human life was reduced to a laboratory experiment. Death itself became an exercise in cost-efficiency, and the slaughterhouses were admirably efficient modern factories. But their business was the slaughter and processing of human beings.

This use of technical means for inhumane ends is Dachau's deep-seated contradiction. In this light, its hygienic restoration is an overstatement rather than a contradiction of its purpose, because Dachau was never as efficient as its present image. The immediate disorder associated with the filth of killing and the systematic rationale for expedient death do not easily converge in our minds. Both conditions existed but only the systematic rationale is portrayed. Ultimately, this image is the most frightening, because it says that efficient decisions can be made without questioning the humanity or inhumanity of the end results. Dachau simply but devastatingly reduces people to a commodity.

The memorial buildings and monuments all express the horror of Dachau's inhumanity, and some memorials symbolize hope for the future. A bronze sculpture by Gild Nander is located at the center axis of the camp on the former assembly grounds.[30] Gaunt human figures with pained faces are entangled in a barbed wire fence upheld with the top curving posts identified with the camps. This sculpture's visual success is its ability to convey both the human suffering and the inhumanity which caused it. The moments of pain and death are portrayed in this sculpture as the real experience of Dachau.

The Jewish shrine, designed by Hermann Guttman, is a spatial reenactment of the Dachau death ritual and the perseverance of Judaic faith.[31] Just inside the entrance to the monument is a ramp bordered by sculpted railings which look like prison fences. The downward ramp and its rails convey the feeling of beginning a walk to hell. At the end of the ramp you enter a dark masonry structure which might be interpreted as being an oven. Once inside, you see candles, and a tablet is inscribed with the word "REMEMBER" in Hebrew. At the center a pilaster rises through an aperture at the structure's peak. Atop the pilaster is a menorah rising above and outside of the building itself. The message here is that Jewish faith, remembrance, and hope have survived the Nazi inferno of Dachau, because the faith is founded upon believing both in God and human dignity.

Catholics and Protestants have built memorial chapels on the prison grounds to remember victims who belonged to these faiths. The Catholic chapel's entrance path is bordered by barbed wire, while the Protestant chapel is surrounded by gravel which represents the prison grounds. The barbed wire and gravel are images of imprisonment while the chapels represent a religious haven from incarceration. Within each structure, the dominant symbol is the Christian cross. The Catholic memorial is somewhat traditional with an altar and suspended cross. On its roof, however, is a black metal crown of thorns which can be interpreted as being made of barbed wire. The prison's history is thus connected with the religious symbols, evoking the sense that these Christian prisoners suffered with Christ. The Protestant chapel was intentionally designed with asymmetrical curved walls to contradict Dachau's systematic linearity, the symbol of the prison's regimented and inhumane ideology. Within the chapel, the visitor is immediately drawn to a small cross sculpture by Fritz Konig on the altar wall. The cross is formed from a bronze block which has been cracked into the shape of a cross.[32] The sculpture's message can be interpreted to mean that amidst the breaking of human spirit, Christianity emerged and survived. The symbolism in these Christian chapels reflects the camp's history. A number of political prisoners at Dachau, such as Martin Niemoller, were clergymen.[33] These Christian leaders used their faith to provide a spiritual haven which helped them to survive the hardships of inhumane imprisonment. These men who held fast to their faith are in sharp contrast to the many Germans who rejected their Christian principles to embrace nazism. The Nazis' moral bankruptcy allowed a Dachau to come to be and made these chapels necessary. Today these chapels are a testament both to the historic failure of nazism and to the faith of its Christian victims.

As a place, Dachau is overwhelming to the visitor. One look at a barbed wire fence calls up the agony and suffering which occurred in this place of horror. The word "REMEMBER" in the Jewish memorial is well intended, but it is redundant to the informed visitor. The cold regimentation of the original camp puts fear into one's mind. Scholars have provided logical explanations of why nazism and the Holocaust occurred, but visitors to Dachau can emotionally understand what no rational explanation can convey. They see how an inhumane ideology was actually implemented, and only the added memorials offer relief from Dachau's artifacts of inhumanity. Beyond relief, the memorials are expressions of the belief that human principles of goodness and justice will overcome evil. The Dachau concentration camp is ultimately a battleground of human dignity versus indignity.

MASSACRE SITES

Massacre sites mark those events and places where victims were killed in their own environs with little or no means of self-defense. While they recall the systematic elimination practiced at the execution factories, these sites possess the added dimension of instantaneous mass murder. Horror is immediate and punctuates the lasting meaning of the tragedy.

Mass killing sites demonstrate our ability to use technology against humankind. From machine guns to bombs, the strategic uses of weaponry illustrate how warring societies can separate technical rationality from philosophical and moral ideals. The dilemma of this dialectic is not simple. An inhumane society may further its war aims through highly technical weaponry. Yet such a society may find the same weapons used against them by their "morally superior" enemies.

These memorials commemorate the horror of an actual event, but their most potent message is fear—the fear that as our technological ability to kill increases, such crimes could happen again even more easily. Frederick Ogburn once theorized that our ability to socialize ourselves to proper uses of technology lags behind the technical innovations themselves.[34] Massacre memorials are a costly tribute to this reasoning.

War massacres memorialize communities rather than a collection of unrelated individuals. The often used phrase "community lost" is not an empty one. The norms, values, and physical symbols of life are obliterated. Community traditions and the accustomed patterns of relationships in space are not necessarily replaced when a war is ended. For better or worse, new patterns of life will emerge as the survivors sustain past customs as best they can.

Oradour-sur-Glane

Oradour is a small village in central France near the city of Limoges. On the afternoon of June 10, 1944, a company from the Reich Division of the Waffen SS killed 642 men, women, and children. "The SS burned every building, leaving behind, as they rolled away in the evening, ruins filled with the stench of burnt human flesh."[35] In total, 254 buildings were destroyed.

Oradour was eliminated as a defenseless target of reprisal. A few days before the massacre, a popular SS officer from the Reich Division was supposedly killed by the French Resistance while driving on a road some miles from the village. Greatly angered, fellow German soldiers wanted revenge, and they received permission from Reich Division officers to have their wish. Aided by Gestapo personnel, the military company brutally took revenge on the village people, who were not responsible for the German officer's death. The massacre was so inhumane and total that some members of the German high command, such as Rommel, wanted to institute court martial proceedings against the Reich Division, but their objections were unheeded.[36]

Long after the war, in 1953, a trial took place in Bordeaux, France, to obtain justice. A number of German enlisted men were prosecuted and executed, but the courts were unable to extradite from Germany the SS officers who were involved in the massacre.[37]

In 1953 a new village at Oradour was built to provide homes for the few remaining survivors and for other people now living in the area. The original village has been left untouched since its destruction, and it stands as a memorial to that fateful day of June 10, 1944.

Oradour is a total war memorial. Every building, street, open space, and remaining artifact within the old village is a symbolic tribute to its devastation. While many monuments seem to be stages, with the visitors as audience, at Oradour everything is the stage. Visitors become actors recapturing the scenes of a tragedy.

Visitors to these ruins have explicit roles to play. At the entrance, a sign instructs them: "REMEMBER." This evokes a reflective, somber response. Once inside the site, the message is repeated. Many signs describe explicit atrocities and punctuate the message with the instruction: "SILENCE." All visitors have the same role, and with everyone performing to the same short script, the visitors reinforce one another's behavior. The symbolic intent is homage to the dead. The signs may seem unnecessary, but the visitor's role of silence is ensured and legitimized by these symbolic cue cards.

There are four basic kinds of scenes that the visitor encounters. They are the execution sites, the burial grounds, the village memorial, and the overall landscape of the remaining village. Each has its own symbolic message.

Of the six execution sites, the church is the most important. Over 400 women and children were crammed inside the church. First the Germans opened fire with machine guns and lobbed grenades, and then they set fire to it. Only one woman escaped and survived. In the ruined church bullet holes, charred walls, and broken religious artifacts starkly mark that moment of horror. The altar still stands but is in disrepair, and the symbolism is startling. A hallowed place used for baptisms, weddings, and everyday religious life was converted into a death chamber. The sign on one of the walls reifies this meaning by describing the tragedy. The church ruins not only represent the massacre of people but also the defamation of sacred ideals beyond the community.

The village men were executed in barns, a bakery, a blacksmith shop, and a garage in the same way as the women and children had been. Markers describing the killings are provided at each site, but the bakery deserves particular mention. In its kitchen, human remains were found inside the ovens. Upon realizing this, an informed visitor can quickly infer: "Oh God, I imagine this is but a small version of the Nazi extermination camps." The execution sites explicitly define the horror of Oradour. Visitors may react calmly or be stunned, but the message is the same: "The worst kind of human endeavor, senseless killing, occurred here."

Oradour's burial grounds include visual messages which convey mixed sensations of hate, the macabre, and mourning. Some family tombs have pictures of family victims placed upon the gravestone. One marker says: "Massacred and killed in the Church by Nazi hordes." While the execution sites symbolize the act of mass killing, the graves convey not only the total

6.7 Deserted Street of Oradour-sur-Glane, France (Author's Collection)

horror but also the individual sacrifice. Death has a name. Claudine, Renee, and Mary are names which cannot be generalized, as with the 6 million Jews who died in the Holocaust. A picture and a name together become a real yet distant human being to the visitor. Within the cemetery, there is a communal grave of black slate upon which is marked in raised letters, 10 June 1944. Upon this crypt are two glass-topped coffins displaying the charred remains of human bones. At the back of the crypt is a memorial column with three French flags at its top. Near the column's base France's colors—red, white, and blue—are wrapped about the column and drawn together with a black band, symbolizing national mourning. Behind this memorial is a walled display of commemorative plaques from various organizations. At the wall's bottom are remembrances to those whose remains are in the communal grave. The cracked porcelain plaque for René Chabert is emblematic of a shattered life. It says: "Our son and dear brother René Chabert, victim of the Nazis." These various grave markers, memorials, and plaques repeatedly tell visitors that the Germans were responsible for the merciless execution of an entire community and that visitors should be saddened by this painful loss of human life.

6.8 Personalized Human Tragedy, Cracked Memorial Plaque in Cemetery, Oradour-sur-Glane, France (Author's Collection)

As a whole, the burial grounds convey a message not unlike that commonly found on a Confederate statue on a courthouse lawn: "Lest we forget," but here there is an additional message, "Remember who did this horrible deed, the Germans." The visitor is encouraged to remember history and contemplate its meaning for the future. But even more, the visitor may be encouraged to hate not only the Nazis but the whole German people.

Between the cemetery and the village is the village memorial. A tree-lined mall leads to stone steps, and then to a low stone arch. Before it is carved "X VI MCMXXXXIV," that is, 10 June 1944. Beyond this point, the cemetery can be seen. The memorial's spatial placement reenacts the passage of life. The village remains are the past life, the arch memorial is a remembrance of the massacre, and the cemetery is a commemoration to those who died and are now with God. The arch is the passage gate from life to death. Beneath the arch and its stone plaza is a memorial museum. Within it are family possessions and children's toys which were not totally destroyed. The artifacts themselves have little value, but the displays immediately make the visitors feel that they are no different than the villagers who were killed. The common life of Oradour-sur-Glane became uncommon for one final, horrible day, and the location and design of the village memorial is the symbolic announcement of that fact.

The remaining areas of Oradour convey disorder and desolation, and these areas symbolize the tragic flight from everyday life. Building ruins, sewing machines, kitchen utensils, a rusting car, and other artifacts of daily life remain as they were after the massacre. The execution sites and burial grounds emphasize the tragedy, but the rest of the village symbolizes the loss of community life.

The aging of Oradour, however, has softened the visual image of its tragedy. Charred walls still exist, but their burnt surfaces are now faded. Tops of some remaining walls are covered with moss, while others are gracefully decorated with vines of ivy. Nature has overlaid the palpable presence of inhumanity with its own patina. The visitor might imagine for a moment that Oradour is the remains of a nineteenth-century village, but such imagination is short-lived. Walking through the village, the visitor cannot escape the desolation. Each building and artifact is a constant physical reminder of human tragedy. Only by leaving the old village entirely can the visitor escape the symbols and relics of this community holocaust. Memories of the wasted village linger with the visitor.

There have been suggestions that the ruins of Oradour should not be preserved, because the ruins perpetuate hatred for Germans more than they commemorate the dead.[38] The German government offered to rebuild the village, but their proposal was refused.[39] Some feel that symbols of injustice should be preserved so that history can instruct future generations. Oradour remains, but its preservation does little to explain how such atrocities could happen.

Hiroshima Peace Park Memorial

On the morning of August 6, 1945, the United States dropped an atomic bomb on Hiroshima, Japan. At least 78,000 people were killed. As many as 200,000 may have died, but the best estimate is about 140,000 people. The total death count is estimated to be between 25 and 50 percent of the city's population, the most devastating loss of life in any one attack in world history. The destruction was so devastating that one Japanese was compelled to say: "I climbed Hijiyama Hill and looked down . . . Hiroshima didn't exist—that was mainly what I saw—Hiroshima just didn't exist."[40]

Hiroshima was a flat city built mainly of wood, and its landscape became a desert of debris. Buildings within a two-mile radius were totally destroyed except for the remains of concrete structures. Between the two to three mile zone 60,000 buildings, one-third of the zone's structures, were reduced to ashes.[41]

Experiencing the human carnage after the bombing was a horror unto itself. Bodies were everywhere amid a deafening silence. Instead of being in panic, "people staggered about in a stupor of adjusting" to the sudden grotesqueness of their city's landscape and the feeling of death in life.[42] The horror was numbing, as Robert Lipton has recorded in his interviews with survivors:

I saw . . . some girls, very young girls, not only with their clothes torn off, but with their skin peeled off as well . . . I had never seen anything which resembled it before . . . should there be a hell, this was it.[43]

I saw blue phosphorescent flames rising from the dead bodies. . . . Yet at that time I had a state of mind in which I feared nothing—though if I were to see those flames now, I might be quite frightened.[44]

The horrors of the bomb continued after the war. Hiroshima's society was confused and debilitated. The bomb's radiation and blast caused innumerable health problems. Beyond the obvious maladies of burns and loss of limb or sight, incidences of leukemia, malignant tumors, and various other forms of cancer were experienced by hibakusha, the survivors. Other nonmalignant, life-threatening diseases were found to be more prevalent among hibakusha.[45] The A-bomb continued to kill people after the war, but the survivors died more slowly and painfully than the immediate victims.

The rebuilding of Hiroshima was a marvel of human endurance and revitalization under stress. Within ten years, the city had been virtually reconstructed, and its financial recovery was so great that its prosperity exceeded many other Japanese communities.

Today, Hiroshima has the appearance of a typical progressive city in a developed country. Underneath this image, its mixed world of immigrants and survivors produces a less confident reality. Hiroshima was shaken from the past, and its survivors have a residual distrust in the nature of human existence.[46]

Hiroshima has resymbolized itself as the City of Peace. Hiroshima was traditionally a military city, and local citizens wanted to change the city's image after the war. They decided that no more war meant no more weapons, and remaining remnants of the military in Hiroshima were deactivated. The postwar mood of pacifism made the symbolic transition to a city of peace an easy one. On August 6, 1949, the law for construction of the Hiroshima Peace Commemorating City was enacted by the National Diet to make Hiroshima ". . . the symbol of the human ideal for eternal peace."[47] Koichi Hasegawa commented: "The spirit which lies at the core of Hiroshima's planning is that the city no longer belongs to the people of Hiroshima or Japan alone, but to the whole human society."[48]

The atomic bomb's catastrophic impact made Hiroshima a common concern for the world, but Hiroshima's citizens were not in agreement regarding design proposals for a memorial. Many people thought that the proposed memorial site might be treated without respect. If large business buildings, such as hotels, were built nearby, the memorial grounds would be profaned, because visitors could look down on the dead. Some proposed memorials were objected to because they lacked Oriental character. One architect—Isamu Noguchi, a second-generation American of Japanese descent—was accused of Americanizing Hiroshima with his memorial designs.[49] This was particularly discomforting to local hibakusha who still had strong anti-American feelings. Citizens felt that memorials in the proposed park had to command a level of honor and humanitarian concern to match Hiroshima's tragedy.

Most of the Peace Park was built in the 1950s, with refinements and additions in the 1960s. In time, the most important memorials have become the Peace Memorial Museum, the Peace Flame, The Children's Atomic Bomb Monument, the A-Bomb Dome, and the Memorial Cenotaph. While numerous other monuments exist, these five memorials express Hiroshima's dominant feelings about their day of infamy.

The Peace Memorial Museum, completed in 1955, has stirred controversy about the bombing of Hiroshima. Photographs and exhibits show the city's devastation, the wastage of the dead, and the human suffering of the injured. Some citizens wish to tone down the portrayal of horror. Commercial businesspeople and some survivors wish to look toward the future rather than the past. However, most hibakusha want the full horror to be known.[50] Yet, the museum's international style of architectural design seems uninspiring and emotionally neutral. On the other hand, the museum is like the A-bomb itself. The A-bomb's nondescript exterior shell does not convey its potential internal content of horror. The museum's interior, like the bombshell's interior, speaks to the horror.

The Peace Flame, built after the other major memorials, reflects the current Japanese architectural trend of using traditional forms in a modern way. The memorial is distinctly Japanese in simplicity and form. Its message, however, is universal. The memorial includes a flame, which visitors recognize as a sign of keeping alive the spirit of those who died. Its simplicity and universal appeal hardly make it a controversial memorial.

The Children's Atomic Bomb Monument, built in 1958, is the most accepted memorial in the park.[51] Its creation was inspired by Sadako Sasaki, a 12-year-old girl who suffered from leukemia. Sadako was two years old when she was critically exposed to the A-bomb's radiation, and later developed leukemia as a result. When the disease began to threaten her life, Sadako decided to help herself by following an old Japanese belief that folding 1,000 paper cranes will cure an illness. Sadako began meticulously to fold her cranes, although she had increasing difficulty making them. She died with 36 cranes left to be made. Her classmates from school prepared the remaining cranes, and all 1,000 were placed in her coffin. The classmates then began a campaign for a memorial. Sadako's story touched the hearts of all Japanese, and paper cranes and financial contributions for the memorial came from all over the country.[52]

Today, the Children's Atomic Bomb Monument is a popular place to visit, and people are still touched by its meaning. Paper cranes are often attached to the monument, and even the visitor who knows nothing of their symbolism suspects a deeper meaning. People willingly accept the intentions behind this monument, because children are always the victims of war rather than its perpetrators. The monument is not just a symbol of peace but also a plea for it. The memorial reminds the Japanese people and others that the story of Sadako and her classmates has a universal message.

In contrast, local citizens have many conflicting feelings about the A-Bomb Dome Monument. Located near the bomb's hypocenter, the memorial is the building remains of the Industry Promotion Hall, one of the few structures standing in Hiroshima after the bombing. Never demolished, it is a grim reminder of the city's destruction. The public controversy has been over whether or not the building should be permanently removed.

Many people object to the fact that the dome is now a tourist site. Tourism itself is not bad, but when business economically extracts profits from past human suffering, tourism is profane. Some Japanese people feel that tourists can never grasp the horror that took place at the dome building site on August 6, 1945. Disfigured bodies laid about the building and in the nearby river.[53] But the tourism will continue unless the citizens of Hiroshima decide to tear down the dome. Others who advocate razing the dome feel that it perpetuates feelings of hostility toward the United States among Hiroshima's survivors.

Many hibakusha want the dome to remain. It is a reminder, a warning, of the bomb's horror and the horror of war itself, and the hibakusha feel that

6.9 A-Bomb Dome as Symbol of Destruction, Hiroshima, Japan (Photograph by Jack Morley)

people should not be allowed to forget or to become complacent. Other hibakusha have considered a compromise which follows a Japanese custom, that is, to let nature take its course over time. Temporarily, however, the decision about what to do with the dome has been resolved. In the late 1960s funds were raised to preserve it as a living reminder.[54] As long as the A-Bomb Dome Monument exists, the Japanese people will be reminded of the costs of atomic warfare.

The Memorial Cenotaph, completed in 1953, is located in the Peace Park's symbolic center and concentrates Japanese emotions about the bombing of Hiroshima. It is a small, modern structure with a traditional Japanese character. Beneath its arch, a stone chest houses the Book of the Past which records the registered names of those killed by the A-bomb. New names of hibakusha are added when they die of diseases resulting from the bomb's radiation. The chest is the intensification of death, and the memorial's ultimate meaning is made explicit by the chest's inscription: "REST IN PEACE. THE MISTAKE SHALL NOT BE REPEATED."[55]

Whose mistake? This is the enduring question and the heart of the cenotaph's equivocal meaning. The inscription permeates all of the other memorials and the park itself. Are the Japanese to blame or are the Americans at fault? Amidst warnings and opportunities to surrender, Japan persisted even though defeat was imminent. Herbert Feis argues that: ". . . the decision to drop the bombs upon Hiroshima and Nagasaki ought not to be censured."[56] U.S. officials felt that the bomb would ultimately result in fewer deaths than would the continuation of the war with conventional weapons.[57] There is evidence that the United States was aware of Japan's willingness to cease hostilities, although unconditional surrender was not acceptable. It is said that President Truman rejected these terms.[58] Clearly, there are differing opinions about whether or not the A-bomb should have been dropped on Hiroshima. These differences will not fade away.

The ethics of means and ends underlie the very existence of Hiroshima's Peace Park. Do the ends justify the means? Saul Alinsky argues that: ". . . in war the end justifies almost any means."[59] The A-bomb, however, was not just any means, and the argument becomes more troublesome since according to Alinsky, ". . . the morality of a means depends upon whether the means is being employed at a time of imminent defeat or imminent victory."[60] There will never be full agreement on the legitimacy of bombing Hiroshima, but there is some consensus about what it means for the future. Hiroshima and its Peace Park have become the cornerstone of the movement against nuclear warfare. August 6 has become an international day for peace demonstrations with Hiroshima as the symbolic center. While the morality of the Hiroshima bombing is the question, certainly its repetition anywhere is seen increasingly to be unacceptable.

NEEDED REMINDERS

There are victim memorials that cannot be strictly classified as prisons, execution factories, or massacre sites. Some memorials are general rather than specific commemorations for an atrocity, and they are not located where the atrocity happened. These memorials appeal to the concern for crimes against humanity as an issue itself rather than merely recognizing any one crime. In other cases, such as when there is a cease-fire, the status of war becomes unclear. In these circumstances, one side may attack a defenseless opponent, resulting in unjustified killing. In this case, victim memorials are provided at the specific site of the crime, but because of the cease-fire, people may not directly associate the tragedy with a war. The memorials discussed earlier in this chapter mainly commemorated victims at the site of the crime under clear conditions of war, but here, these conditions are not met. When either the tragedy's location or clarity of warfare is suspended as a memorial criterion, there are varying and even conflicting interpretations of the resulting commemorations of victims.

There is no better example of inhumanity in war than the Holocaust. In Jerusalem, there is a memorial to all Jewish martyrs of the Holocaust, Yad Vashem. Its exterior is simple, as is its interior, which focuses on a bronze sculpture of a flame. At its base, a flame burns constantly. Nothing else need be said to Jews who visit here. The flame represents the eternal light above every ark that holds a torch in a synagogue. Martyrs were often consumed by fire, but the fire of their spirit and memories stays within us.

One of the best general monuments is the Memorial des Martyrs de la Deportation in Paris which is located behind Notre Dame Cathedral.[61] Built to remember French victims of the Holocaust, its symbolism goes beyond national boundaries. Its power resides in replaying the Holocaust experience. Behind Notre Dame is a walk leading to an entranceway, and at the entrance is a set of descending steps. Here the visitor can see, at one end of a high wall, a stylized sculpture of barbed wire. Descending the walled stairway into the plaza gives the immediate feeling of imprisonment. The visitor grasps that this is a Holocaust memorial, but not all is made clear. The visitor then encounters a small structure with an inconspicuous entrance, and human curiosity tells one to walk inside and investigate. Once inside the chamber, there is the realization that the visitor has been symbolically executed. At one end of the chamber is a deep rectilinear space covered by bars, reminiscent of an oven. At its base is a slab of black slate, and on the sides are 200,000 small glass tiles which are lit from behind. Each tile is symbolic of a person burned in the oven while the slate symbolizes their collective remains. Above the symbolic oven is inscribed in French: "IN MEMORY OF THE TWO HUNDRED THOUSAND FRENCH VICTIMS EXTERMINATED IN THE NIGHT AND THE FOG IN THE NAZI CAMPS." The visitor is forced into the horror of the victims' historical tragedy.

6.10 Symbolic Chamber and Oven to Executed Victims of the Holocaust, Memorial des Martyrs de la Deportation, Paris, France (Author's Collection)

Other memorials capture the historical tragedy of victims but on a smaller scale. A good example is the Anne Frank house in Amsterdam, made famous by her published diary. Anne Frank was a Jewish teenager who was protected by a Dutch family. Living in a hidden room, she wrote of her day-to-day experiences and her inability to live a full life. The Nazi's eventually found her family's hideout, and she was taken away and ultimately executed. The apartment was made a memorial after the war, and it is frequently visited by tourists from many countries. In a small open area near the apartment, there is a statue of her, and it is marked quite simply, "ANNE FRANK, 1929-1945." The horror of the Holocaust is made real through the story of how one person was forced into confinement, tried to survive, wanted desperately to lead the life of a normal teenage girl, and was ultimately treated as a parasite by the Nazis. The visitor is confronted with the suffering of an actual victim. This personalizes the experience of suffering more than any collective memorial to the many unknown ever could.

Holocaust memorials in the United States have been rare, but one of the first monuments was dedicated in 1980 at the Toledo, Ohio, Jewish Community Center. Entitled "For This the Earth Mourns," the monument was built to remember the tragedy as a whole. It is an ensemble of sculpted figures standing upon a bed of broken bricks. Both young and old people are portrayed with gaunt faces and slumped shoulders.[62] The facial expressions convey not only the dulling pain of physical hardship but also despair. Many memorial statues give viewers the impression that they are about to speak or move, but the Holocaust figures at Toledo give the visitor the opposite feeling. The figures appear to be aware, but without the energy or motivation to speak or move. Symbolically, the sculpture ensemble is a political statement of forced alienation without human recourse, because the figures do not visually express an appeal for help to the viewer. There is a social distance between the depiction of their suffering and a visitor's presence. "For This the Earth Mourns" forces people to realize that they must not distance themselves from a tragedy that should never have occurred and that must not be allowed to happen again.

While the Toledo memorial has the sanctity of being on Jewish property, the Holocaust Memorial in San Francisco does not. Designed by the well-known sculptor, George Segal, the San Francisco Holocaust Memorial is located in Lincoln Park opposite the California Palace of the Legion of Honor. The monument has caused controversy among Jews and non-Jews. Jews have been concerned about potential vandalism in the public park, but they have also been critical about the monument's definition of victims. A Jewish art professor at the University of California at Berkeley commented: "Our monument singles out Jews, but in the Holocaust they were not the only ones killed. There were communists, gays, gypsies, Poles."[63] Criticism by non-Jews ranged from feelings of harassment to anti-Semitism. One person said: "OK, what happened to the Jews was terrible, but this constant harping is getting to be a bore."[64] The memorial's public location has caused people to voice their opinions, and old prejudices have emerged along with valid arguments.

If the memorial's very existence caused controversy, then its actual design added fuel to it. The sculpture is an ensemble of figures behind a barbed wire fence, and it attempts to portray what the Nazi concentration camps were really like. A mound of naked figures lie dead, piled on a concrete slab. They look as if they had just been killed in the gas chambers and were ready for the ovens. Facing away from these bodies, a gaunt man in rags stands holding the barbed wire fence with an expressionless look of dull pain. Surrounded by death and full of suffering, the standing man represents the survivors.[65] For many people the San Francisco Holocaust Memorial is just too horrible. It is so realistic that they are unable to see any symbolism or expression of justice. The sculpture's virtue rests with its interpretations of historical horror. It says that to sterilize the horror of the Holocaust is to begin to forget, and that must not happen.

Atrocities during cease-fires in war are not commemorated when the victors find it convenient to forget history. The Sand Creek Massacre of the

6.11 Holocaust Memorial, Toledo, Ohio (Courtesy of Lois Dorfman)

6.12 Holocaust Memorial, San Francisco, California (Photograph by Leonard Schwab)

Southern Cheyenne tribe by Union soldiers in 1864 demonstrates this. The war between the United States and the American Indians led to atrocities on both sides, but cease-fires created the potential for crimes in which one side attacked the other unexpectedly and unfairly. Verbal agreements to stop fighting without a peace treaty created a middle world of no war but no peace. In September 1864, the Southern Cheyenne tribe committed to U.S. officials that they would stop future raids, although most fighting came from other tribes.[66] They were peacefully settled near Camp Weld, Colorado, on Sand Creek. Some skirmishes with other tribes occurred in the meantime. The commander of the U.S. Third Colorado Regiment, Colonel John Chivington, actively hated all Indians, regardless of tribe.[67] On November 29, 1864, from 400 to 500 Southern Cheyennes were killed and mutilated by an unexpected and unprovoked attack by the Third Regiment.[68] Congressional hearings were later held due to public outcry, but no action was taken.[69] Eventually, Indian lands were confiscated by legislative mandate, and today, few Americans know about the atrocities at Sand Creek.

The Sand Creek Massacre site has barely been marked, and there is little for visitors to learn there. On Colorado State Highway 96 is a state road marker which reads: "SAND CREEK BATTLE OR MASSACRE." Beyond this sign is a gravel road and for miles there is no further marker identifying the route. Eventually the visitor comes to a small hill, and on it is a simple earthmound about three feet in height. Atop the mound is a very small stone marker which simply reads: "SAND CREEK BATTLE GROUND NOV. 29 & 30, 1864." Both historical markers are compromising, because no blame is assessed. Much confusion does surround the massacre, but the compromising inscriptions are negligent. Women, children, and old men were brutally killed, disembodied, and then looted by armed U.S. soldiers. The immensity of the crime is not matched by the memorial's physical stature or care. The memorial at the massacre site is so small that visitors at Sand Creek might think that the event was only incidental. Yet, most visitors must go out of their way to visit Sand Creek, and those that do are probably aware of its history. The massacre was a historical event that most Americans have forgotten, and the nondescript memorials for Sand Creek are evidence of this attitude.

Victim memorials can bring forth memories of horror, albeit some more powerfully than others. They can drain the emotions we feel toward the atrocities they commemorate and can alter the way we view the future. But a nation, particularly a victorious nation, can choose to avoid providing memorials to commemorate their war crimes. It is easy for us to say "never again" to war crimes, but it is less clear for us to decide how to commemorate them properly, and more importantly, how to avoid their repetition. Victim memorials shake our comfortable conceptions of victimization. They can make us face what we believe about ourselves and humanity, and they can allow us to face true horror. If this happens, victim memorials serve their most important purpose.

CHAPTER SEVEN
REMEMBRANCE AS POLITICAL CRITIQUE

THE COMMEMORATION OF WAR reshapes how a society views its political history. The good can be made to appear better, and the bad can be presented in its best light. America's wars of justice enable us to feel righteous, while those for Manifest Destiny allow us to feel that the United States did only what was necessary. Wars of defeat are redeemed by honoring those who fought. But memorials can falsely separate past history from existing political realities. Monuments can conveniently allow people to put the past behind them. If bad political motives and questionable values led to a war, people can falsely assume that these causes have been eliminated. More simply, war memorials can be treated as symbolic grave markers to past political action. Nations, however, often repeat their political past. A country and its citizens may be unwillingly drawn into an unjustified war, and if they are victorious, the people may falsely assume that the political problems have been resolved. Memorials often represent how people saw their nation's political aims. As time passes, later generations of citizens may accept these memorials as valid assessments of war memory whether they are accurate or not.

Democracy brings with it more than political pluralism. It also brings open questioning, and this can encourage people to examine the truth or falseness of the country's commemoration of war. Remembering the past need not be an exercise in false consciousness. Authentic memory has been pursued and realized many times in the American experience.

Three points need to be understood in the formation of authentic memory. First, how are sacred memorials developed and maintained to honor the American past? Second, how have humanitarian concerns reached beyond history to make retrospective remembrance more meaningful? Finally, what is the future of war and the memorials which may follow? By answering these questions, a better understanding of what has been and should be remembered becomes possible.

HONORING THE PAST

Providing sacred memorials for past wars poses a twofold question: how to create authentic memory and how to preserve it. The lack of understanding regarding these separate issues and their interrelationships has often resulted in the improper commemoration of war and the loss of remembrance. These two concerns must be addressed for the present American experience to be understood.

Commemoration of U.S. wars in the twentieth century has generally included three patterns. First, communities remember their local warriors, and this interest evolves into a demand for national recognition. Second, memorials are created at the national level, culminating in the enshrinement of an unknown soldier. Finally, a few communities learn from these previous attempts and build memorials that articulate the meaning of a war more accurately than earlier attempts. One pattern gives way to the next as Americans try to articulate their understanding of the war more clearly.

Local communities often provide memorials immediately following a war, and their efforts create the demand for more commemoration. They use memorial plaques in courthouses or modest monuments. Communities use patriotic inscriptions to remember local people who served, and while their efforts are sincere, these memorials are usually very simple statements about the past. Veterans begin to want more profound monuments than these simple, local memorials. They begin campaigns for national recognition, especially for recognition in Washington, D.C. Armed service branches often update the memorials they erected for previous wars, and this remembrance creates a more focused demand for war memory. The move from local to national concern results from practicality and justification. Communities can build memorials more quickly than the U.S government can, which makes decisions slowly and is expected to be more careful about approving memorial designs. Local memorials are votes of approval that justify the demand for national war memorials.

Some national memorials are built without difficulties, although the federal bureaucratic process may result in delays. Armed services memorials in Washington, D.C., are updated as are memorials in U.S. national overseas cemeteries. These types of war memorials have been institutionalized, and while commemoration may be slow, it is inevitable.

Veterans can face difficulties in their attempts to have national memorials built. Those who fought want to be singularly remembered with their own memorial. Fund-raising campaigns begin for building a monument, and a process for choosing a memorial design is articulated. The process can be smooth, but that is not necessarily the case. The USS *Arizona* Memorial in Hawaii and the Vietnam Memorial in Washington were deluged with problems from getting governmental support to choosing a final memorial design. The Vietnam Memorial provides a good example of conflicts between the general citizenry and veterans. Those who fought in Vietnam rejected the perceptions of people who remained at the homefront. Veterans did not want a memorial that reflected current design trends. They saw themselves as different, and they did not wish to be identified with design motifs which were considered to be the norm. Since the Second World War, memorials had become either streamlined monuments or utilitarian buildings. Vietnam veterans wanted a contradiction to this image. This desire for contradiction was felt earlier by veterans from both world wars, who did not want the grand monuments which had become standard. Instead, these veterans tended to opt for utilitarian memorials to demonstrate that remembrance should serve a constructive purpose rather than a purely symbolic one, which had been the case with many memorials. Eventually, the conflict between veterans and the public results in a compromise which is satisfactory to both groups.

While national memorials and cemeteries enhance American memory, the ultimate commemoration is the interment of the remains of an unidentified warrior into the Tomb of the Unknown Soldier at Arlington National Cemetery. Past memory is projected into the present by treating all who have fought as honorable. It is more than collective memory. Honorable remembrance is treated wholistically rather than as a remembrance for the many individual soldiers who died. This seamless memory enables Americans to overlook differences between wars of justice and defeat. Although no soldiers from wars of Manifest Destiny are now buried in the tomb, their implicit presence is a part of the salute to past endeavors. Memory is seen as timeless and no one war is singled out or criticized as just or unjust.

After national memory has been formalized, more intricate memorials are often then developed in some communities. The World War I memorials in Indianapolis and Kansas City, erected long after the war, reflect a deeper perception than the Doughboy statues built soon after the war. While communities built fewer monuments after the Second World War, museums and utilitarian memorials were built that reflected more than the memorial plaques which some communities quickly erected. The Korean War has been mainly ignored, but the Milwaukee War Memorial Building does reflect a conscious local attempt to remember this war after the Unknown Soldier ceremonies had already been held in Arlington National

Cemetery in 1958. The New York City and Kansas City memorials for Vietnam are designed to embody the contradictory aspects of that war by taking advantage of the problems experienced with the Vietnam Memorial in Washington D.C. Learning from earlier efforts to commemorate the recent past enables communities who wait to have more meaningful memorials than those which erect memorials soon after a war.

The overall pattern of memory is one of anticipation and response. As time passes, wars are increasingly commemorated, and by learning from past mistakes, memory becomes more articulate. Sometimes design techniques used to commemorate previous wars are borrowed. When this is done, the result is often a rubber-stamp memorial which neither realizes explicit war history nor offers new artistic means to convey it. Even when memorials are designed without superficially borrowing from the past, people have difficulties in determining how to commemorate a specific war. Designs and inscriptions used in other memorials for that war are examined, and some of those concepts are used along with new ideas. This analysis of other designs, both old and new, and the articulation of the war's meaning constitute the anticipation phase. The integration that is made between the design and the interpretation is the response.

Honoring the past has little worth if meaning is not maintained. Rituals do continue past memory, but as honorable events, they can fade in time as the veterans die. Reinforcement of meaning must ultimately come from the living, or it will disappear. Holidays, such as Memorial Day, do keep honor intact, but preservation of memory also includes the physical maintenance of memorials and a renewal of historic knowledge to understand why wars were fought.

The preservation of war memorials as artifacts and rituals ultimately reflects a war's perceived importance. The American Revolution, the Civil War, and the world wars have come to be seen as this nation's most important wars. The first two are exemplified by the number of places which have been designated as historic sites. The National Park Service, which emerged in the twentieth century, maintains those memorials and keeps their landscapes, which are reconstructed in historical context, in pristine condition. Time seems to have stopped in these places, and war memory is made explicit. While commemorations for the world wars are prominent in Arlington National Cemetery and Washington, D.C., the national memorials and cemeteries overseas best demonstrate the preservation of memory. They are immaculately kept by the American Battle Monuments Commission. All First World War sites in France would officially qualify as sites for historic preservation in the United States, but there is nothing to restore. Their memorial chapels and grounds are so well maintained that these sites look as if construction was just completed. Those wars which Americans value the most have the finest war memorials and the best preserved landscapes.

Memorials for less popular wars tend to receive less attention for the preservation of memory. Historic sites for these wars under the care of the National Park Service do exist, and while they are well maintained, they tend to have fewer memorials. Some memorials for the War of 1812, the Mexican wars, the American Indian wars, and the Spanish-American War do attract visitors, but many battle sites and monuments to these wars are simply ignored. The Honolulu Memorial National Cemetery of the Pacific has provided grounds and commemoration to soldiers from Korea and Vietnam, but the cemetery's symbolic identity with World War II is so great that these two wars are overlooked. Commemoration of battle sites for them is nonexistent and virtually impossible. Lack of physical maintenance for less popular wars typically occurs at the local level. While the same may hold true for all war memorials, the less popular wars often have smaller and less intricate memorials which are made of less expensive materials. As a result, less care is taken to maintain them.

While certain wars have continuing national importance, some wars have retained specific local significance. The Mexican wars have never attracted a great deal of national attention, but in Texas, memories of the fight for state independence still thrive. Texans treat their revolution as an integral part of their state's history. A war's true historical importance may not bear any resemblance to its perceived importance in popular memory. Wars of Manifest Destiny now receive less attention than most other American wars, even though they resulted in more territorial gains than the popular wars. The preservation and importance of war memory strongly depends upon what messages people wish to retain as part of their national heritage.

Perhaps the best example of how past memory of American wars is structured is neither famous nor exceptionally well designed. As part of the bicentennial celebration in 1976, the Veterans of Foreign Wars in the United States dedicated a war memorial on the grounds of its headquarters in Washington, D.C., to commemorate the nation's war endeavors. It is a measuring stick of structured memory. The monument is comprised of 12 plaques which are evenly distributed in groups of four on all sides of a triangular marble pylon. American war history is depicted from its earliest wars at the bottom to its most recent ones at the top on all three sides, but not all sides are treated equally. The positions of plaques on the monument typify how America has come to value its historic wars.

The main facade portrays the nation's most popular wars with a commemorative plaque on the base. This side faces Maryland and Constitution Avenues on the building's triangular lot where these two streets join. Constitution Avenue physically borders the Washington Mall, making this facade the most important side for the monument, because it symbolically connects it to other memorials on the Mall. The bottom plaque begins with the Spirit of 76 image of the familiar fife player, two drummers, and an American flag to symbolize the American Revolution. Above it is a scene of

Appomattox, representing the end to the Civil War. Atop these two plaques, a battle scene depicts U.S. soldiers fighting in World War I, and on top is the famous Second World War scene of U.S. Marines raising the flag at Iwo Jima. All these memorial plaques depict America's most popular wars at their best. All the wars of victory as justice are shown, and the Civil War is portrayed in its most victorious light, as a nation justly reunited.

The Second Street side of the monument is next in importance, and it contains a mixture of images. On the bottom is a scene depicting the Battle at Yorktown which symbolizes victory in the American Revolution. Next, a scene of Confederate leaders looks much like the relief on Georgia's Stone Mountain. Above these plaques is a World War II scene depicting the war in Europe. Finally, a scene from the Korean War rests on top. Victory is mixed evenly with defeat on the Second Street side, but the main message can be seen as the willingness to fight independent of the factors that led to these wars.

The nation's less popular wars are relegated to the back facade, which faces the building but is not readily visible. At the base the War of 1812 is depicted through the battle at Fort McHenry. Next, a battle scene portrays the Union's role in the Civil War, and above it, the Spanish-American War is represented with an illustration of the Rough Riders. The top plaque commemorates the Vietnam War, showing soldiers on a gunboat near a riverbank. With the exception of the depiction of the Union in the Civil War, the other three wars represent Manifest Destiny and defeat. These three are wars that must be remembered, but they are not the great wars. To accurately illustrate how Americans view these wars, one might justifiably conclude that the Confederate scene might be better placed here, because the South was defeated. The plaque display of the less desirable war causes would then be visually unified. On the other hand, the Union scene which is actually there redeems these other three war endeavors. The American public has accepted that all of these wars should be remembered, but the War of 1812, the Spanish-American War, and the Vietnam War are not valued as much as other wars. Their placement on the back side of the Veterans of Foreign Wars Memorial is evidence of that attitude.

The V.F.W. Memorial is not a totally accurate measure of how Americans remember their nation's wars, but it comes close. The wars that Americans are proudest of are displayed up front, and the less popular wars are less visible on the memorial. Not all of the nation's wars are represented on this monument. There are no plaques for the Mexican War or the American Indian wars, although together these wars account for the nation's largest territorial gains resulting from war. The monument demonstrates what past wars Americans wish to honor as well as those that they are willing to forget.

Preservation of memory in war memorials is easily transformed into only the desirable images of the past. Some wars were more important than others, but importance is a political interpretation as well as a vote for

7.1 Veterans of Foreign Wars Memorial as Political Measuring Stick, Washington, D.C. (Author's Collection)

popularity. The legitimate commemoration of America's wars of justice and of the Civil War as reuniting the country obscures the fact that these wars are also the most popular in the public mind. On the other hand, the less popular wars often receive little attention for many reasons. Fewer people were killed in these wars, and Americans also do not feel as strongly about the reasons for fighting in these wars. This may explain why Americans tend to ignore them, but this inattention makes it difficult to differentiate between what should be justifiably honored and what needs to be deplored in the American political past. A war's lack of popularity can become forgetfulness of wrongdoing.

HUMANITARIAN CRITIQUE OF THE PAST

The social purpose of most sacred memorials is to express honor, but some go beyond honor to a questioning of the past. Not all those who fought were treated as equal partners in battle. Prejudice was often present. Memories of this darker side of war memory finally emerge when history is documented. Commemorating victims can be more than documenting their pain through monuments. Educational interpretations teach people about the past while commemorating it. Critique goes even further by questioning the legitimacy of war itself. All these examinations bring forth an assessment of what ought to be remembered beyond the battlefront. By posing questions and offering interpretations of past wars, people can achieve a deeper understanding of injustices which should not be repeated.

Not all soldiers who fought have been remembered for their contributions, but recognition of this past neglect is slowly emerging. Some U.S. Army museums now recognize the contributions of the nineteenth-century black cavalrymen that the Indians called "the Buffalo Soldiers."[1] Such displays destroy the myth that the West was won solely by whites. Blacks in military service were only allowed to serve in backline positions and suffered other forms of prejudice, but the Second World War by necessity brought down many racial barriers. In 1983, the National Air and Space Museum in Washington, D.C., included a temporary exhibit of the Black Eagles, a fighter squadron which was a pioneer in demonstrating blacks' ability and courage in battle.[2] The display presented scenes from their training and fighting days, and a video program told more fully about prejudices that they faced. Black visitors were immediately drawn to the exhibit, but others gave their attention as well. Black veterans themselves have gone beyond the official portrayals of the past. When the Vietnam Memorial wall was dedicated, they identified themselves as a group and voiced their objections to racism at the battlefront. When the Vietnam Memorial statue was finally built, a black man was one of three soldiers in the composition. Minority groups such as blacks are honored more now than they were in the past, because these groups have insisted on being included. In addition, a changing social climate has made other Americans more willing to honor all those who fought. The civil rights movement has brought about a more integrated America. It has begun to influence how America sees minorities, including how their contributions to war should be commemorated.

The lack of commemoration for black Americans is best typified by a single memorial in downtown Baltimore, Maryland, which attempts to recall their contributions. Ironically, it was dedicated in 1971 while black servicemen were fighting and losing their lives in disproportionate numbers in the Vietnam War. A further irony is its location on the same square as the Battle Monument for the War of 1812, which is considered to be this nation's first major war memorial. The monument depicts a black soldier in a contemporary Army uniform. Standing in a military pose, he is reading a scroll inscribed with the dates of the many wars in which black Americans have fought, from the American Revolution to the present. The scroll is more than remembrance. The symbolic reading of the dates symbolizes what many Americans have forgotten or ignored. Atop the scroll is a simple wreath symbolizing honor. The inscription wholistically and explicitly encompasses past accomplishments. It reads:

DEDICATED TO THE
MEMORY OF
THE NEGRO HEROES
OF THE UNITED STATES

"SLEEP IN PEACE
SLAIN IN THE COUNTRY'S WAR"

While blacks are the most obvious example of prejudice, Japanese-Americans who fought and received numerous unit citations have been ignored. With their efforts forgotten by the nation, Japanese-Americans have found it necessary to remember themselves. At the site of the former prison camp in Rohwer, Arkansas, they have built a monument which honors those who fought by making clear the hardships that Japanese-Americans faced. Although interned in the camps, men volunteered or were drafted into military service while their families were prisoners. Unjustly imprisoned and deprived of the basic rights of citizens, these soldiers still distinguished themselves in combat.

Women are another group which has been treated as a minority. Although they have received some commemoration, their wartime efforts have not been fully recognized by many Americans. Nurses have received the most recognition. The Nuns of the Battlefield Monument in Washington, D.C., honors those Catholic nuns who cared for the sick and wounded during the Civil War.[3] In Arlington National Cemetery there is a memorial for nurses who served in the Spanish-American War. Arlington also has the Jane A. Delano Memorial, which is dedicated not only to Delano but also to the 18,000 women who joined the Army Nurse Corps during World War I. Another Jane Delano Monument stands in the garden of the Red Cross Headquarters in Washington, D.C., and it is dedicated to Delano and the 296 nurses who died while serving during the First World War. Also in the nation's capital, there is the Red Cross Men and Women Killed in Service Monument, which shows two men and a woman carrying an injured man. The poses in this memorial are intended to portray service in peace or war.[4] While all of these memorials recognize women's efforts, they are few in comparison to the memorials for men felled in battle, and most people must actively seek them out.

Attempts have been made to make women's wartime efforts more visible. In 1986 the U.S. Congress passed a bill that approved construction of a memorial in the nation's capital to commemorate the women veterans of American wars. Like the memorial to the black soldier in Baltimore, this monument to women is an attempt to atone for earlier oversights. Increasingly, war museums include portrayals of the woman's role in war. Such displays can help to break down stereotypical images of women and commemorate the wartime hardships they have faced. Undoubtedly, these attempts to commemorate women in war are due in part to the women's movement which has legitimately argued for recognition of their efforts.

Even with those efforts, it is necessarily true that masculine images persist. Overwhelmingly, the armed services personnel who have been killed in war have been men. Most people never even consider that women who served in the nation's wars might be buried in Arlington National Cemetery. In fact, women who served in the armed services are buried at Arlington, and in other military cemeteries as well. In 1984, a veteran's reunion was held in Normandy, France, to celebrate the fortieth anniversary of D-Day. During the celebration, Nancy Reagan, wife of the U.S. president, placed flowers at the graves of the four women who are buried in the Normandy American Cemetery. Admittedly, honoring four members of the armed services seems insignificant when compared to the 9,376 bodies buried at Normandy; but honoring these four women reminds all Americans that men's lives are not the only cost of war.

Perhaps the most neglected form of recognition is the remembrance of women on the homefront. During the Second World War, women constructed an enormous number of weapons used in the war. While their efforts are recorded in books and film, many of the factory buildings which marked their efforts have been converted to other uses or have been demolished. The sacred monuments which commemorate war in the American townscape unquestionably commemorate the endeavors of men, while the nonsacred memorials of old factories—if they even exist—go unnoticed as historical evidence of women's achievements.

Although some redress for past prejudices has been made, there are still few memorials commemorating the minority experience in war. Minorities, especially when they are poor, are rarely able to afford monuments. More damningly, they often do not have immediate access to documents that prove racism took place.[5] Verbal objections by minority groups have either been ignored or regarded as the invalid oral accounts of a few disgruntled individuals. Minority groups have often suffered from lack of recognition after a war as much as they suffered from prejudice during that war. The lack of memorials built for minorities is a historic testament to American prejudice.

Remembering victims in war raises the question of why they were allowed to suffer. Wrongdoings committed by the Confederacy at Andersonville Prison in Georgia have been addressed in a small way, but no museum accounts for Union atrocities in Elmira, New York. In more recent times,

Japanese-Americans have been modestly remembered at the Eastern California Museum in Bishop, California. Life at the Manzanar Camp is illustrated through artifacts and photographs, and some description is offered to explain the discrimination that Japanese-Americans suffered. To honor all these victims is not sufficient, because conveying honor only shifts attention away from the causes and people responsible for these injustices. Americans may not want to know that President Franklin D. Roosevelt signed the document that enabled Japanese-Americans to be imprisoned, but the fact remains that he did. A nation's leadership and its complying citizenry must accept responsibility for their unjustified acts if they are to become more humanitarian. When they do not, their future generations must recognize past inhumanity so that such crimes will not be repeated, in victory or in defeat.

The greatest crime against humanity in any war was undoubtedly the Holocaust during the Second World War which resulted in the death of millions. Historically, it has been viewed as being beyond the American experience, because the death camps and their memorials are in Europe. This perception is changing. The killing of Jews in concentration camps ultimately persecutes the spirit of American Jews whose relatives were executed. The history of the Holocaust should not only be remembered but also documented so that its causes and its reality are better understood. A few American Holocaust monuments have been built, but as memorials, they can only commemorate the past. American Jews felt that a deeper probing of meaning was necessary, and they have begun the task of articulating this dark chapter in human history.

Throughout the United States local Holocaust centers are being established to account fully for this tragic chapter in history. Two themes are consistently woven together in these centers. They include a historical museum and also function as educational centers. Photographs, ghetto scenes, prison artwork, and artifacts from the camps provide historical evidence of crimes against humanity. Many of these museums are arranged to tell the full story of the Holocaust. The historical roots of anti-Semitism are presented to demonstrate that the ultimate horror began long before the Second World War. Prewar abuses under the Third Reich are then used to demonstrate the withering away of human rights. Finally, the horror of the concentration camps is told and some form of commemoration is made for those who were killed. These museums do clarify the past, but founders of these centers thought that continuing education was also necessary to further understanding of the inhumane principles behind the Holocaust. The centers provide films, libraries, educational seminars, and other means to enlighten those who want to know more. As a research center, oral histories from living survivors are being gathered to probe more deeply into the past. As part of their services, living survivors can come and receive psychological care which they are unable to obtain elsewhere.[6]

Humanitarianism is expressed in these centers by contradicting myths, having philosophical debates over history and human decisions made within it, and caring for living survivors. These centers are open to Jews and non-Jews alike, and their active presence prevents the Holocaust from being forgotten. Mere remembrance is insufficient, because the greater aim of Holocaust centers is to educate people so that society will not repeat crimes against humanity under any circumstances.

The dual themes of history and education in Holocaust Centers are exemplified by the Martyrs Memorial and Museum to the Holocaust in Los Angeles, California. Upon entering the center, visitors see people studying and doing research in a small library thoroughly filled with books and documents. In nearby administrative offices, workers are constantly involved in aiding and informing visitors to the center. The museum presents a short history of the Holocaust along with commemorative art. In the very center of the main display space is a model of the Sobibor death camp. A guide explains how Jews were unknowingly led through this factory line of death. Artifacts, such as the unforgettable striped prison suit, are displayed to convey how prisoners were forced to live. There is a seminar space where people can gather to view films and to discuss Holocaust history. One of the most significant historical artifacts is a symbol of the horror. On one wall of the main display room, the remains from a bolt of cloth show an uncut sheet of the yellow stars that Jews were forced to wear under the Nazi tyranny. Row after row of identical stars vividly conveys the message that to the Nazis all Jews were identical and worthy of nothing. The mass-manufactured stars symbolize the mass manufacture of the false belief. This small sheet captures this Holocaust center's entire purpose. The center exists to prevent the systematic development of inhumane ideology by learning history through humanitarian education.

The themes of history and humanitarian education are spiritually joined in the center's Martyrs Memorial to commemorate Holocaust victims. At its entranceway, the memorial begins with an inscription in English and Hebrew from Psalm 30:1 which says: "I WILL EXTOL THEE, O LORD; FOR THOU HAST LIFTED ME UP, AND HAST NOT MADE MY FOES TO REJOICE OVER ME." Once inside visitors immediately realize that they are in a memorial that represents the cattle cars which were used to haul Jews to the concentration camps. The wooden slats along the cars' walls are marked with commemorative plaques for particular people that close friends wish to remember. Interspersed among these plaques are ones which simply but piercingly say "UNKNOWN CHILD." the unavoidable, disconcerting fact is that while some victims are known, many remain unnamed, and of these, many were defenseless children. After leaving these cattle carriers, visitors enter a memorial chapel. At its front is a crypt, and at the crypt's center is a black marble sarcophagus above a pit that represents a grave. Above the

7.2 Memorial Room at Martyrs Memorial and Museum of the Holocaust, Los Angeles, California (Author's Collection)

sarcophagus is a shallow urn holding six lights commemorating the 6 million who were killed in the Holocaust. The floor has a radial pattern leading to the sarcophagus, and small plaques with the names of all the concentration camps are placed on the floor and surround the sarcophagus. Behind the sarcophagus is an altar bounded by Hebrew numbers on two vertical spaces to symbolize the Ten Commandments. At the center is a yellow Star of David surrounded by a chrome pipe arch interlaced with barbed wire. Above the altar are iron bars with a skylight above this encagement. The altar space articulates the Holocaust's inhumanity, but more importantly, it conveys the perseverance of the Jewish faith to survive under terror and persecution. From the cattle car memorial to the crypt, visitors are engaged in a dialectic between historical inhumanity and humanitarian remembrance.

The Martyrs Memorial and Museum not only represents fully how the Holocaust should be remembered but also indicates local limitations. Its library, museum, and memorial are a combined statement that people must study the past, see the physical evidence of history, and value the past through thoughtful commemoration. One advantage of Holocaust centers is also a disadvantage. They are primarily local institutions. City and even regional residents have access to them, but many people live too far from these centers located in major metropolitan cities. Moreover, there are limits to what a local center can accomplish. This is especially true considering the expense of maintaining a comprehensive museum and library as well as focusing the American public's attention on the Holocaust.

The United States Holocaust Memorial Museum in Washington, D.C., is being built to bring national attention to the Holocaust. The national center has three distinct aims. First, it is to be an in-depth museum which fully documents the Holocaust. Second, as an educational institution, the center will be a clearinghouse of historical documents, and will provide workshops, and encourage scholarly study. Last, the Holocaust Memorial is responsible for seeing that the Days of Remembrance of the Victims of the Holocaust are commemorated as approved by the U.S. Congress in 1979.[7] When completed, this Holocaust Memorial will be a sacred statement of humanity on national hallowed ground. The Holocaust as a historical experience beyond U.S. boundaries will symbolically become part of what the nation is obligated to remember, inhumanity to humanity.

The dedication ceremony in 1983 for the Holocaust Memorial, which is to open in 1989, helped gain public attention for how war can be used as the means for crimes greater than aggression. Numerous speeches were made by survivors who recalled the horror of prison life and witnessed the unjustifiable killing in the execution factories. Second-generation Jews accounted for the pain that they suffer by having their heritage stripped from them, as if relatives were nothing more than anonymous human beings. Amidst all these vivid accounts, it was U.S. Vice President George Bush who perhaps best addressed the critical importance of the United States Holocaust Memorial Museum and Education Center when he spoke officially for all Americans:

Remember, that from the whispers from those lost in the Holocaust, the world must not repeat the hate; we must remember instead to teach tolerance, to teach respect and dignity for every man, regardless of race, color or creed.

The Holocaust Memorial Museum will house this lesson you bring here with you today. Yes, it will document the horrible, the unmentionable. Yes, it will point the blame. And it will credit the saviors. But, most of all, it will, because of you, teach. This museum will show what can happen when humanitarian goals are forsaken and the hellish forces that emanate when an Adolf Hitler comes to power.

The Holocaust serves as a universal warning. It is not to be sentimentalized; not abstracted. Its impact must not be diluted. The Holocaust is no metaphor; it is truth.[8]

All people who have been mistreated as warriors or victims in war need to be remembered as a warning for the future. Even though the wars in Korea and Vietnam produced no clear victory, Americans have grown accustomed to being victors, and they have often seen themselves as virtuous because of it. But the concern for humanitarianism goes beyond victory and defeat. It is the recognition that all war deeds are subject to critique regardless of the merits of engaging in war.

Past wars are often questioned through the medium of art. A multitude of war art in specific public and military museums reflects past American endeavors.[9] While most of these works glorify the past rather than questioning it, art is often also used as social criticism. Rather than merely reflecting on war, some artists openly challenge accepted premises about war. Their art is a philosophical critique of the past, and humanitarian concerns are their points of focus. Prison camp art may be seen as critique, but such works typically are ledgers of past wrongdoings more than an interpretation of them. The most famous example of art as critique of war is probably Pablo Picasso's *Guernica*, which he painted as a protest against Nazi involvement in the Spanish War of 1936. Equivalent expressions have been created by American artists who seriously question the past. Art often criticizes war by demonstrating its inhumanity.

Roger Shimomura was interned as a boy in the Japanese-American Relocation Center at Minidoka, Idaho, and his painting reflects upon prison life there. Instead of relying upon his own memories, he has used the diaries his grandmother kept before, during, and after being in Minidoka. Using passages from her diaries, Shimomura created a series of paintings which interprets prison life. Each painting accounts for a specific entry from the diary for a given day. Rather than making prison life timeless, he portrays it as time actually spent. These scenes are interpreted using traditional Japanese painting techniques, known as ukiyo-e. Shimomura's painting *July 25, 1942* demonstrates the subtle messages that he attempts to convey. The diary entry for the painting is: "They said on Monday we are to bring all our books that are written in Japanese to the main office. Fortunately this will not inconvenience me as I only brought a Bible and some religious books."[10]

Shimomura's grandmother is portrayed as a member of two cultures who has been victimized by one of them. She wears the traditional Japanese hairstyle and kimono. Her perspective is both Western and Eastern as she holds a Bible to symbolize the West and is symbolically framed by a traditional Japanese screen. The mixture of these symbols depicts the cultural crossovers which typify Japanese-Americans. But in the far distance behind the screen is a barbed wire fence which symbolizes prison life. The intertwining of cultural cues—the Japanese dress and the Bible— suggests how his grandmother was forced to turn inward to find meaning in life; the fence shows the physical limitations which were imposed by prison life. The physical prison seems to be echoed by a kind of personal prison. Inhumanity is not shouted out, but it is expressed through little events, such as checking books to ferret out enemies among a people who never were a

7.3 *July 25, 1942* by Roger Shimomura (Photograph by Roger Shimomura)

threat. Shimomura's painting demonstrates that victimization can be subtle as well as blatant.

Artistic interpretations of war can be about how it is memorialized. No other artist has critiqued the American war memorial as vividly as Edward Kienholtz. As an antiwar statement Kienholtz sculpted *The Portable War Memorial*. When read from left to right, the sculpture presents three successive themes. The first one portrays traditional American symbols of patriotism—an "I WANT YOU" Uncle Sam poster and a sculpture group recreating the scene of the Iwo Jima flag-raising. The second scene has a blackboard with the names of some 475 countries which no longer exist. Attached to it is an inverted cross with an American eagle on the vertical

7.4 *The Portable War Memorial* by Edward Kienholtz, Ludwig Museum, Cologne, West Germany (Courtesy of the Rheinische Bildarchiv, Cologne)

brace, and on the horizontal portion of the cross is the inscription: "A PORTABLE WAR MEMORIAL COMMEMORATING V___ DAY, 19___." This center section's theme is remembrance, but it is offered as a challenge. The names of countries represent what we have forgotten, and the inscribed, inverted cross with an American eagle tells the viewer that Americans are willing to honor war but do not remember the history behind it. The empty blanks in the inscription tell us that we can put in the name of any war at any time without questioning the purpose of war itself. The final scene portrays business as usual. Wars come and go, but Americans are indifferent. What is important in life is eating a hot dog and getting a Coke from a machine. Daily life does not include a questioning of war.[11] To some people, Kienholtz's memorial sculpture may seem cynical, but he is attempting to illustrate how indifference to war is a loss of humanity. The war memorial in critical art can be used to challenge the principles that memorials commemorate, such as justice and honor.

These artists and others like them seek more than to use war as a unique topic for art. They ". . . seek to illuminate . . . and to solidify the broader political movements of which they are integral parts."[12] These works ultimately aim to deal with social justice amidst circumstances of war and peace which the public can accept or ignore. Art is offered as a societal challenge, and humanitarian concerns are the foundation for these visual arguments.

Remembering prejudice and victimization as well as having artful interpretations of war shake people into realizing the inhumanity which wars can so easily provide. Honoring the past is not enough. Yet, war memorials are often limited in what is remembered. Many memorials are justifiably limited to honor. Remembering those who fought is necessary, such as national cemeteries in which war dead are buried. Some people may argue that there are enough memorials to remember past wars. Yet, minority groups still go unrecognized and Japanese-American camps are largely left abandoned. The Holocaust memorial movement, on the other hand, is a good sign that truly terrible instances of inhumanity will not be forgotten. Artful interpretations of war most often glorify the past, and even artists who critique war often do so without a clear understanding of the subject. Others, however, do provide genuine insight, and while the humanitarian critique of past wars has been uneven, this neglect need not continue. People can strive for interpretations of war history that go beyond victory and defeat, and these will enable people to recognize those who suffered from prejudice and victimization. As that knowledge emerges, humanitarian commemoration for all people becomes more possible.

HONOR WITHHELD: THE FUTURE OF WAR AND MEMORIALS

No event in modern times so changed the face of war as when the American B-29 bomber, *Enola Gay*, dropped the atomic bomb on Hiroshima, Japan, to end the Second World War. Before this time, war had consisted largely of long, continuous attacks on cities and battles for territory. Its evolution had involved the introduction of more and more sophisticated weapons to be used at the battlefront. Soldiers dug in to protect themselves and wore special equipment. The bombing of cities was actually found to increase the willingness of the citizens to continue the fight. But all this changed with the dropping of the atomic bomb. A nuclear war on a world scale will be so devastating that civilization as we now know it would come to an end.

The war memorial which embodies the birth of this horror is the Bradley Science Museum in Los Alamos, New Mexico. The atomic bomb was largely developed at Los Alamos, and it was actually tested there before being used on Japan. Casings of the two bombs used at Hiroshima and Nagasaki are on display at the museum. They are childishly referred to as Fat Man and Little Boy. While exhibits do explain their development, the bomb casings are the critical symbols of nuclear warfare. They are quite large, and unknowing visitors could see them simply as big machines; but for those who are aware that they represent the consequences of nuclear war, the bombs' message of destruction is potent.

The overwhelming power of nuclear weapons changes not only the meaning of horror in war but also how it can ultimately be remembered. Past remembrance of inhumane treatment in prison camps and execution factories recognizes those people who died so painfully; but nuclear warfare accomplishes the same inhumane ends with much greater efficiency. Barbed wire fences, gas chambers, and ovens to process victims are pale next to the devastation that would be wrought by a nuclear Holocaust.

Remembrance after a nuclear war would be remembrance by default rather than commemoration. Instead of having a neatly kept memorial park as in Hiroshima, the model of remembrance would be large-scale versions of Oradour-sur-Glane without memorial upkeep or ceremonies. The few survivors would be constantly reminded of the nuclear war by living in rubble without the means provided by civilization to repair the damage. These unreconstructed remains would be a disgraceful testament to the inability of developed nations to arrive at peaceful solutions.

Since World War II, people have come to recognize this potential horror, and they have been both angered and discouraged by it. "Ban the bomb" demonstrations reflect a cry for humanity, and peace institutes have been created to educate societies as a form of prevention against a nuclear war. Amidst these efforts, there is a combined sense of fatalism, criticism, and hope about it all. Youngsters interviewed on the streets of Chicago told Studs Terkel:

LINDA: It used to bother me to think about what happens if the bomb comes and I die and I'm young. It doesn't bother me now, 'cause I'm happy. I figure as long as I'm happy, whatever happens, it happens.

FRANKIE: The bomb is your enemy, 'cause that's the one that's gonna put the hurts on you. You're gonna feel it. (Laughs.) For a little while. Everything hurts for a little while. That's all, man, for a little while.

ETHEL: I wanna see if I'm gonna grow up first. I mean, I might not live to be grown up. 'Cause I don't know when my time is up. I don't know when I'm gonna die yet. I never know if I could die overnight from the bomb or somethin'. So the day wasn't promised to me. (Laughs.) I don't know what may happen, uh, my life weren't promised to me.[13]

Since the bombing of Hiroshima and Nagasaki, nations have so far acknowledged the unthinkable consequences of a nuclear war. But this has not prevented them from engaging in what has come to be called "limited warfare." U.S. involvement in Korea, Vietnam, and more recently in Grenada demonstrates a willingness to engage in war without using the nation's full military potential. These wars employ the tactics of imposing geographical limitations, limiting the war's objectives, and constraining the types of military targets sought and the weaponry used.[14] These restraints not only prevent the complete destruction that would result from a nuclear war but also enable war itself to continue to be used as a partial means to confront political problems. But these limitations also mean that, even for a world power like the United States, victory itself becomes limited. There are seldom clear winners in these highly constrained conflicts.

Limited warfare has reshaped how war memory can be commemorated.

There are few large memorials for such wars, and there are fewer casualties to be remembered. The Tomb of the Unknown Soldier symbolically unites all those who have fought and died in American wars, and Korea and Vietnam have been explicitly remembered there. Yet smaller wars, such as Grenada, are forgotten. They may receive a small local commemoration, but they have not become part of national remembrance. The issue is not that all those who fought in these wars should be honored but that what can be honored has changed. Such wars are now euphemistically referred to as police actions, and while people are made aware of those who died, they are often less willing to honor those who fought. American limited warfare has so far resulted in a stalemate in Korea, a loss in Vietnam, and a questionable victory in Grenada. Americans tend not to see these wars as wars of justice which resolve conflicts. Veterans and those who gave their lives in these wars are often given lower status than those who fought in the world wars, although they were just as courageous. Honor is sometimes withheld because the American people question the humanitarian issues behind these wars at a philosophical level or become shallowly disgruntled when a clear victory was not attained. The political acceptance of feasible war has muddled the clarity of commemorating those who fought. The American people have found it difficult to honor soldiers from wars for questionable causes and with no clear results.

Regardless of the changes brought about by limited warfare and the threat of nuclear war, war memorials of all types will continue to be part of the American scene. Heightened concern over the expression of humanitarian values will bring these remembrances under more criticism, but this questioning will not eliminate businesses which rely on war-related artifacts, nor will it stop collectors or re-creationists from participating in their pastimes. Pluralism in a democracy allows people to pursue their own interests when such pursuits do not interfere with the freedom of others. The gap between sacred memorials with a humanitarian purpose—the highest level of social purpose—and the identity of nonsacred memorials—the lowest level of social purpose—will remain. The conflict is one of consciousness, not legality, and it is a conflict which leads proponents of each group to question the other. Can those who use war for collections, reenactments, and games realize the inhumanity of war? Can people who believe that humanitarian concerns should prevail see that not all collectors and re-creationists embrace war just as a personal fantasy? The answers can be yes, but when the contemplation of past wars is not informed by humanitarian principles, there is insufficient consciousness to permit people to judge either political history or current events. As a result, they are unprepared to critique or to fully appreciate how war is remembered through memorials, whether sacred or nonsacred.

To understand fully how war memorials create and symbolize meaning in American life, they must be seen politically. Wars are drastic political and moral acts, and history before and within these conflicts is inextricably linked to how they are remembered. War memorials are political memory, sacred or not. The expression of this meaning in everyday life can be quite naive. Sacred places of remembrance can be reduced to simplistic notions of American heritage. Although war memorials may appear to have little impact on the life of the nation, they give meaning to place which we may accept without question. To ignore a nation's history is to ignore its political evolution. To ignore war memorials is to ignore how political history symbolizes and morally justifies the American landscape, rightly or wrongly.

NOTES

CHAPTER ONE: WAR MEMORIALS AS SYMBOLIC MESSAGES

1. Bernard Barber comments that college scholarships have been established as war memorials. This nonspatial commemoration is not considered here since the aim of this discussion is to relate memorials to the built environment. See Barber, Bernard. "Place, Symbol and Utilitarian Functions in War Memorials," *Social Forces*, vol. 28, 1949, p. 67.

2. Tuan, Yi-Fu. "The Significance of the Artifact," *Geographical Review*, vol. 74, no. 4, 1980, pp. 465-66.

3. Whittick, Arnold. *War Memorials*. London: Country Life, 1946, pp. 6-8.

4. Ibid., p. 12.

5. Ibid., p. 7.

6. Ibid., p. 13.

7. Ibid., p. 8.

8. Ibid., p. 13; Fletcher, Bannister, *A History of Architecture*. New York: Scribners, 1961, pp. 225-27.

9. Fletcher, *History of Architecture,* pp. 221-25.

10. Curl, James Stevens. *A Celebration of Death*. New York: Scribners, 1980, pp. 87, 96-97.

11. Whittick, *History of Architecture,* pp. 71, 93.

12. Durkheim, Emile. *The Elementary Forms of the Religious Life*. New York: The Free Press, 1965, p. 52.

13. Eliade, Mircea. *The Sacred and the Profane*. New York: Harcourt, Brace and World, 1959, pp. 23-24.

14. Robinson, Brian S. "Some Fragmented Forms of Space," *Annals of the Association of American Geographers,* vol. 67, no. 4, 1977, p. 551.

15. Barber, "Place, Symbol and Utilitarian Functions," p. 332.

16. Ibid., p. 330; Lethaby, W.R. *Form in Civilization.* London: Oxford University Press, 1957, pp. 46-53.

17. Mayo, James M. "Resymbolization of a Symbol." *Dimensions.* vol. 2, no. 2, 1981, pp. 14-17.

18. Hubbard, William. "A Meaning for Monuments." *The Public Interest,* no. 74, Winter 1984, p. 28.

19. Coombs, Rose B. *Before Endeavors Fade.* London: Battle of Britain International, 1983.

20. Ibid., pp. 61, 92.

21. Tuan, "The Significance of the Artifact," p. 463.

22. Alexander, Christopher, et al. *A Pattern Language.* New York: Oxford University Press, 1977, p. 132.

23. Jackson, J. B. *Landscapes.* (Edited by E. H. Zube.) Amherst, MA: University of Massachusetts Press, 1970, p. 158.

CHAPTER TWO: WAR MEMORIALS IN THE LANDSCAPE: EVOCATIONS OF HISTORY

1. Jackson, John B. *Discovering the Vernacular Landscape.* New Haven, CT: Yale University Press, 1984, p. 152.

2. Tuan, Yi-Fu. *Segmented Worlds and Self.* Minneapolis, MN: University of Minnesota Press, 1982, p. 169.

3. Ibid., p. 167.

4. Ruesch, Jurgen, and Weldon Kees. *Nonverbal Communication.* Berkeley, CA: University of California Press, 1956, pp. 142-43.

5. Rapoport, Amos. *House Form and Culture.* Englewood Cliffs, NJ: Prentice-Hall, 1969, p. 54.

6. Mayo, James M. "Propaganda with Design: Environmental Dramaturgy in the Political Rally," *Journal of Architectural Education.* vol. 34, no. 2, 1978, pp. 24-27, 32.

7. Lyndhurst, Joseph. *Military Collectibles.* New York: Crescent Books, 1983, p. 6.

8. Wright, Talmadge. "Marketing Culture, Simulation and the Aesthetization of Work and War," Paper presented at the Popular Culture Conference of the American Culture Association, 1985, pp. 4-5.

9. Ibid., pp. 13-18.

10. Jackson, *Discovering the Vernacular Landscape,* p. 27.

11. Clay, Grady. *Close Up: How to Read the American City.* Chicago: University of Chicago Press, 1973, pp. 172-73.

12. Lowenthal, David. "Age and Artifact: Dilemmas of Appreciation," in D. W. Meinig (ed.) *The Interpretation of Ordinary Landscapes.* New York: Oxford University Press, 1979, p. 111.

13. Reed, John Shelton. "The Heart of Dixie: An Essay in Folk Geography," *Social Forces,* vol. 54, no. 4, 1976, pp. 933-44.

14. Lowenthal, "Age and Artifact," p. 110.

15. Widener, Ralph W. *Confederate Monuments: Symbols of the South and the War Between the States.* Washington D.C.: Andromeda Associates, 1982, pp. 86, 158.

16. Ibid., pp. ix-xi.

17. Gay, Vernon, and Marilyn Event. *Discovering Pittsburgh and Sculpture.* Pittsburgh, PA: University of Pittsburgh Press, 1983, pp. 26, 147, 282, 288, 293, 295, 296, 301.

18. Widener, *Confederate Monuments,* pp. 277-79, 281.

19. Goode, James M. *The Outdoor Sculpture of Washington D.C.: A Comprehensive Historical Guide.* Washington, D.C.: Smithsonian Institution Press, 1974, pp. 278-79, 283, 384.

20. Lowenthal, "Age and Artifact," p. 123.

21. Steinburg, Rolf, and Manfred Hamm. *Dead Tech.* San Francisco, CA: Sierra Club Books, 1982, pp. 89-102.

22. Ibid., p. 90.

23. As a boy, the author distinctly remembers the scene of B-29 nose shells being used as temporary greenhouses. At the time, it was both a joy and sadness. One could actually take a glimpse of a part of the real thing, but it was frustrating not to experience the whole aircraft, especially for a youngster who loved planes.

24. Allan, Douglas A. "Ch. 1: the Museum and Its Functions," in L.H. Evans (ed.). *The Organization of Museums: Practical Advice.* Paris: UNESCO Press, 1978, pp. 13-27.

25. Manchester, William. *American Caesar: Douglas MacArthur 1880-1964.* New York: Dell Publishing Co., 1982, p. 842.

26. Cary, Norman Miller. *Guide to U.S. Army Museums and Historical Sites.* Washington, D.C.: U.S. Government Printing Office, 1975. This book is the most comprehensive public guide in the United States which describes the location and contents of these museums.

27. Gleed, Edward C. "The Story of America's Black Air Force," *Tony Brown's Journal,* January/March 1983, pp. 4-11. The article gives an overall history of those airmen who have come to be known as the Black Eagles.

28. Jackson, John B. *The Necessity for Ruins.* Amherst, MA: University of Massachusetts Press, 1980, p. 12.

29. Ibid., p. 27.

30. Lowenthal, "Age and Artifact," p. 124.

31. Relph, Edward. *Place and Placelessness.* London: Pion, 1976, p. 85.

32. Ibid., p. 87.

33. Ibid., p. 95.

34. Davis, William C. *Gettysburg: The Story Behind the Scenery.* Las Vegas, NV: K.C. Publications, 1983, p. 42.

35. These and following quotes are from tourist pamphlets provided by these commercial museums.

36. Tuan, *Segmented Worlds and Self,* p. 7.

37. Jackson, *The Necessity for Ruins,* p. 102.

38. Warner, Samuel Bass. *The Living and the Dead.* New Haven, CT: Yale University Press, 1959, p. 266.

39. Bryan, C.D.B. "Memorial Day in Stony Creek, Conn.," *New York Times,* May 30, 1977, p. 15.

40. Davis, *Gettysburg,* p. 33.

41. Miller, Tom. "After Delay, Vets Pay Their Tribute," *The Kansas City Times,* June 7, 1984, pp. A1, A12.

42. Davis, *Gettysburg,* p. 34.

43. Koury, Michael J. *To Consecrate This Ground: The Custer Battlefield 1876-1976.* Ft. Collins, CO: Old Army Press, 1978, pp. 43-45.

44. Norton, Bill. "Byron's Wars," *Kansas City Star Sunday Magazine,* September 29, 1985, pp. 1, 12-17.

45. Jackson, *The Necessity for Ruins,* p. 102.

46. Lowenthal, "The American Scene," *Geographical Review,* vol. 58, no. 1, 1968, p. 76.

47. Tuan, *Topophilia.* Englewood Cliffs, NJ: Prentice-Hall, 1974, pp. 100-2.

48. Tuan, Yi-Fu. *Space and Place.* Minneapolis, MN: University of Minnesota Press, 1977, p. 159.

CHAPTER THREE: MONUMENTS TO VICTORY AS JUSTICE

1. Kammen, Michael. *A Season of Youth.* New York: Knopf, 1978, p. 37.

2. Warner, Samuel Bass. *The Living and the Dead.* New Haven: Yale University Press, 1959, pp. 133-34.

3. Kammen, *A Season of Youth,* p. 37.

4. Lancaster, Bruce. *The Revolution.* New York: American Heritage Publishing, 1958, pp. 64-65.

5. Lyndon, Donlyn, "Public Buildings: Symbols Qualified by Experience," *The Public Interest,* no. 74, Winter 1984, p. 84. The Boston Massacre is also remembered in the Boston Commons with a bronze plaque illustrating the scene, especially Crispus Attucks who was black and the first soldier killed by the British. Touching the hand of Crispus Attucks on the plaque is considered locally to bring good luck. See Weston, George F., Jr. *Boston Ways: High, By and Folk.* Boston, MA: Beacon Press, 1957, p. 136.

6. Boatner, Mark M. *Landmarks of the American Revolution.* Harrisburg, PA:Stockpole Press, 1973, pp. 142-43.

7. Lancaster, *The Revolution,* p. 101.

8. Kent, Louise A. *Village Greens of New England.* New York: Barrows and Company, 1948, p. 109.

9. Ibid., p. 110.

10. Ibid., p. 115.

11. In the summer, the city of Lexington has young guides available on the green to enable visitors to learn its history. The author's guide told the tale about the sculptor for the Minuteman statue.

12. Kent, *Village Greens,* p. 109.

13. Lancaster, *The Revolution,* p. 20.

14. Kammen, *A Season of Youth,* p. 29.

15. Ketchum, Richard M. *Decisive Day: The Battle for Bunker Hill.* Garden City, NY: Doubleday, 1962, pp. xiv-xv.

16. Boatner, *Landmarks of the American Revolution,* p. 148.

17. Morris, Richard B. *Independence: A Guide to Independence National Historic Park.* Washington, D.C.: National Park Service, Division of Publications, 1982, pp. 59-60.

18. Relph, Edward. *Place and Placelessness.* London: Pion, 1976, pp. 101-3.

19. Law, Frank P. "The Washington Memorial Chapel." Valley Forge, PA, unpublished pamphlet, n.d., p. 2.

20. Ibid., p. 5.

21. Sternlieb, George. "Cities: Fantasy and Reality," *Journal of Architectural and Planning Research.* vol. 1, no. 3, 1984, p. 211.

22. Goode, James M. *The Outdoor Sculpture of Washington, D.C.: A Comprehensive Historical Guide.* Washington, D.C.: Smithsonian Institution Press, 1974, pp. 53, 62.

23. Klein, Milton M. "Commemorating the American Revolution: The Bicentennial and Its Predecessors," *New York History,* vol. 58, no. 1, 1977, p. 274.

24. Ibid., p. 260.

25. Lemisch, Jesse. "Bicentennial Schlock," *The New Republic,* vol. 175, November 6, 1976, pp. 21-23.

26. Kammen, *A Season of Youth,* pp. xv-xvi.

27. Fishel, Lester H. "The Past Invades the Present," *New York History,* vol. 58, no. 1, 1977, pp. 4-15.

28. To review a variety of Doughboy style memorials, see Friedlander, Lee. *The American Monument.* New York: Eakins Foundation Press, 1976.

29. Curl, James Stevens. *A Celebration of Death.* New York: Charles Scribner's Sons, 1980, pp. 3-9.

30. Craven, Wayne. *Sculpture in America.* New York: Cornwall Books, 1984, p. 491; and Price, Willadene. *Gutzon Borglum: Artist and Patriot.* Chicago: Rand McNally, 1961, pp. 122-23.

31. Catanese, Anthony J., and James C. Snyder. *Introduction to Urban Planning.* New York: McGraw-Hill, 1979, p. 21.

32. Scott, Mel. *American City Planning Since 1890.* Berkeley, CA: University of California Press, 1969, p. 45.

33. Ibid., p. 45.

34. Leary, Edward A. *Indianapolis: The Story of a City.* Indianapolis: Bobbs-Merrill, 1971, p. 191. George Kessler, a well-known planner during the City Beautiful movement, helped in selecting the Memorial Plaza Site and designing its street boulevards.

35. Ibid., pp. 191-92.

36. Madison, James H. *Indiana Through Tradition and Change.* Indianapolis: Indiana Historical Society, 1982, p. 39.

37. The author would like to thank Thomas V. Hull, librarian for the National Headquarters of the American Legion, for historical insight to veteran's attitudes toward the Indiana War Memorial.

38. Brown, Genevieve, et al. *Indiana: 1930.* Indianapolis, IN: Board of Public Printing, 1930, p. 79.

39. Ibid., p. 80.

40. Ibid., pp. 82-83.

41. Mayo, James M. "Resymbolization of a Symbol," *Dimensions,* vol. 2, no. 2,

1981, pp. 14-18. In Kansas City, Missouri, the Liberty Memorial has had a similar transformation of meaning to a city symbol.

42. Wilson, William H. *The City Beautiful Movement in Kansas City.* Columbia, MO: University of Missouri Press, 1964, p. 119.

43. McPherson, J. E. *The Liberty Memorial.* Kansas City, MO: Spencer Press, 1929, pp. 34-36.

44. Ibid., p. 28.

45. Ibid., p. 25.

46. Mayo, "Resymbolization of a Symbol," p. 15.

47. Federal Writers Project. *San Francisco: A Guide to the Bay and Its Cities.* New York: Hastings House, 1973, pp. 159-66.

48. *Tennessean Rotogravure*, August 26, 1928, p. 28.

49. Emerson, William, "Bridges as Memorials," *Architectural Forum*, vol. 45, no. 6, 1926, pp. 337-44.

50. Magonigle, H. Van Buren. "Architects—War Memorials—Competitions," *Journal of the American Institute of Architects*, vol. 8, no. 4, 1920, p. 163.

51. Swarthout, Egerton. "Memorial Buildings," *Architectural Forum*, vol. 45, no. 6, 1926, p. 330.

52. Whittick, Arnold. *War Memorials.* London: Country Life, 1946, p. 3.

53. McPherson, *The Liberty Memorial*, pp. 13-14.

54. Whittick, *War Memorials*, pp. 1-2.

55. Goode, *Outdoor Sculpture of Washington, D.C.*, p. 133.

56. Ibid., p. 137.

57. Ibid., p. 207.

58. Ibid., p. 208.

59. Ibid., pp. 462-63.

60. Ibid., p. 200.

61. Hinkel, John V. *Arlington: Monument to Heroes.* Englewood Cliffs, NJ: Prentice-Hall, 1965, p. 140.

62. Ibid., pp. 138-39.

63. Hinkel, *Arlington*, p. 136.

64. Pershing, John, J. "Our National War Memorials in Europe," *National Geographic Magazine*, vol. 65, no. 1, 1934, pp. 1-2. For a historical analysis of the commission's work on World War I memorials, see: Grossman, Elizabeth G. "Architecture for a Public Client: The Monuments and Chapels of the American Battle Monuments Commission," *Journal of the Society of Architectural Historians*, vol. 43, May 1984, pp. 119-43.

65. Cret, Paul P. "Memorials—Columns, Shafts, Cenotaphs and Tablets," *Architectural Forum*, vol. 45, no. 6, 1926, p. 333.

66. Pershing, "Our National Memorials in Europe," p. 5.

67. Ibid., p. 17.

68. Ibid., p. 10.

69. Coombs, Rose B. *Before Endeavors Fade.* London: Battle of Britain International, 1983, pp. 70-73.

70. Ibid., pp. 85-87.

71. Ibid., pp. 54-63, 132-41. There are some exceptions for American memorials. Belleau Wood behind the Aisne-Marne Chapel, Mont Faucon Monument, and Sommepy Monument all have some remaining ruins and trenches.

72. Whittick, *War Memorials*, p. 40.

73. De Busscher, J. M. *Les Folies de L'industrie*. Brussels: Archives d'Architecture Moderne, 1981, p. 19.

74. Ibid., p. 77.

75. Ibid., p. 10.

76. Curl, *A Celebration of Death*, p. 324; Whittick, *War Memorials*, p. 41.

77. Whittick, *War Memorials*, p. 41.

78. Mayo, "Resymbolization of a Symbol," p. 15.

79. Fussell, Paul. *The Boy Scout Handbook and Other Observations*. New York: Oxford University Press, 1982, p. 231.

80. American Battle Monuments Commission. *Cambridge American Cemetery and Memorial*, 1979, p. 20.

81. North, Thomas. "In Proud Remembrance: American Memorials and Military Cemeteries of World War II," *National Sculpture Review*, vol. 14, no. 1, 1965, p. 5.

82. American Battle Monuments Commission, *Cambridge American Cemetery and Memorial*, pp. 18-19. To review other pamphlets by the Commission on World War II memorials, see: *Rhone American Cemetery and Memorial*, 1958; *Honolulu Memorial National Cemetery of the Pacific*, 1964; *Florence American Cemetery and Memorial*, 1977; *Henri-Chapelle American Cemetery and Memorial*, 1977; *Ardennes American Cemetery and Memorial*, 1978; *Lorraine American Cemetery and Memorial*, 1978; *Sicily-Rome American Cemetery and Memorial*, 1978; *Brittany American Cemetery and Memorial*, 1980; *Manila American Cemetery and Memorial*, 1980; *Epinal American Cemetery and Memorial*, 1982; and *Luxembourg American Cemetery and Memorial*, 1983.

83. American Battle Monuments Commission, *Cambridge American Cemetery and Memorial*, p. 22.

84. For a basic understanding of parterre design in the French tradition, see: Thacker, Christopher. "The Formal French Garden," *The History of Gardens*. Berkeley, CA: University of California Press, 1979, pp. 138-45.

85. American Battle Monuments Commission. *Rhone American Cemetery and Memorial*, p. 10.

86. Many chapels were originally designed with a Christian motif. To embrace the Jewish faith, Ten Commandment tablets have been added and are typically set to one side of the altar. In some World War I chapels, soldiers' names on chapel walls were prefaced by symbols of high decorations which they received. For example in the Somme Chapel, some soldiers have a Distinguished Service Cross carved and enameled before their name. After World War II, honoring valor was focused on remembering Medal of Honor winners. On Walls of the Missing, a recipient's name has the Medal of Honor star before it. The biggest change was that Medal of Honor winners each received a specially designed cross inlaid with gold leaf to mark their graves.

87. North, "In Proud Remembrance," pp. 7-24.

88. Curl, *A Celebration of Death*. New York: Scribners, 1980, p. 325.

89. American Battle Monuments Commission. *Honolulu National Cemetery of the Pacific*, pp. 21, 24.

90. Craig, Lois. *The Federal Presence: Architecture, Politics and Symbols in United States Government Building*. Cambridge: MIT Press, 1978, p. 515.

91. Sulzberger, C.L. *World War II*. New York: Simon and Schuster, 1966, p. 154.

92. Slackman, Michael. *Remembering Pearl Harbor: The Story of the USS Arizona Memorial*. Honolulu, HI: Arizona Memorial Museum Association, 1984, p. 63.

93. Ibid., p. 52.

94. Ibid., p. 73.

95. Ibid., p. 74.

96. Ibid., p. 86. Slackman provides an excellent account of the trials and tribulations of getting congressional approval for a war memorial.

97. Goode, *The Outdoor Sculpture of Washington, D.C.:* pp. 409-10.

98. Ibid., p. 184.

99. Ibid., p. 199.

100. Ibid., pp. 191-92.

101. Ibid., p. 189.

102. Fussell, *The Boy Scout Handbook,* p. 233.

103. Editorial Staff. "Living Memorials," *Architectural Forum,* vol. 82, no. 8, 1945, p. 141.

104. Hudnut, Joseph. "The Monument Does Not Remember," *Atlantic,* September 1945, p. 58.

105. Doezema, Marianne, and June Hargrove. *The Public Monument and Its Audience*. Cleveland, OH: Cleveland Museum of Art, 1977, pp. 45-47.

CHAPTER FOUR: MONUMENTS TO VICTORY AS MANIFEST DESTINY

1. Horsman, Reginald. *The War of 1812*. New York: Alfred A. Knopf, 1969, p. 268.

2. Blum, John M., et al. *A History of the United States: The National Experience*. New York: Harcourt, Brace and World, 1963, p. 183.

3. Horsman, *The War of 1812,* p. 85.

4. Ibid., pp. 100-102.

5. Kelleran, Ann. *Old Fort Niagara: Adventures in Western New York History: Vol. I*. Buffalo, NY: Buffalo Historical Society, 1960, p. 15.

6. Doezema, Marianne, and June Hargrove. *The Public Monument and Its Audience*. Cleveland, OH: Cleveland Museum of Art, 1977, p. 23. A bronze replica is now in Cleveland along Lake Erie.

7. Oliver Hazard Perry is also remembered fervently in Rhode Island. He lived in Newport, and his house is marked as a historic structure. There is a commemorative statue of him at the State Capitol in Providence. In addition, a statue of Perry stands in Buffalo, New York, at the Front, a local park.

8. In Vergennes, Vermont, there is a Greek classical monument with Doric columns which commemorates Thomas MacDonough. If there is any symbolism to derive from it, MacDonough is honored with a Greek temple to commemorate him as the classical hero.

9. There are lesser known memorials from the War of 1812 in New York at Sackett's Harbor, Oswego, and Ogdenburg.

10. Horsman, *The War of 1812,* pp. 194-214.

11. Rukert, Norman G. *Fort McHenry: Home of the Brave*. Baltimore, MD: Bodine and Associates, 1983, pp. 91-93.

12. Papenfuse, Edward C., et al. *Maryland: A New Guide to the Old Line State.* Baltimore: Johns Hopkins University Press, 1976, p. 410. Other memorials not discussed here are the Aquila Randall Monument and the Wells McComas Monument. See Papenfuse et al., pages 37 and 414.

13. Ibid., p. 396.

14. Ibid., p. 416.

15. Ibid., p. 369.

16. Alexander, Robert L. *The Architecture of Maximilian Godefroy.* Baltimore: Johns Hopkins University Press, 1974, pp. 101-12.

17. Although the Chalmette Monument is simple in design, the history of its construction is a saga of struggle. See Haber, Leonard V., *The Battle of New Orleans and Its Monument.* New Orleans, LA: Louisiana Landmarks Society, 1983.

18. Huber, Leonard V. *New Orleans: A Pictorial History.* New York: Crown Publishers, 1971, p. 105.

19. Horsman, *The War of 1812,* pp. 215-36.

20. This proposal is documented in the National Park Service's news release entitled: "Monument at Horseshoe Bend 60 Years Old." See p. 4.

21. Hamilton, Virginia V. *Seeing Historic Alabama: Fifteen Guided Tours.* University, AL: University of Alabama Press, 1982, p. 175.

22. This observation was confirmed in January 1984 by the Bureau of Historic Preservation, Department of State, the State of Florida. This agency keeps all records of state historic markers.

23. To review the history of "The Star-Spangled Banner," see Rukert, *Fort McHenry,* pp. 37-48.

24. Goode, James M. *The Outdoor Sculpture of Washington, D.C.* Washington, D.C.: Smithsonian Institution Press, 1974, p. 377.

25. Commission of Control for Texas Centennial Celebrations. *Monuments Commemorating the Centenary of Texas Independence.* Austin, TX: Steck Publishers, 1938, pp. 9-13. This book was a Texas Centennial edition to document what monuments were built for the Texas Revolution, and it is the best single source in identifying these monuments.

26. Federal Writers Project. *Texas: A Guide to the Lone Star State.* New York: Hastings House, 1940, pp. 330-32.

27. Commission of Control for Texas Centennial Celebrations, pp. 84-85.

28. Ibid., pp. 86-87.

29. Ibid., pp. 77-83.

30. Stilgoe, John R. *Common Landscape of America, 1580 to 1845.* New Haven, CT: Yale University Press, 1982, p. 29.

31. Federal Writers Project. *South Carolina: A Guide to the Palmetto State.* New York: Oxford University Press, 1941, pp. 222-23.

32. Federal Writers Project. *Kentucky: A Guide to the Bluegrass State.* New York: Harcourt, Brace and World, 1939, p. 165.

33. Federal Writers Project. *Utah: A Guide to the State.* New York: Hastings House, 1954, p. 246.

34. Very few local memorials for individuals were found in the Federal Writers Project books on the states. Elizabeth, New Jersey, dedicated a park to its hometown hero, General Winfield B. Scott. In Camden, South Carolina, the Dickinson Monument was built in honor of James Polk Dickinson, colonel of the Palmetto Regiment. A statue of John Drake Sloat is located at the entrance of the

Presidio at Monterey, California, to remember him as the commander of U.S. forces that took Monterey. See Federal Writers Project. *New Jersey: A Guide to Its Past and Present.* New York: Hastings House, 1977, p. 177; *South Carolina: A Guide to the Palmetto State.* New York: Oxford University Press, 1941, p. 180; and *California: A Guide to the Golden State.* New York: Hastings House, 1967, p. 235.

35. California Department of Parks and Recreation. *California Inventory of Historic Resources.* Sacramento, CA: State of California, 1976, pp. 181-82, 185, 187-88.

36. Goode, *Outdoor Sculpture of Washington, D.C.,* pp. 287, 341.

37. U.S. Military Academy. *The West Point Guide.* New Windsor, NY: Commercial Offset Printers, n.d., pp. 37-38.

38. Hinkel, John V. *Arlington: Monument to Heroes.* Englewood Cliffs, NJ: Prentice-Hall, 1965, p. 126.

39. American Battle Monuments Commission. *American Memorials and Overseas Military Cemeteries,* 1983, p. 8.

40. American cemeteries do exist in Italy for those Americans who died in World War II. While Italy was an Axis power, the United States technically defines Italy as a co-belligerent since its people supported the Allied cause immediately after the fall of Mussolini and after Allied troops had forced out the German forces.

41. The author's source for the old inscription is the American Battle Monuments Commission, March 1985.

42. Brown, Dee. *Bury My Heart at Wounded Knee.* New York: Bantam Books, 1971, p. 8.

43. Brandon, William. *Indians.* New York: American Heritage Publishing, 1961, p. 362.

44. Ferris, Robert C. *Soldier and Brave.* Washington, D.C.: U.S. Department of the Interior, 1971, pp. 45-49.

45. Jackson, J. B. *The Necessity for Ruins.* Amherst: University of Massachusetts, 1980, p. 14.

46. Stilgoe, John R. *Common Landscape of America, 1580 to 1845.* New Haven, CT: Yale University Press, 1982, pp. 103-7. Hart, Herbert M. *Tour Guide to Old Western Forts.* Ft. Collins, CO: Old Army Press, 1980.

47. Ferris, *Soldier and Brave,* p. 57.

48. Utley, Robert M. *Fort Davis.* Washington, D.C.: U.S. National Park Service Historical Handbook Services, 1965, p. 27.

49. Ferris, *Soldier and Brave,* pp. 46-47.

50. Ibid., p. 60.

51. Stands in Timber, John, and Margot Liberty. *Cheyenne Memories.* New Haven, CT: Yale University Press, 1967, pp. 203-7.

52. McCollough, Alameda. *The Battle of Tippecanoe: Conflict of Cultures.* Lafayette, IN: Tippecanoe County Historical Association, 1980, pp. 3-7.

53. Ibid., p. 30.

54. DeWall, Robb. *Korczak: Storyteller in Stone.* Crazy Horse, SD: Korczak's Heritage, 1983.

55. National Park Foundation. *The Complete Guide to America's National Parks.* New York: Viking Press, 1981, p. 164; Koury, Michael J. *To Consecrate This Ground: The Custer Battlefield 1876-1976.* Ft. Collins, CO: Old Army Press, 1978, p. 5.

56. Koury, *To Consecrate This Ground,* p. 26.

57. Ibid., pp. 9-45.

58. Blum et al., *A History of the United States,* p. 498.

59. Ibid., p. 500.

60. O'Toole, G.J.A. *The Spanish War.* New York: W. W. Norton, 1984, p. 17.

61. Blum et al., *A History of the United States,* p. 502.

62. Ibid., pp. 497-99.

63. This dilemma did not go unnoticed as a number of American politicians and dignitaries formed the Anti-Imperialist League during the Spanish-American War. See Blum et al., p. 509.

64. Young, Louis Stanley. *Life and Heroic Deeds of Admiral Dewey and Battles in the Philippines.* Philadelphia, PA: Globe Bible Publishing, 1899, pp. 527-44. Young gives a flourished description of all the events surrounding New York City's celebrations for Dewey.

65. Ibid., p. 534; and Craven, Wayne. *Sculpture in America.* New York: Cornwall Books, 1984, p. 479.

66. Federal Writers Project, Ray Bearse, ed. *Vermont: A Guide to the Green Mountain State.* Boston: Houghton Mifflin, 1966, p. 290; and Eastman, John. *Who Lived Here: A Biographical Guide to Homes and Museums.* New York: Facts on File, 1983, p. 64. Personal mementos belonging to Admiral Dewey are now kept by the Vermont Historical Society in its museum collection. While a serious effort by a citizen group to raise money for the Dewey House took place, the preservation movement was not strong in Vermont in 1969. According to the society's librarian, such a campaign five years later would have probably saved the Dewey House.

67. Federal Writers Project. *The Ohio Guide.* New York: Oxford University Press, 1940, p. 224.

68. Trask, David F. *The War with Spain in 1898.* New York: Macmillan, 1981, pp. 135-36.

69. Proctor, Alexander Phimister. *Sculptor in Buckskin: An Autobiography.* Norman, OK: University of Oklahoma Press, 1971, pp. 242-43.

70. Davies, A. Mervyn. *Solon H. Borglum.* Chester, CT: Pequot Press, 1974, pp. 105-10. The O'Neill monument was well accepted and popular among the Rough Riders and President Roosevelt. Aesthetically, it is perhaps the most successful design among all Spanish-American War memorials.

71. Hinkel, *Arlington,* p. 126. It is interesting to note that neither the Rough Riders nor any U.S. troops were commemorated with a monument in Tampa, Florida, which was the debarkation point to Cuba. However, two state historical road markers describe this event. This was confirmed by the Florida State Parks Department in January 1985.

72. Ibid., p. 127.

73. The use of the *Maine*'s anchor for veteran pins was verified by Beulah Cope, Adjutant General for the United Spanish War Veterans in February 1985.

74. Federal Writers Project. *South Carolina: A Guide to the Palmetto State.* New York: Oxford University Press, 1941, p. 223.

75. Federal Writers Project. *Massachusetts: A Guide to the Pilgrim State.* Boston: Houghton Mifflin, 1971, p. 459.

76. Federal Writers Project, *The Ohio Guide,* p. 186.

77. Gay, Vernon, and Marilyn Evert. *Discovering Pittsburgh's Sculpture.*

Pittsburgh, PA: University of Pittsburgh Press, 1983, pp. 18-19, 49-50.

78. Santovenia, Emeterio S. *Libro Commemorativo de La Inauguracion de La Plaza del Maine en La Habana*: Secretario de Obra Publicas, 1928, pp. 130, 147-62; and Roberts, W. Adolphe. *Havana: The Portrait of a City*. New York: Coward-McCann, 1953, p. 190.

79. The removal of the eagle from the Plaza del Maine was confirmed by Professor Emeritus Jose Juan Arrom, Yale University, March 1985.

80. Stern, Robert A. M., Gregory Gilmartin, and John M. Massengale. *New York 1900*. New York: Rizzoli International Publications, 1983, p. 125; and Fried, Frederick, and Edward V. Gillon, Jr. *New York Civic Sculpture: A Pictorial Guide*. New York: Dover Publications, 1976, pp. 100-1.

81. O'Toole, *The Spanish War,* pp. 397-400.

82. Ibid., p. 400.

83. Goode, *Outdoor Sculpture of Washington, D.C.*, p. 194.

84. Federal Writers Project. *Nebraska: A Guide to the Cornhusker State*. New York: Viking Press, 1939, p. 249.

85. Federal Writers Project. *Oregon: The End of the Trail*. Portland, OR: Binfords and Mort, 1940, pp. 217-18.

86. Alden, John D. *The American Steel Navy*. New York: American Heritage Press, 1972, p. 349.

CHAPTER FIVE: MONUMENTS TO DEFEAT

1. Catton, Bruce. *The Civil War*. New York: American Heritage Publishing, 1960, p. 359.

2. Warren, Robert Penn. *The Legacy of the Civil War*. Cambridge: Harvard University Press, 1983, p. 103.

3. Ibid., p. 108.

4. Widener, Ralph W. *Confederate Monuments: Symbols of the South and the War Between the States*. Washington, D.C.: Andromeda Associates, 1982, p. viii.

5. Ibid.

6. Craven, Wayne. *The Sculptures at Gettysburg*. Gettysburg, PA: Eastern Acorn Press, 1982, p. 37.

7. Davis, William C. *Gettysburg: The Story Behind the Scenery*. Las Vegas, NV: KC Publications, 1983, p. 23.

8. Ibid., p. 21.

9. Widener, *Confederate Monuments,* pp. 167-70.

10. Ibid., pp. 125-29. While Mississippi was one of the first states to build a large memorial, many state legislators who were Confederate veterans opposed a monument of any kind in Vicksburg. "They believed that it would be a shame and a disgrace for Mississippi to erect a memorial on federal property to commemorate a Union victory." See Walker, Steve, and David F. Riggs. *Vicksburg Battle Monuments*. Jackson, MS: University Press of Mississippi, 1984, pp. 42-43.

11. Craven, *The Sculptures at Gettysburg,* pp. 19-30; pp. 79-95.

12. Ibid., p. 90.

13. Ibid., p. 91.

14. Walker and Riggs, *Vicksburg Battle Monuments,* pp. 44-45.

15. Ibid., pp. 60-61.

16. Ibid., pp. 32-33.

17. Davis, *Gettysburg,* p. 42.

18. Pantenburg, Leon. "Enough Gunpowder in Vicksburg?" *Vicksburg Evening Post,* July 4, 1983, p. 1.

19. Goldberger, Paul. *The City Observed: New York.* New York: Random House, 1979, p. 223; and Fletcher, Bannister. *A History of Architecture.* New York: Scribners, 1961, p. 139.

20. Goldstone, Harmon H., and Martha Dalrymple. *History Preserved: A Guide to New York Landmarks and Historic Districts.* New York: Simon and Schuster, 1974, p. 409.

21. Wilson, Richard G. *McKim, Mead, and White.* New York: Rizzoli, 1983, pp. 148-51.

22. Doezema, Marianne, and June Hargrove. *The Public Monument and Its Audience.* Cleveland, OH: Cleveland Museum of Art, 1977, pp. 34-38.

23. Ibid., p. 39.

24. Ibid., pp. 35-36.

25. Ibid., p. 39.

26. Grimaldi, Anthony E. *The Indiana Soldiers and Sailors Monument and Its Dedication: A Study of a Nineteenth Century American Monument and Its Allied Arts.* Ph.D. diss., Ohio University, 1982, pp. 19-20.

27. Ibid., pp. 32-93. Grimaldi's analysis of the symbolic meaning of the Indiana Soldiers and Sailors Monument is both thorough and excellent.

28. Ibid., p. 23.

29. Ibid., pp. 41-42.

30. Ibid., p. 44.

31. Ibid., p. 43.

32. Goode, James M. *The Outdoor Sculpture of Washington, D.C.: A Comprehensive Historical Guide.* Washington, D.C.: Smithsonian Institution Press, 1974, p. 360.

33. Widener, *Confederate Monuments,* pp. 277-83. According to Widener's documentation, Richmond has 19 Confederate monuments.

34. Goode, *Outdoor Sculpture of Washington, D.C.,* p. 27.

35. Civil War memorials, especially those dedicated to generals and admirals, were used in traffic circles, squares, and other critical locations as focal elements to embellish Washington's city plan by L'Enfant.

36. Goode, *Outdoor Sculpture of Washington, D.C.,* pp. 243-48. The sculptor, Henry M. Shrady, spent most of his professional career on the Grant Memorial. As Goode describes him, Shrady went to great lengths to portray authentic battle schemes and the essence of General Grant himself.

37. Ibid., p. 245.

38. Ibid., p. 193.

39. Ibid., p. 197.

40. Hinkel, John V. *Arlington: Monuments to Heroes.* Englewood Cliffs, NJ: Prentice-Hall, 1965, pp. 123, 133.

41. Goulden, Joseph C. *Korea: The Untold Story of the War.* New York: Times Books, 1982, p. 3.

42. Ibid., p. xv.

43. Ibid., p. xvi.

44. Goode, *Outdoor Sculpture of Washington, D.C.,* p. 137.

45. Hinkel, *Arlington,* pp. 140-43.

46. American Battle Monuments Commission. *Honolulu Memorial National Cemetery of the Pacific,* 1964, p. 4.

47. Ibid., pp. 18-20.

48. Other memorials for remembering the Korean War have been built. For example, a memorial statue of General Douglas MacArthur was dedicated at Inchon in 1957 to commemorate his offensive to drive back the North Koreans in 1950.

49. Richard, George. *Milwaukee County War Memorial,* Milwaukee, WI: Milwaukee County War Memorial, 1968, pp. 16-17.

50. Welsh, Douglas. *The History of the Vietnam War.* New York: Galahad Books, 1981, pp. 180-81.

51. Wilson, Richard M. "Vietnam Veterans Peace and Brotherhood Chapel," *DAV,* vol. 19, no. 7, 1977, pp. 12-13.

52. Keller, Tom. "The DAV Vietnam Veterans National Memorial," *DAV,* vol. 25, no. 2, 1983, p. 16.

53. Some visitors feel that the chapel's design suggests the wings of a fallen angel. See Westphall, Victor, "Vietnam: The Hinge of Destiny," commemorative program, 1972, p. 12.

54. Wilson, "Vietnam Veterans Peace and Brotherhood Chapel," p. 12.

55. Scruggs, Jan C., and Joel L. Swerdlow. *To Heal a Nation: The Vietnam Veterans Memorial.* New York: Harper and Row, 1985, pp. 81-82. For a full account of the controversy surrounding the Vietnam Memorial, this book offers the most complete description of the conflicting events.

56. Arnbeck, Bob. "Monumental Folly," *The Progressive,* vol. 46, no. 6, 1982, p. 46.

57. Vietnam Veterans Memorial Fund. *The Vietnam Veterans Memorial Design Competition.* Washington, D.C., 1980, p. 5.

58. Hess, Elizabeth. "A Tale of Two Memorials," *Art in America,* vol. 71, no. 4, 1983, pp. 122-23; and Arnbeck, "Monumental Folly," p. 47.

59. Scruggs and Swerdlow, *To Heal a Nation,* pp. 81-82.

60. Ibid., pp. 106, 130-34.

61. Hess, "A Tale of Two Memorials," p. 125.

62. Ibid.

63. WGBH Educational Foundation, "Vietnam Memorial," *Frontline,* no. 118, 1983, pp. 5-6.

64. Karnow, Stanley. *Vietnam: A History.* New York: Viking Press, 1983, p. 9.

65. WGBH Educational Foundation, "Vietnam Memorial," pp. 4, 11, 15.

66. Ibid., pp. 3, 11.

67. Hess, "A Tale of Two Memorials," p. 126.

68. Scruggs and Swerdlow, *To Heal a Nation,* p. 133.

69. The symbolism for the Kansas City Vietnam Veterans Memorial Fountain is described by David M. Baker in his statement of design and in the literature provided by the fund-raising committee.

CHAPTER SIX: MEMORIES OF HORROR

1. In California, camps were located at Manzanar and Tule Lake, and Idaho had the Minidoka Camp. Arizona had camps at Poston and Gila River while Utah had

Topaz. In Wyoming, there was Heart Mountain, Colorado had Amanche, and Arkansas had Rohwer and Jerome.

2. Weglyn, Michi. *Years of Infamy: The Untold Story of America's Concentration Camps.* New York: William Morrow and Company, 1976, p. 27.

3. Residents of Minidoka Relocation Center. *The Minidoka Interlude.* Hunt, ID: Minidoka Residents, 1943, p. 3.

4. Jackman, Norman R. "Collective Protests in Relocation Centers," *American Journal of Sociology,* vol. 63, no. 3, 1957, pp. 264-72.

5. Weglyn, *Years of Infamy,* pp. 156-73.

6. Girdner, Audrie, and Anne Loftis. *The Great Betrayal.* London: Collier-Macmillan, 1969, pp. 209-36.

7. The Manzanar plaque is inscribed: "In the early part of World War II, 110,000 persons of Japanese ancestry were interned in relocation centers by Executive Order No. 9066, issued on February 19, 1942. Manzanar, the first of ten such concentration camps, was bounded by barbed wire and guard towers, confining 10,000 persons, the majority being American citizens. May the injustices and humiliation suffered here as a result of hysteria, racism and economic exploitation never emerge again."

8. Garrett, Jessie A., and Ronald C. Larson. *Camp and Community.* Van Nuys, CA: Delta, 1977, pp. xvi, 229-30.

9. Baker, Raymond F. *Andersonville.* Washington, D.C.: U.S. Department of the Interior, 1972, pp. 7-10.

10. Ibid., pp. 10, 16.

11. Futch, Ovid L. *History of Andersonville Prison.* Gainesville, FL: University of Florida Press, 1968, p. 45.

12. Baker, *Andersonville,* p. 16.

13. Futch, *History of Andersonville Prison,* p. 119.

14. Baker, *Andersonville,* pp. 18-19.

15. Futch, *History of Andersonville Prison,* p. 66.

16. Thompson, William J., "The Story of the Andersonville Sculpture," mimeograph, n. d.

17. Futch, *History of Andersonville Prison,* p. 40.

18. Ibid., pp. 49-54.

19. Widener, Ralph W. *Confederate Monuments: Enduring Symbols of the South and the War Between the States.* Washington, D.C.: Andromeda Associates, 1982, p. 42.

20. Robertson, James I. "The Scourge of Elmira," in W. B. Hesseltine (ed.), *Civil War Prisons.* Kent, OH: Kent State University Press, 1962, p. 80.

21. Zipfel, Friedrich, Eberhard Aleff, Hans L. Schoenthal, and Wolfgang Gobel. *Plotzensee Memorial.* Berlin: Informationzentrum, 1981, p. 2.

22. Rothfels, Hans. *The German Opposition to Hitler.* Hinsdale, IL: Regneny Co., 1948.

23. Zipfel et al., *Plotzensee Memorial,* p. 29.

24. Rieth, Adolf. *Monuments to the Victims of Tyranny.* New York: Praeger, 1968, p. 13.

25. Feig, Konnilyn G. *Hitler's Death Camps.* New York: Holmes and Meier, 1979, p. 43.

26. Ibid., p. 47.

27. Ibid., p. 50.

28. Ibid., pp. 47-48.

29. Ibid., p. 44.

30. Rieth, *Monuments to the Victims,* p. 21.

31. Ibid., pp. 26-27.

32. Ibid., p. 26.

33. Feig, *Hitler's Death Camps,* p. 51.

34. Ogburn, Frederick W. *Social Changes with Respect to Culture and Original Nature.* New York: Viking Press, 1927, p. 196.

35. Beck, Philip. *Oradour: Village of the Dead.* London: Leo Cooper, 1979, p. vii.

36. Ibid., p. 56.

37. Ibid., pp. 70-82.

38. Ibid., pp. 84-86.

39. Ibid., p. 10.

40. Kawasaki, Shoichiro, ed. *A Call from Hibakusha of Hiroshima and Nagasaki.* Tokyo: Asahi Evening News, 1978, p. 61.

41. Lifton, Robert J. *Death in Life: Survivors of Hiroshima.* New York: Random House, 1967, p. 29.

42. Ibid., p. 20.

43. Ibid., p. 27.

44. Ibid., p. 29.

45. Ibid., pp. 31-32.

46. Ibid., p. 256.

47. Hasegawa, Koichi. "Hiroshima Resurrected as a Mecca of Peace," *The American City,* vol. 67, no. 4, 1952, p. 96.

48. Ibid., p. 96.

49. Lifton, *Death in Life,* pp. 271-72.

50. Ibid., p. 273.

51. Ibid., pp. 271-72.

52. Ibid., p. 104.

53. Ibid., pp. 276-77.

54. Ibid., p. 279.

55. Ibid., p. 274.

56. Feis, Herbert. *The Atomic Bomb and the End of World War II.* Princeton, NJ: Princeton University Press, 1966, p. 200.

57. Ibid., p. 192.

58. Kawasaki, *A Call from Hibakusha,* pp. 99-100.

59. Alinsky, Saul D. *Rules for Radicals.* New York: Random House, 1979, p. 29.

60. Ibid., p. 34.

61. Curl, James Stevens. *The Celebration of Death.* New York: Charles Scribner's Sons, 1980, pp. 351-54.

62. Dorfman, Lois. "For This the Earth Mourns," *Shoah,* vol. 3, no. 1, 1982, pp. 25-26, 38.

63. Coffelt, Beth. "The Holocaust and the Art of War," *California Living Magazine,* in *The San Francisco Examiner,* October 23, 1983, p. 12.

64. Ibid., p. 12.

65. Ibid., p. 14.

66. Hoig, Stan. *The Sand Creek Massacre.* Norman, OK: University of Oklahoma Press, 1961, pp. 110-28.

67. Ibid., pp. 141-42.

68. Ibid., pp. 145-62.

69. Ibid., pp. 163-76.

CHAPTER SEVEN: REMEMBRANCE AS POLITICAL CRITIQUE

1. Utley, Robert M. *Fort Davis.* Washington, D.C.: U.S. National Park Service Historical Handbook Series, 1965, pp. 21-22. A special exhibit of the Buffalo Soldiers is also part of the U.S. Army's Museum at Fort Riley, Kansas.

2. Gleed, Edward C. "The Story of America's Black Air Force," *Tony Brown's Journal,* January/March 1983, pp. 4-11.

3. Goode, James M. *The Outdoor Sculpture of Washington, D.C.: A Comprehensive Historical Guide.* Washington, D.C.: Smithsonian Institution Press, 1974, p. 102.

4. Ibid., pp. 200, 462-63.

5. Bach, Ira J., and Mary L. Gray. *A Guide to Chicago's Public Sculpture.* Chicago: University of Chicago Press, 1983, p. 216. The World War I Black Soldiers' Memorial in Chicago is one of the few classical memorials strictly devoted to commemorating blacks in war.

6. Busis, Sidney, et al. "Holocaust Remembrance in Local Communities," *Shoah,* vol. 3, no. 1, 1982, pp. 17-22.

7. Wiesel, Elie. *President's Commission on the Holocaust.* Washington, D.C., U.S. Government Printing Office, 1983, pp. 9-16.

8. United States Holocaust Memorial Council. *Days of Remembrance, 1983.* Washington, D.C., 1983, p. 30.

9. Meredith, Roy. *The American Wars: A Pictorial History from Quebec to Korea.* New York: World Publishing, 1955. This book accounts for better known paintings of past wars and where they are located.

10. Lew, William W., et al. *Journey to Minidoka: The Paintings of Roger Shimomura.* Orden, UT: Collett Art Gallery, 1983, p. 14.

11. Von Blum, Paul. *The Critical Vision: A History of Social and Political Art in the U.S.* Boston, MA: South End Press, 1982, pp. 113-15.

12. Ibid., p. 158.

13. Terkel, Studs. *The Good War.* New York: Pantheon Books, 1984, pp. 586-88.

14. Johnson, James Turner. *Just War Tradition and the Restraint of War.* Princeton, NJ: Princeton University Press, 1981, pp. 193-94.

BIBLIOGRAPHY

Alden, John D. *The American Steel Navy*. New York: American Heritage Press, 1972.

Alexander, Christopher, et al. *A Pattern Language*. New York: Oxford University Press, 1977.

Alexander, Robert L. *The Architecture of Maximilian Godefroy*. Baltimore: Johns Hopkins University Press, 1974.

Alinsky, Saul D. *Rules for Radicals*. New York: Random House, 1979.

Allan, Douglas A. "Ch. 1: The Museum and Its Functions," in L. H. Evans (ed.). *The Organization of Museums: Practical Advice*. Paris: UNESCO Press, 1978, pp. 13-27.

American Battle Monuments Commission. *Aisne-Marne American Cemetery and Memorial*, 1983.

_____. *American Memorials and Overseas Military Cemeteries*, 1983.

_____. *Ardennes American Cemetery and Memorial*, 1978.

_____. *Brittany American Cemetery and Memorial*, 1980.

_____. *Cambridge American Cemetery and Memorial*, 1979.

_____. *Epinal American Cemetery and Memorial*, 1982.

_____. *Florence American Cemetery and Memorial*, 1977.

_____. *Henri-Chapelle American Cemetery and Memorial*, 1977.

_____. *Honolulu Memorial National Cemetery of the Pacific*, 1964.

_____. *Lorraine American Cemetery and Memorial*, 1978.

_____. *Luxembourg American Cemetery and Memorial*, 1983.

_____. *Manila American Cemetery and Memorial*, 1980.

_____. *Meuse-Argonne American Cemetery and Memorial*, 1971.

_____. *Netherlands American Cemetery and Memorial*, 1973.

_____. *Normandy American Cemetery and Memorial,* 1975.

_____. *North Africa American Cemetery and Memorial,* 1971.

_____. *Oise-Aisne American Cemetery and Memorial,* 1978.

_____. *Rhone American Cemetery and Memorial,* 1958.

_____. *Saint Mihiel American Cemetery and Memorial,* 1971.

_____. *Sicily-Rome American Cemetery and Memorial,* 1978.

_____. *Suresnes American Cemetery and Memorial,* 1971.

Arnbeck, Bob. "Monumental Folly," *The Progressive,* vol. 46, no. 6, 1982, pp. 46-47.

Bach, Ira J., and Mary L. Gray. *A Guide to Chicago's Public Sculpture.* Chicago: University of Chicago Press, 1983.

Baker, Raymond F. *Andersonville.* Washington, D.C.: U.S. Department of the Interior, 1972.

Barber, Bernard. "Place, Symbol and Utilitarian Functions in War Memorials," *Social Forces,* vol. 28, 1949, pp. 64-68.

Beck, Philip. *Oradour: Village of the Dead.* London: Leo Cooper, 1979.

Blum, John M., et. al. *A History of the United States: The National Experience.* New York: Harcourt, Brace and World, 1963.

Boatner, Mark M. *Landmarks of the American Revolution.* Harrisburg, PA: Stockpole Press, 1973.

Brandon, Williams. *Indians.* New York: American Heritage Publishing, 1961.

Brown, Dee. *Bury My Heart at Wounded Knee.* New York: Bantam Books, 1971.

Brown, Genevieve, A. N. Bobbitt, and J. Otto Lee. *Indiana: 1930.* Indianapolis, IN: Board of Public Printing, 1930.

Bryan, C.D.B. "Memorial Day in Stony Creek, Conn.," *New York Times,* May 30, 1977, p. 15.

Busis, Sidney, et al. "Holocaust Remembrance in Local Communities," *Shoah,* vol. 3, no. 1, 1982, pp. 17-22.

California Department of Parks and Recreation. *California Inventory of Historic Resources.* Sacramento, CA: State of California, 1976.

Cary, Norman Miller. *Guide to U.S. Army Museums and Historical Sites.* Washington, D.C.: U.S. Government Printing Office, 1975.

Catanese, Anthony J., and James C. Snyder. *Introduction to Urban Planning.* New York: McGraw-Hill, 1979.

Catton, Bruce. *The Civil War.* New York: American Heritage Publishing, 1960.

Clay, Grady. *Close Up: How to Read the American City.* Chicago: University of Chicago Press, 1973.

Coffelt, Beth. "The Holocaust and the Art of War," *California Living Magazine,* in *The San Francisco Examiner,* October 23, 1983, pp. 12-15.

Commission of Control for Texas Centennial Celebrations. *Monuments Commemorating the Centenary of Texas Independence.* Austin, TX: Steck Publishers, 1938.

Coombs, Rose B. *Before Endeavors Fade.* London: Battle of Britain International, 1983.

Corbett, Harvey W. "The Value of Memorial Architecture," *Architectural Forum,* vol. 45, no. 6, 1926, pp. 321-24.

Craig, Lois. *The Federal Presence: Architecture, Politics and Symbols in United States Government Building.* Cambridge: The MIT Press, 1978.

Craven, Wayne. *The Sculptures at Gettysburg*. Gettysburg, PA: Eastern Acorn Press, 1982.

———. *Sculpture in America*. New York: Cornwall Books, 1984.

Cret, Paul P. "Memorials—Columns, Shafts, Cenotaphs and Tablets," *Architectural Forum*, vol. 45, no. 6, 1926, pp. 331-36.

Curl, James Stevens. *A Celebration of Death*. New York: Scribner's, 1980.

Davies, A. Mervyn. *Solon H. Borglum*. Chester, CT: Pequot Press, 1974.

Davis, William C. *Gettysburg: The Story Behind the Scenery*. Las Vegas, NV: KC Publications, 1983.

De Busscher, J. M. *Les Folies de L'industrie*. Brussels: Archives d'Architecture Moderne, 1981.

DeWall, Robb. *Korczak: Storyteller in Stone*. Crazy Horse, SD: Korczak's Heritage, 1983.

Doezema, Marianne, and June Hargrove. *The Public Monument and Its Audience*. Cleveland, OH: Cleveland Museum of Art, 1977.

Dorfman, Lois. "For This the Earth Mourns, The Making of a Holocaust Memorial," *Shoah*, vol. 3, no. 1, 1982, pp. 25-26, 38.

Durkheim, Emile. *The Elementary Forms of the Religious Life*. New York: The Free Press, 1965.

Eastman, John. *Who Lived Here: A Biographical Guide to Homes and Museums*. New York: Facts on File, 1983.

Eliade, Mircea. *The Sacred and the Profane*. New York: Harcourt, Brace and World, 1959.

Emerson, William. "Bridges as Memorials," *Architectural Forum*, vol. 45, no. 6, 1926, pp. 337-44.

Federal Writers Project. *California: A Guide to the Golden State*. New York: Hastings House, 1967.

———. *Kentucky: A Guide to the Bluegrass State*. New York: Harcourt, Brace and World, 1939.

———. *Massachusetts: A Guide to the Pilgrim State*. Boston: Houghton Mifflin, 1971.

———. *Nebraska: A Guide to the Cornhusker State*. New York: Viking Press, 1939.

———. *New Jersey: A Guide to Its Past and Present*. New York: Hastings House, 1977.

———. *The Ohio Guide*. New York: Oxford University Press, 1940.

———. *Oregon: The End of the Trail*. Portland, OR: Binfords and Mort, 1940.

———. *San Francisco: A Guide to the Bay and Its Cities*. New York: Hastings House, 1973.

———. *South Carolina: A Guide to the Palmetto State*. New York: Oxford University Press, 1941.

———. *Texas: A Guide to the Lone Star State*. New York: Hastings House, 1940.

———. *Utah: A Guide to the State*. New York: Hastings House, 1954.

———. *Vermont: A Guide to the Green Mountain State*. Boston: Houghton Mifflin, 1966.

Feig, Konnilyn G. *Hitler's Death Camps*. New York: Holmes and Meier, 1979.

Feis, Herbert. *The Atomic Bomb and the End of World War II*. Princeton, NJ: Princeton University Press, 1966.

Ferris, Robert C. *Soldier and Brave.* Washington, D.C.: U.S. Department of the Interior, 1971.

Fishel, Lester H. "The Past Invades the Present," *New York History,* vol. 58, no. 1, 1977, pp. 4-15.

Fletcher, Bannister. *A History of Architecture.* New York: Scribners, 1961.

Fried, Frederick, and Edward V. Gillon, Jr. *New York Civic Structure: A Pictorial Guide.* New York: Dover Publications, 1976.

Friedlander, Lee. *The American Monument.* New York: Eakins Foundation Press, 1976.

Fussell, Paul. *The Boy Scout Handbook and Other Observations.* New York: Oxford University Press, 1982.

Futch, Ovid L. *History of Andersonville Prison.* Gainesville, FL: University of Florida Press, 1968.

Garrett, Jessie A., and Ronald C. Larson. *Camp and Community.* Van Nuys, CA: Delta, 1977.

Gay, Vernon, and Marilyn Evert. *Discovering Pittsburgh's Sculpture.* Pittsburgh, PA: University of Pittsburgh Press, 1983.

Girdner, Audrie, and Anne Loftis. *The Great Betrayal: The Evacuation of the Japanese-Americans During World War II.* London: Collier-Macmillan, 1969.

Gleed, Edward C. "The Story of America's Black Air Force," *Tony Brown's Journal,* January/March 1983, pp. 4-11.

Goldberger, Paul. *The City Observed: New York.* New York: Random House, 1979.

Goldstone, Harmon H., and Martha Dalrymple. *History Preserved: A Guide to New York City Landmarks and Historic Districts.* New York: Simon and Schuster, 1974.

Goode, James M. *The Outdoor Sculpture of Washington, D.C.: A Comprehensive Historical Guide.* Washington, D.C.: Smithsonian Institution Press, 1974.

Goulden, Joseph C. *Korea: The Untold Story of the War.* New York: Times Books, 1982.

Grimaldi, Anthony E. *The Indiana Soldiers' and Sailors' Monument and Its Dedication: A Study of a Nineteenth Century Monument and Its Allied Arts.* Ph.D. diss., Ohio University, 1982.

Grossman, Elizabeth G. "Architecture for a Public Client: The Monuments and Chapels of the American Battle Monuments Commission," *Journal of the Society of Architectural Historians.* vol. 43, May 1984, pp. 119-43.

Gurney, Gene. *Arlington National Cemetery.* New York: Crown Publishers, 1965.

Hamilton, Virginia V. *Seeing Historic Alabama: Fifteen Guided Tours.* University, AL: University of Alabama Press, 1982.

Hart, Herbert M. *Tour Guide to Old Western Forts.* Ft. Collins, CO: Old Army Press, 1980.

Hasegawa, Koichi. "Hiroshima Resurrected as a Mecca of Peace," *The American City,* vol. 67, no. 4, 1952, p. 96.

Hess, Elizabeth. "A Tale of Two Memorials," *Art in America,* vol. 71, no. 4, 1983, pp. 121-26.

Hinkel, John V. *Arlington: Monument to Heroes.* Englewood Cliffs, NJ: Prentice-Hall, 1965.

Hoig, Stan. *The Sand Creek Massacre.* Norman, OK: University of Oklahoma Press, 1961.

Horsman, Reginald. *The War of 1812.* New York: Alfred A. Knopf, 1969.

Hubbard, William. "A Meaning for Monuments," *The Public Interest,* no. 74, Winter 1984, pp. 17-30.

Huber, Leonard V. *New Orleans: A Pictorial History.* New York: Crown Publishers, 1971, p. 105.

_____. *The Battle of New Orleans and Its Monument.* New Orleans, LA: Louisiana Landmarks Society, 1983.

Hudnut, Joseph. "The Monument Does Not Remember," *Atlantic,* September 1945, pp. 55-59.

Jackman, Norman R. "Collective Protests in Relocation Centers," *American Journal of Sociology,* vol. 63, no. 3, 1957, pp. 264-72.

Jackson, J. B. *Discovering the Vernacular Landscape.* New Haven, CT: Yale University Press, 1984.

_____. *Landscapes.* (Edited by E.H. Zube). Amherst, MA: The University of Massachusetts Press, 1970.

_____. *The Necessity for Ruins.* Amherst, MA: The University of Massachusetts Press, 1980.

Johnson, James Turner. *Just War Tradition and the Restraint of War.* Princeton, NJ: Princeton University Press, 1981.

Kammen, Michael. *A Season of Youth.* New York: Knopf, 1978.

Karnow, Stanley. *Vietnam: A History.* New York: Viking Press, 1983.

Keller, Tom. "The DAV Vietnam Veterans National Memorial," *DAV,* vol. 25, no. 2, 1983, pp. 16-17.

Kent, Louise A. *Village Greens of New England.* New York: Barrows and Company, 1948.

Ketchum, Richard M. *Decisive Day: The Battle for Bunker Hill.* Garden City, NY: Doubleday, 1962.

Klein, Milton M. "Commemorating the American Revolution: The Bicentennial and Its Predecessors," *New York History,* vol. 58, no. 1, 1977, pp. 257-76.

Koury, Michael J. *To Consecrate This Ground: The Custer Battlefield 1876-1976.* Ft. Collins, CO: Old Army Press, 1978.

Lancaster, Bruce. *The Revolution.* New York: American Heritage Publishing, 1958.

Law, Frank P. "The Washington Memorial Chapel." Valley Forge, PA, unpublished pamphlet, n.d.

Leary, Edward A. *Indianapolis: The Story of a City.* Indianapolis: Bobbs-Merrill, 1971.

Lemisch, Jesse. "Bicentennial Schlock," *The New Republic,* vol. 175, November 6, 1976, pp. 21-23.

Lethaby, W. R. *Form in Civilization.* London: Oxford University Press, 1977.

Lew, William W., et al. *Journey to Minidoka: The Paintings of Roger Shimomura.* Ogden, UT: Collett Art Gallery, 1983.

Lifton, Robert J. *Death in Life: Survivors of Hiroshima.* New York: Random House, 1967.

Lowenthal, David. "Age and Artifact: Dilemmas of Appreciation." in D. W. Meinig (ed.) *The Interpretation of Ordinary Landscapes.* New York: Oxford University Press, 1979, pp. 103-28.

———. "The American Scene," *Geographical Review,* vol. 58, no. 1, 1968, pp. 61-88.

Lyndhurst, Joseph. *Military Collectables.* New York: Crescent Books, 1983.

Lyndon, Donlyn. "Public Buildings: Symbols Qualified by Experience," *The Public Interest,* no. 74, Winter 1984, pp. 77-97.

Madison, James H. *Indiana Through Tradition and Change.* Indianapolis: Indiana Historical Society, 1982.

Magonigle, H. Van Buren. "Architects—War Memorials—Competitions," *Journal of the American Institute of Architects,* vol. 8, no. 4, 1920, pp. 162-63.

Manchester, William. *American Caesar: Douglas MacArthur 1880-1964.* New York: Dell Publishing Co., 1982.

Marshall, S.L.A. *World War I.* New York: American Heritage Publishing, 1964.

Mayo, James M. "Propaganda with Design: Environmental Dramaturgy in the Political Rally," *Journal of Architectural Education,* vol. 34, no. 2, 1978, pp. 24-27, 32.

———. "Resymbolization of a Symbol," *Dimensions,* vol. 2, no. 2, 1981, pp. 14-18.

McPherson, J.E. *The Liberty Memorial.* Kansas City, MO: Spencer Press, 1929.

Meredith, Roy. *The American Wars: A Pictorial History from Quebec to Korea.* New York: World Publishing, 1955.

Miller, Tom. "After Delay, Vets Pay Their Tribute," *The Kansas City Times,* June 7, 1984, pp. A1, A12.

Morris, Richard B. *Independence: A Guide to Independence National Historic Park.* Washington, D.C.: National Park Service, Division of Publications, 1982.

National Park Foundation. *The Complete Guide to America's National Parks.* New York: Viking Press, 1981.

North, Thomas. "In Proud Remembrance: American Memorials and Military Cemeteries of World War II," *National Sculpture Review,* vol. 14, no. 1, 1965, pp. 5-26.

Norton, Bill. "Byron's Wars," *Kansas City Star Sunday Magazine,* September 29, 1985, pp. 1, 12-17.

Ogburn, Frederick W. *Social Change with Respect to Culture and Original Nature.* New York: Viking Press, 1927.

O'Toole, G.J.A. *The Spanish War.* New York: W. W. Norton, 1984.

Pantenburg, Leon. "Enough Gunpowder in Vicksburg?" *Vicksburg Evening Post,* July 4, 1983, p. 1.

Papenfuse, Edward C., et al. *Maryland: A New Guide to the Old Line State.* Baltimore: Johns Hopkins University Press, 1976.

Pershing, John J. "Our National War Memorials in Europe," *National Geographic Magazine,* vol. 65, no. 1, 1934, pp. 1-36.

Price, Willadene. *Gutzon Borglum: Artist and Patriot.* Chicago: Rand McNally, 1961.

Rapoport, Amos. *House Form and Culture.* Englewood Cliffs, NJ: Prentice-Hall, 1969.

Reed, John Shelton. "The Heart of Dixie: An Essay in Folk Geography," *Social Forces,* vol. 54, no. 4, 1976, pp. 933-44.

Relph, Edward. *Place and Placelessness.* London: Pion, 1976.

Residents of Minidoka Relocation Center. *The Minidoka Interlude*. Hunt, ID: Minidoka Residents, 1943.

Richard, George. *Milwaukee County War Memorial*. Milwaukee, WI: Milwaukee County War Memorial, 1968.

Rieth, Adolf. *Monuments to the Victims of Tyranny*. New York: Praeger, 1968.

Robertson, James I. "The Scourge of Elmira," in W. B. Hesseltine (ed.), *Civil War Prisons*. Kent, OH: Kent State University Press, 1962.

Robinson, Brian S. "Some Fragmented Forms of Space," *Annals of the Association of American Geographers,* vol. 67, no. 4, 1977, pp. 549-63.

Rothfels, Hans. *The German Opposition to Hitler*. Hinsdale, IL: Regneny Co., 1948.

Ruesch, Jurgen, and Weldon Kees. *Nonverbal Communication*. Berkeley: University of California Press, 1956.

Rukert, Norman G. *Fort McHenry: Home of the Brave*. Baltimore, MD: Bodine and Associates, 1983.

Russell, Don. *Custer's Last*. Ft. Worth, TX: Amon Carter Museum of Western Art, 1968.

Santovenia, Emeterio S. *Libro Commemorativo de La Inauguracion de la Plaza del Maine in La Habana*. Habana, Cuba: Secretario de Obra Publicas, 1928.

Scott, Mel. *American City Planning Since 1890*. Berkeley, CA: University of California Press, 1969.

Scruggs, Jan C., and Joel L. Swerdlow. *To Heal a Nation: The Vietnam Veterans Memorial*. New York: Harper and Row, 1985.

Slackman, Michael. *Remembering Pearl Harbor: The Story of the USS* Arizona *Memorial*. Honolulu, HI: Arizona Memorial Museum Association, 1984.

Stands in Timber, John, and Margot Liberty. *Cheyenne Memories*. New Haven, CT: Yale University Press, 1967.

Steinberg, Rolf, and Mannfred Hamm. *Dead Tech*. San Francisco, CA: Sierra Club Books, 1982.

Stern, Robert A.M., Gregory Gilmartin, and John M. Massengale. *New York 1900*. New York: Rizzoli International Publications, 1983.

Sternlieb, George. "Cities: Fantasy and Reality," *Journal of Architectural and Planning Research,* vol. 1, no. 3, 1984, pp. 209-15.

Stilgoe, John R. *Common Landscape of America, 1580-1845*. New Haven, CT: Yale University Press, 1982.

Sulzberger, C. L. *World War II*. New York: Simon and Schuster, 1966.

Swarthout, Egerton. "Memorial Buildings," *Architectural Forum,* vol. 45, no. 6, 1926, pp. 325-30.

Terkel, Studs. *The Good War*. New York: Pantheon Books, 1984.

Thacker, Christopher. *The History of Gardens*. Berkeley: University of California Press, 1979.

Trask, David F. *The War with Spain in 1898*. New York: Macmillan, 1981.

Tuan, Yi-Fu. *Segmented Worlds and Self*. Minneapolis: University of Minnesota Press, 1982.

————. "The Significance of the Artifact," *Geographical Review,* vol. 74, no. 4, 1980, pp. 462-72.

_____. *Space and Place: The Perspective of Experience.* Minneapolis: University of Minnesota Press, 1977.

_____. *Topophilia.* Englewood Cliffs, NJ: Prentice-Hall, 1974.

United States Holocaust Memorial Council. *Days of Remembrance, 1983.* Washington, D.C., 1983.

U.S. Military Academy. *The West Point Guide.* New Windsor, NY: Commercial Offset Printers, n.d.

Utley, Robert M. *Fort Davis.* Washington, D.C.: U.S. National Park Service Historical Handbook Series, 1965.

Vietnam Veterans Memorial Fund. *The Vietnam Veterans Memorial Design Competition.* Washington, D.C., 1980.

Von Blum, Paul. *The Critical Vision: A History of Social and Political Art in the U.S.* Boston, MA: South End Press, 1982.

Walker, Steve, and David F. Riggs. *Vicksburg Battlefield Monuments.* Jackson, MS: University Press of Mississippi, 1984.

Warner, Samuel Bass. *The Living and the Dead.* New Haven: Yale University Press, 1959.

Warren, Robert Penn. *The Legacy of the Civil War.* Cambridge: Harvard University Press, 1983.

Weglyn, Michi. *Years of Infamy: The Untold Story of America's Concentration Camps.* New York: William Morrow and Company, 1976.

Welsh, Douglas. *The History of the Vietnam War.* New York: Galahad Books, 1981.

Weston, George F., Jr. *Boston Ways: High, By and Folk.* Boston, MA: Beacon Press, 1957.

WGBH Educational Foundation. "Vietnam Memorial," *Frontline,* no. 118, 1983.

Whittick, Arnold. *War Memorials.* London: Country Life, 1946.

Widener, Ralph W. *Confederate Monuments: Enduring Symbols of the South and the War Between the States.* Washington, D.C.: Andromeda Associates, 1982.

Wiesel, Elie. *President's Commission on the Holocaust.* Washington, D.C.: U.S. Government Printing Office, 1983.

Wilson, Richard G. *McKim, Mead, and White.* New York: Rizzoli, 1983.

Wilson, Richard M. "Vietnam Veterans Peace and Brotherhood Chapel." *DAV,* vol. 19, no. 7, 1977, pp. 12-13.

Wilson, William H. *The City Beautiful Movement in Kansas City.* Columbia, MO: University of Missouri Press, 1964.

Wright, Talmadge. "Marketing Culture, Simulation and the Aestheticization of Work and War," Paper presented at the Popular Culture Conference of the American Culture Association, 1985.

Young, Louis Stanley. *Life and Heroic Deeds of Admiral Dewey and Battles in the Philippines.* Philadelphia, PA: Globe Bible Publishing, 1899.

Zipfel, Friedrich, Eberhard Aleff, Hans L. Schoenthal, and Wolfgang Gobel. *Plotzensee Memorial.* Berlin: Informationszentrum, 1981.

INDEX

306   INDEX

ABOUT THE AUTHOR

JAMES M. MAYO is a professor in the School of Architecture and Urban Design at the University of Kansas. He received his bachelor of architecture and master of urban planning from Texas A&M University. His Ph.D. is in sociology from Oklahoma State University. Dr. Mayo has published articles in the *Journal of Architectural Education, Environment and Behavior, Journal of the American Planning Association,* and numerous other journals. He is on the editorial boards of the *Journal of Architectural and Planning Research* and the *Journal of Architectural Education.* His research is particularly known for relating political ideology to the built environment and design practice. In preparation for this book, Dr. Mayo drove 27,000 miles on the roads and back roads of the United States and Europe to make visual accounts for both known and lesser known American war memorials.